NOTHING LEFT TO STEAL

Jailed for telling the truth

MZILIKAZI WA AFRIKA

PENGUIN BOOKS

First published by Penguin Books (South Africa) (Pty) Ltd, 2014
A Penguin Random House company

Registered Offices: Block D, Rosebank Office Park, 181 Jan Smuts Avenue,
Parktown North, Johannesburg 2193, South Africa

www.penguinbooks.co.za

Reprinted 2014 (twice)

ISBN 978-0-14-353892-9
eISBN 978-0-14-353140-1

Text design and typesetting by Triexie Smit in 11/14.5 pt Minion Pro
Cover design by Hanneke du Toit
Cover photograph by Kevin Sutherland at the *Sunday Times*
Printed and bound by CTP Printers, Cape Town

MIX
Paper from
responsible sources
FSC
www.fsc.org   FSC™ C017578

I dedicate this book to the men who opened my eyes,
Nathaniel Makanete and Ripho Machate; without you
I would have been blind for years.

To my late parents, Simon Ndzhukula and Ilina Nxumalo,
without you I wouldn't be here, thanks a million for
giving me life, love and wisdom.

Last but not least, Jocelyn Maker, my second mother
and former *Sunday Times* investigations unit editor, for
giving me freedom to use my pen and wings to fly.

Preface

Just days after I joined the *Sunday Times* as a rookie reporter in January 1999, I was stripped naked, brutally assaulted and thrown into the lion's den.

On my first investigative assignment with the newspaper, I had infiltrated a modern-day slave trade syndicate operating between South Africa and Mozambique.

I had arrived in the Mozambique capital, Maputo, dressed in my oldest clothes. Since *eu não falo português* (I don't speak Portuguese), I managed to manoeuvre around by speaking my home language, Xitsonga, which is close to Xilandi, one of the Mozambican languages.

Within hours, I was recruited by the syndicate's runners and taken to a safe house in Rosana Garcia, a small Mozambican town near the South African border in Komatipoort.

The dark was strong, paving the way for the stars to blossom, indicating that the night had just begun. As these stars decorated the sky, the earth was struggling to cope with the nightmares as the wind blew strongly, bringing with it the elements of coldness.

Under usual circumstances, this was supposed to be bedtime for normal folk, but it was the beginning of a night of horror for me.

That night I became a slave smuggled to my homeland South Africa, ready to be sold to the masters for a price I didn't even know.

As we weathered the coldness and darkness waiting for the moment of truth, deep inside my mind, apart from being nervous, I was pondering the big story that would finally emerge once I had completed my undercover assignment.

But little did I know that my cover was about to be busted. The slave master, John Nkuna, found my passport and cash stashed in my underwear during a strip search at one of the South African safe houses.

The slave trade might have ended in the eighteenth century thanks to the introduction of colonialism in Africa, but almost two hundred years later in Mozambique, a country that battled many wars even after ousting Portuguese colonialists in 1975, the practice was still going on, though in a new form called human trafficking.

Nkuna went berserk, picking up a hoe handle and clobbering me brutally as he interrogated me. When he was satisfied that I was physically broken, Nkuna and his assistants dragged me into a bakkie (pick-up-truck) parked outside.

With two AK-47 assault rifles pointed in my face, they drove me around before dumping me in the middle of Kruger National Park in the hopes that lions or leopards would finish what they had started.

Through the grace of God, I survived to tell the story, exposing the slave ring. Nkuna would eventually be arrested and sent to jail.

This was not the first time that I had been brutally assaulted and had guns shoved in my face. I was arrested on 9 October 1989, just weeks before I was to sit my matric examination, after an *ipimpi* (police informer) told the police that I had a couple of AK-47 rifles stashed somewhere in my house. I was not a gunrunner but a political activist whose house was often used as a "base" – a secret place where underground political activities were taking place – to move weapons.

After I was arrested, a police officer put a 9-millimetre pistol into my mouth and threatened to blow my brains out.

I was then assaulted. My uncle's house where I was staying alone at the time was raided and ransacked and everything turned upside down. But no guns were found, not even a single bullet.

Little did they know that the guns were hidden inside a coal stove in the corner of the house; the cooking pots on top were just a disguise. The stove had not been used for months. Had the guns been found, I would have faced potential treason charges and possible life imprisonment.

I had a duty as one of the oppressed citizens of this country to make a contribution, no matter how small or big, to our struggle. Young as I was, my conscience would not allow me to fold my arms and wait for miracles to happen and for our freedom to fall from the sky.

Che Guevara said it loud and clear: "The revolution is not an apple that falls when it is ripe. You have to make it fall."

That excruciating chapter of our history must be told, repeatedly, to the young and future generations so that they may know where we came from as a nation and how the price of our freedom in this beautiful country was paid for with tears, pain and the blood of the innocent.

Our pain and agony lies buried in our memories. Some of us might have forgiven our tormentors, but not all of us will forget what happened.

My second arrest on 4 August 2010 made international headlines. I was arrested in front of television cameras and members of the South African National Editors' Forum (SANEF) on trumped-up charges.

This illegal arrest was designed to intimidate me, harass me and humiliate me. Worst of all it was an attempt to get me fired from the job that was integral to everything that I am.

I was arrested without a warrant and my house was raided and ransacked without a search warrant. I was literally kidnapped, bundled into an unmarked police vehicle surrounded by heavily armed guards and then smuggled to Mpumalanga, more than 300 kilometres away from Johannesburg, in another unmarked police vehicle, without the knowledge of my lawyer, my family or my bosses.

My release was only secured with a late-night High Court application, more than 30 hours later, when a judge ordered my immediate release.

For years, many people have been trying to get a glimpse into my life. I had kept it private to protect myself as an investigative journalist and to keep my children and family safe from any retaliation to my work. I have always resisted any temptation to be a celebrity socialite.

Those who knew me from my childhood want to know how I raised myself from squalor to become the fearless and passionate journalist that I am today.

After long soul-searching and robust debate with my family and friends, they won and I agreed to weave together a story of my life, hopefully told with wit and always with candour.

Writing a memoir is like ascending a theatre stage naked, watching the audience in stitches but still giving a prodigious performance. While some of the patrons might snigger at first, before the end of the show some of them may be in tears as the story of your life hits home.

One of the biggest problems about writing a memoir is that it opens old wounds, exposes the skeletons in your cupboard and rubs salt into fresh sores. Sometimes the pain is too much to bear but that is what makes you stronger and defines your character. A child must first crawl in order to learn to walk.

As a child, I grew up in appalling conditions, flirting with hunger, toying with poverty and surrounded by bastions of racism. Things turned for the worse when my parents divorced and I was forced to live with relatives and was denigrated and kicked like a football from one house to the other.

I was called names, labelled a thief, stupid and lazy; I was often abused, physically and mentally. It was the small price I had to pay for the roof over my head and food in my stomach.

From an early age I had to learn to amaze my enemies and dazzle my admirers. It was the best skill to survive another day.

Even though I went through this torturous journey, today every scar in my body has healed and every pain inflicted has eased. As it is said, what won't kill you will definitely make you stronger.

My hope is that this book will inspire a new generation of young men and women to take the struggle for investigative journalism to another level.

But investigative journalism is not all moonlight and roses. It demands the best of you: you need courage, zeal and the heart of stone. As an investigative journalist you will be forced to walk where angels fear to tread, forced to swim with crocodiles in the river and dance with lions in the jungle to get to the truth.

Life as an investigative journalist has no glamour but only blood, sweat and tears.

I have been declared *persona non grata* in Zimbabwe and detained for 15 hours at Libreville International Airport, Gabon, simply because I am a journalist dangerously armed with a pen and a notebook.

If I weren't a patriot, I would have been an émigré and settled in Nebraska, United States of America, after honorary citizenship was bestowed upon me on 30 August 2001. But I chose Africa, more especially my home, South Africa, where my heart is.

Even though I wasn't born with a pen in my hand, deep down I believe I was born to write and this is my candid confession.

Mzilikazi wa Afrika
Johannesburg
1 April 2014

THE FIRST TESTAMENT

"In the beginning God created the heavens and the earth."
– Genesis 1:1

Chapter 1

NGHUNYUPESU: The writing is on the wall

"Even in the jungle there are those that hunt the hunters." – Mzwakhe Mbuli

A compromise verdict was reached. There was no other way: I must hang. I had to be flushed out and destroyed. I was the notorious party pooper who everybody loved to hate.

I was like a mosquito, the jury said, causing people sleepless nights and disturbing their peace.

I was sniffing around in the wrong places, like a stray dog. I was an *agent provocateur*. I had my probing eyes on the wrong people, very powerful people with political connections.

My pen had become more dangerous than a loaded gun; it was vicious and malicious; it spat venom and caused havoc. I had become their worst nightmare.

My name was discussed in boardrooms and whispered in the corridors of power. It had become a swear word: some people puked at the sound of it, and others cursed it.

A plan was cooked: they had brought in the best chefs, graduates from the University of Propaganda and Public Manipulation. The aroma from the kitchen was appetizing and permeated the air. Their buffet was delicious and the public would swallow it without asking about the ingredients or the recipe. There would be enough food for everyone, even for the hobos on the street.

For starters, they legally bugged my phone. They went to a High Court judge for the order. The poor judge was told that I was a dangerous criminal, involved in cross-border gun smuggling. My passport records showed more than a dozen entrances in and out of South Africa travelling to Mozambique

3

and Swaziland in less than six months and this was enough to convince the judge.

The judge issued the order. It seemed the right thing to do. Anybody suspected of being a dangerous criminal, smuggling weapons that were used to arm the dangerous gangs involved in cash heists and bank robberies, should, if an application is made, have his phone bugged, the judge was told.

Besides telling the judge lies, their real motive was different. They wanted to know who my sources were and what they were telling me. They were also hoping that they would get something, a secret perhaps, that they could use to blackmail me. They had unleashed the dogs; they followed me around; they set up honey traps: beautiful women sent to seduce me and then scream, "Rape!"

After blowing a small fortune of the taxpayers' money there was nothing to show from this costly exercise. My sources and I were talking in codes they could not crack. They couldn't make head or tail of the text messages intercepted on my phone and their bevy of women were returning untouched and with nothing to report back.

The ammunition they needed to execute their plan came on 1 August 2010.

The *Sunday Times* on that day published a front-page story exposing the former national police commissioner General Bheki Cele in a R500 million property lease scandal.

My colleague Stephan Hofstatter and I broke that story.

Cele wanted to move the police head offices into a building owned by businessman Roux Shabangu, who is close to President Jacob Zuma. (Shabangu was a VIP guest at Zuma's inauguration ceremony.) And Cele wanted to move without following prescribed government tender procedures, thus violating Treasury rules.

Numerous phone calls were made to Cele after the newspaper hit the streets, followed by meetings, and the police boss was hooked. There was a mouth-watering meal on their menu and I was the main course. My head would be delivered on a platter, but only if Cele came on board and was hungry enough for revenge.

Cele did not need anybody to whet his appetite. He was more than hungry: he was a wounded lion and our story hurt his pride. No journalists had ever written such a damning story about him as he was the darling of the media in KwaZulu-Natal, his home province. He was also a powerful politician. He did not think twice before ordering his meal from the menu.

He started his offensive in the media, calling a press conference two days after the story was published to test the waters. The conference was well attended and Ndosi (Cele's clan name) seized the opportunity to denounce our story as "incorrect, worse and misleading".

The maverick politician resorted to a personal onslaught at the press conference, calling me "a very shady journalist".

The plan was in progress and the ball was rolling. They decided to pounce.

Six people were called to a secret meeting in Witbank, a vibrant Mpumalanga coal-mining town east of Johannesburg, the day before I was to be arrested. They were each given special assignments and a collection of calumnies against me.

Later a team of police officers handpicked to execute the task at hand were told that my arrest must achieve maximum impact.

"It must be felt in all the four corners of South Africa," was their instruction, claimed one of the people who attended the meeting in Witbank.

I was arrested on 4 August 2010 at my place of work, the *Sunday Times* offices in Rosebank, Johannesburg, in full view of other journalists and distinguished members of SANEF who, ironically, had come to the building to discuss matters that affect the lives of journalists in this country.

The arrest was nothing but a daylight kidnapping of a man who is almost two metres tall. I had become a thorn in the flesh of many politicians. I had exposed their devious shenanigans on the front pages of one of Africa's biggest and most influential newspapers.

I was taken from the office under the pretext that I was being taken to Rosebank police station, a stone's throw away, to be charged with whatever charges they had concocted and would then be released on bail. But to everybody's surprise including the *Sunday Times* lawyer, Eric van den Berg, who was handling the matter, I was handcuffed, bundled into an unmarked police vehicle parked on the road outside and whisked away to no man's land. Not even my lawyer or my bosses or any member of my family were told of my whereabouts.

Instead of taking me to Rosebank police station, the team – led by General Shadrack Sibiya, who was based at the head offfice of the elite investigations unit, the Hawks, in Silverton, Pretoria at the time, and the investigating officer Colonel Christopher Mabasa, then the station commander for Kabokweni police station, outside White River in Mpumalanga – went straight to my house and ransacked it without a search warrant. They confiscated my notebooks, some dating back ten years, my new MacBook and my eight-year-old son's laptop.

While my bedroom was being searched, Hawks' spokesperson Musa Zondi was taking photos of me like paparazzi who had caught a celebrity with his pants down. He scornfully questioned me about a briefcase they had been told I had, which was supposedly "full of documents".

I told Zondi that I did not have such a briefcase.

He became angry. "We were instructed to find it and bring it to the office for scrutiny," he screamed.

"I wish you the best of luck finding such a briefcase in my house," I retorted.

Zondi's attitude left a bitter taste in my mouth: he behaved as if I was a felon, a convicted criminal; yet I was just arrested on flimsy charges which I believed he knew had no bearings on me.

When I had been arrested back at the office, Zondi was running down the street like a maniac, shouting and trying to prevent journalists from taking photos of my melodramatic arrest. He wanted to be the only photographer taking photos of "the great moment".

"I will supply you with these photos later," Zondi told everyone at the time.

This was the same Zondi, a former colleague, who used to work at our offices but was fired after an internal investigation found him guilty of misconduct, fraud, corruption and misappropriation of intellectual property. Zondi appealed his leaving the company and failed.

It was alleged at the time that Zondi would report for work and use his workstation to conduct his private business during working hours. It was also alleged that he abused his position to influence his business deals, a direct conflict of interest.

Back at my house, Zondi was gloating that I was finished and that their elaborate plan to obliterate my journalism career was in full swing. He couldn't hide his hatred and thirst for vengeance.

"*Sikubambe ngamasende.* [We've got you by the balls.] You are finish and klaar," he told me.

The incursion into my house was actually a sinister plot, hatched at the meeting in Witbank, to plant drugs and guns to help make their "case" against me stronger. Two officers part of this plot have told me this in the presence of two of my colleagues, even giving details of the whole operation. One of the officers spoiled these plans by threatening to go public with the information that they were framing an innocent man. The officer who was part of the team that searched my house later suffered the consequences of his honesty. He was fired from police service.

After the police were satisfied that they had taken whatever they wanted from my house, although they had been prevented from planting drugs and guns and failed to find any briefcase full of classified and sensitive documents, I was taken to the Hawks' head office, still without the knowledge of my lawyer or bosses.

At the Victoria and Griffiths Mxenge Building, as the Hawks' head office is known, I was transferred to another unmarked police car, escorted by four police officers led by Mabasa, and driven more than 300 kilometres to Mpumalanga, the undisputed capital of political killings in this country, where an evil plot had been hatched to kill me.

Mabasa blew the whistle on the plot to kill me, however, after he and his team dropped me off at Waterval Boven police station in Mpumalanga. He took a unilateral decision to lock me up for the night, for my own safety.

Before handing me over to the Waterval Boven police, Mabasa, accompanied by one of his teammates, had pulled me aside and warned me.

"This is very sensitive and dangerous. We have been discussing it with this comrade," he said pointing to a fellow police officer, who was his junior in rank. "You seem to be a good person and we both like you. We are just doing our job."

As I was puzzling over his statement, Mabasa dropped the bombshell. "We have decided to drop you off here for the night for your own safety. We can't give you more information because we would be in danger. I just want to warn you that these guys want to kill you. They want you dead, Mzilikazi. Make no mistake about it.

"While you are here in Mpumalanga, just do yourself a favour: don't eat or drink anything. We know they are going to try and poison you – that's one of their plans. These people want you dead."

The news shattered me. I was stunned, shocked and paralyzed to the bone. I begged Mabasa to phone Van den Berg and make him aware of where I was just in case I was killed that night. After a lot of persuasion Mabasa obliged. It was only then, around 5:30 p.m., for the first time since I was arrested, that my lawyer was made aware of my whereabouts.

I thanked Mabasa and his colleague from the bottom of my heart for the warning and the phone call to my lawyer. I was then locked into a small stinky cell with a blocked toilet along with three other prisoners.

I was paranoid, not sure whether the three prisoners were also part of this elaborate plot and were recruited to kill me in the dead of night.

Ask anyone who has been locked up: the first universal question you are asked when you are thrown into a police or prison cell is, "What are you in here for?"

That was the question that I was asked and my honest answer was, "I don't know."

The three guys thought I was trying to pull the wool over their eyes and did not buy my story until I explained to them what had transpired earlier in the day.

One of the guys who called himself Mathanzima started boasting about his crimes, including the fact that he had killed two women and a man.

"Those women were prostitutes and the man was just a punk. They deserved to die. Nobody messes with Mathanzima," he said, trying to justify his crimes.

I am not sure whether Mathanzima was trying to make me wet my pants with his criminal chronology or whether he was indeed a killer with no remorse. One thing is for certain: Mathanzima looked like a dangerous man and his face was an exhibition of all sorts of scars. If there was a person who was hired to kill me in that cell, Mathanzima was the one, I told myself. Mathanzima and the other cellmate were brazenly smoking dagga (cannabis) there in the police cell.

One of the other three was a man with big eyes like an owl who was reserved and quiet and did not interrogate me. His eyes were red and shining like he was drunk.

For about 30 minutes I paced around the cell, swimming in a sea of confusion. I rattled my brain but failed to make sense or logic of the events that had happened that day. I was lost in a jungle of questions: why was I arrested, who wanted me dead and was my family safe out there?

One thing I was certain about was that my arrest was designed to intimidate me, assassinate my character and portray me as a crook and an unethical journalist.

They had sent a team of armed policemen to arrest me like I was some kind of dangerous criminal or at least a wanted hoodlum, but I neither owned a gun nor did I have any ambition to own one.

My arrest, without any shadow of doubt, had the reminiscence of the dark days of apartheid when police used to pick up anybody they suspected of being involved in any criminal activity. At that time, being a political activist or speaking your mind was a criminal offence. These were the times when four people gathered together could be regarded as an "illegal gathering" and lead to an arrest.

My arrest held a lot of implications and connotations. It came a day after Cele called his press conference. It also came at the time when there was robust national debate over proposed legislation to curtail press freedom, proposals for a new Protection of Information Act and the ANC's proposal to establish a media tribunal.

Many South Africans were up in arms against these draconian proposals, especially the Protection of Information Bill better known as the Secrecy Bill.

The Bill was initially aimed at sending whistle-blowers and journalists to jail for 25 years for passing on and reporting about so-called classified information. It was seen as a shield behind which the ANC was trying to protect its corrupt members from being scrutinised and investigated by journalists like myself.

Coincidentally, on the day of my arrest SANEF was meeting to discuss, among other things, the ANC's onslaught against media freedom.

After I disappeared without trace, kidnapped by men of so-called law and order who refused to tell my lawyer or any member of my family of my whereabouts, the *Sunday Times* editor at the time, Ray Hartley, was forced to go public and he issued a press statement.

In his statement Hartley said, "A member of the *Sunday Times* staff, Mzilikazi wa Afrika, was arrested this morning. We have assigned lawyers to represent him and we are trying to establish what the charges against him are and where he is being held, so far without any success. Our lawyers have been unable to get a clear answer from the police on either of these two questions.

"I am deeply concerned at the fact that a journalist can be arrested and held at an undisclosed location in a country where the rule of law ought to apply.

"He was arrested by a large number of policemen in an operation which was clearly designed to intimidate and I can only conclude that this was the true motive for what took place today.

"Mzilikazi was one of the authors of the story which we published on Sunday about the rental of new police headquarters at the cost of R500 million without following the usual tender procedures. I hope, for the sake of our country, that he was not arrested on spurious charges in order to punish him for what he wrote.

"We are doing everything in our power to have him released and we are doing all that we can to assure his wellbeing."

Zackie Achmat, a human rights activist, also issued a statement saying, "This arrest is an assault on the Constitution and every person in South Africa including those who arrested him, for they too can suffer the consequences of dictatorship should government be allowed to succeed with intimidating the media. Mzilikazi wa Afrika's arrest must serve as the catalyst that unites our society to defeat the Protection of Information [Secrecy] Bill."

While the news about my arrest made headlines around the globe, I was in the dark, cut off from the world of communication. I was not even aware of the outrage and anger it had caused.

As I was being driven around by the police the propaganda machinery kicked in and conspiracy theories started crawling out like cockroaches after dark.

One of the allegations that surfaced was that there was a conspiracy to frame me for bribery. The allegation was that I had accepted money to destroy Mpumalanga Premier David Mabuza and Cele.

Most people do not understand the world of investigative journalism, more especially how we, Hofstatter and myself, as members of the *Sunday Times* investigation unit, work.

We work as a team, share our sources, interrogate each other's information and attend secret meetings with sources together. If we go alone, we brief each other about the meeting and share notes of that particular meeting. At the end of any investigation, our stories are checked by our editor who interrogates every line in the story and all the documents. There is no room for bribery or outside influence, political or otherwise. We do not serve as anybody's blunt influence.

Just before 9:00 p.m. that night, before Mathanzima could kill me as I was thinking he was going to, I was fetched from my cell by two plain-clothes police officers who informed me that they had been given strict instructions to deliver me to General Leroy Mapiyane, the head of the Hawks in Mpumalanga whose offices are in Nelspruit.

I was handcuffed with my hands behind my back and pushed into the third unmarked police car of the day. I wasn't sure whether these men were my hitmen or real policemen. I also did not understand who wanted to see me in Nelspruit at night.

One of the officers was furious and asked me, "Who are you and what is so special about you that we had to stop what we were doing and drive you at this time of the night to Nelspruit? I am tired and I was supposed to be sleeping now after spending the day chasing criminals like you."

I reminded the officer that I was not a criminal and snapped, "I also didn't expect to be driven around in the middle of the night by armed police officers wasting state resources and handcuffed like I were some criminal."

The other officer, who introduced himself as Jabu Mndebele, called for peace and quiet in the car to curb the screaming match. As we were driving in silence, the 9:00 p.m. news bulletin came on the car radio. There was Zondi saying the reason they sent six police vehicles and armed officers to arrest me was because I had "run away" and refused to co-operate with the investigating officer.

The police officers turned in unison and looked at me, and Mndebele asked, "Are you this famous journalist?"

"I am the journalist. I am not sure about being famous," I responded.

"My man," Mndebele said, "you have been on the news the whole day, every radio station and TV channel. Why were you arrested?"

"Ask your boss that question, maybe you will get the answer because I honestly don't know," I answered.

Mndebele picked up his phone and called someone. "Tell me why was this journalist Mzilikazi wa Afrika arrested?"

And the answer was, "I don't know."

"So now you see, not even your colleague knows. I also don't know," I protested.

When we arrived in Nelspruit at 10:00 p.m., Mndebele phoned Mapi-yane to inform him that we had arrived and to check whether I could be delivered.

"Don't bring him to the office right away; there is someone here who I don't want him to see. Keep him in the car and I will call you when the coast is clear," I heard Mapiyane say.

And that "someone" who Mapiyane did not want me to see in his office happened to be Mabuza, the premier of the province. What the premier was doing in Mapiyane's office at that time of the night is a subject for speculation. I also do not know.

We drove around the block until Mndebele, the driver, was told the coast was clear.

Unfortunately for Mapiyane, we spotted the premier leaving the building as his car was parked right at the building's entrance on the main street.

"What is DD [as Mabuza is affectionately known] doing here?" I asked, but nobody answered.

As I was ushered into Mapiyane's office, he had a simpleton's smile on his face, and said, "Ah, my man, Mzilikazi wa Afrika!"

I fired my first salvo of questions, "Why am I arrested and why am I here?"

"Let's talk about it later," Mapiyane said. He instructed Mndebele and the officers to take me away as he was expecting someone who he also did not want me to see.

I am still not sure if it was the same someone I spotted leaving the building or if it was another someone, as I was taken to a place where I could not see anybody moving in and out of Mapiyane's office or the building itself. I was kept waiting for more than three hours.

At about 1:40 a.m. I was taken back to Mapiyane's office, where he told me that I was going to be charged with fraud and defeating the ends of justice. And he read me my rights.

I asked, "What did I do? What fraud did I commit here?"

Mapiyane said I had been writing bad stories about the province and Mabuza.

"Is that fraud?" I asked.

"There are nine provinces and nine premiers, why are you only writing about Mpumalanga and Mabuza?"

"Is that defeating the ends of justice?" I asked him.

"You have written a story stating that the premier of this province has resigned," Mapiyane explained.

"Look, man," I said annoyed, "there is your laptop. Can you please google and see if I have ever written such a story and stop wasting my time."

"Look," he said, "we have prepared a statement for you; just sign it to make things easier."

"General," I asked, "honestly speaking, do you think I am an idiot or a moron? I am not signing anything without my lawyer."

Mapiyane tried every trick in the book to get me to sign that statement and I refused point blank. I did not even want to touch it or read it.

After Mapiyane realised that I would not budge, he instructed his officers

12

to take me to the nearby Nelspruit police station, where I was booked in at 3:20 a.m.

The cell in Nelspruit was bigger and tidier compared to the one at Waterval Boven, but it was overcrowded.

Since I had arrived in the wee hours of the morning, I was not allocated a mattress or a blanket, not that I needed one, so I sat against the wall and eventually fell asleep.

Around 8:00 a.m. on 5 August 2010, I was woken up to the good news that Van den Berg and his team, lawyer Renier Spies and candidate attorney Christopher Picas, were at Nelspruit police station to see me and they had been granted access.

We met in a small office near the holding cells and they had brought with them the daily newspapers. The news about my arrest was in every newspaper in the country, and for the first time I realised how this whole controversy had caused a national outrage. Of course I had expected some public outcry, as my arrest was a clear case of abuse of power and a threat to the journalism fraternity, but for the life of me, I had underestimated the magnitude of the anger and impact it was going to make.

After all, I was one of the most hated journalists in this country: the native causing all the problems for politicians – as my friends call me – because I refuse, like many other journalists, to be a praise-singer for a certain political party or its politicians.

After a brief meeting with the lawyers, Van Den Berg left to have a word with Mabasa about my possible bail application while Spies went to the state prosecutors to look at the charge sheet. He found it was empty.

Three senior state prosecutors called an urgent meeting with Mabasa to decide on his case against me. After more than an hour the prosecutors told Mabasa that I had no case to answer to as there was not enough evidence to put my case on the roll. The police officer, obviously taking instructions from "someone", said he was adamant that I be taken to court.

Mabasa had been given a simple order: arrest Mzilikazi and by hook or by crook haul him before any magistrate and you will get a promotion. Most of all you'll be in the good books of the premier of the province.

Conflicted as he was, Mabasa turned a deaf ear to the three senior state prosecutors' words of wisdom as he was aiming for the possible promotion he had been promised, and wished to remain in Mabuza's good books.

That was not the only drama of the day: after the police were informed the matter could not be placed on the roll, they made a public announcement that I was to appear at Kabokweni Magistrate's Court, 35 kilometres outside Nelspruit, sending journalists and members of my family, including my lawyers, on a wild goose chase.

I was taken in yet another unmarked police vehicle, this time a minibus taxi accompanied by eight police officers, to Kabokweni Magistrate's Court. When we arrived at the court building, the officers were told that they must take me back and deliver me to Mapiyane's office in Nelspruit.

This was justice, I guess, or wasting state resources in the name of justice.

I was kept at Mapiyane's office, like his trophy, until 5:00 p.m. when he and his team began to interview me in front of my lawyers.

The interview was surreal to say the least. One of the questions I was asked by Mapiyane was whether I had "directly or indirectly been discrediting senior office bearers of the ANC in Mpumalanga".

After this mundane interview, Mapiyane refused to release me into the custody of my legal team and insisted that I be taken back to Nelspruit police station.

Van Den Berg asked Mapiyane what good reason he had to refuse to release me into his custody, but the policeman did not have an answer. My legal team immediately brought an urgent court application to the Pretoria High Court for my release and to appear in court the following day for an official bail application or for the case to be withdrawn.

As the legal battle was raging in the Pretoria High Court, I was back in the police cell, where I found out that I was the only prisoner without a cellphone; every one of my cellmates had one.

We were listening to the radio via one of the cellphones when the leading news item on the 10:00 p.m. news was that a High Court judge had ordered the police to release me immediately.

Acting Judge Johan Kruger said, "One minute spent in police custody is one minute too many. The freedom of the individual is a constitutionally protected value and so is due process. In the constitutional state, the Constitution reigns supreme. I am of the view that justice will be served if he is released. It is unlikely that a few hours of freedom should cause irrevocable harm to the state's case. If we err, we err on the side of freedom."

Van Den Berg arrived at the police station armed with the court order and I was released and ordered to report to the Nelspruit Magistrate's Court the following morning.

As I walked out of the police station I was greeted by a group of cheering journalists, and I told them that I was happy to be out. "The truth has set me free and it will continue to set me free. They don't have a case against me."

The following day I was released on R5000 bail in a packed Nelspruit Magistrate's Court. A crowd wearing ANC T-shirts had been sent to the court to insult me and to threaten me with violence.

While I was out on bail, we established that Mabuza was the official complainant in my case. Mabuza's collaborators were two journalists, Riot Hlatshwayo and Alfred Moselakgomo, who were working for our sister publication, the *Sowetan*, and based in Nelspruit, as well as Mabutho Sithole, who was the spokesperson for the premier at the time.

Mabuza, Sithole, Hlatshwayo and Moselakgomo's statements were riddled with contradictions and inconsistencies. Advocate Christopher Macadam, deputy director of public prosecutions at the time, wrote a strongly worded letter after studying the dockets and raised the matter regarding the inconsistencies. He advised the state that should the matter go to court Mabuza and Sithole's contradictions would be "a source of considerable embarrassment".

On 8 September 2010, the National Prosecuting Authority (NPA) officially withdrew the charges against me and I immediately sued the state for wrongful arrest. My legal suit was not about money but a matter of principle.

The State settled the matter out of court, in my view to avoid further embarrassment, and paid me R100 000 plus all my legal costs.

Police minister, Nathi Mthethwa, admitted that my arrest was wrongful.

Hartley, in a statement about the settlement, said, "No case was ever brought against Wa Afrika in court and the *Sunday Times* believes that he was the victim of an outrageous act of intimidation by the police.

"This was a full-frontal assault on the freedom to report on corruption and it is comforting that the minister has acknowledged the arrest was wrongful. However, no amount of money can make up for the pain and suffering experienced by Mzilikazi."

A lot of innocent people were used on my case, a clear abuse of power, and some of them came forward to explain the roles they were forced to play. A lot of lies were said and told to the public.

The former minister of police, Nathi Mthethwa, also made statements about my arrest, which it transpired were not correct.

During a parliamentary debate on 31 August 2010, Mthethwa was grilled about the circumstances under which I was arrested. The minister said, "Madam Deputy Speaker, according to the reports I have received, the arrest was made by the local Rosebank police station after the investigating officer from Mpumalanga waited for more than two hours at the Rosebank station for the person to hand themselves over to the police."

This is incorrect. I was arrested by members of the Hawks, who had come from Pretoria. And I had never refused or delayed handing myself over to any officer.

Mthethwa, who is now the minister of arts and culture, continued to the National Assembly: "When the suspect failed to present himself the investigating officer and two other officers proceeded in one vehicle to the place where this person works. At his workplace a commotion broke out and other vehicles were dispatched to establish the problem. The costs for any arrest are not calculated on an individual basis but are part of the South African Police Service (SAPS) operational budget."

What Mthethwa failed to tell Parliament was that when I walked out of our offices there were already six cars from Pretoria parked outside.

Mthethwa was also incorrect when he said to Parliament: "The person's lawyer was present at the time of arrest and therefore, there was no time delayed in contacting his lawyer."

I was arrested just before 11:00 a.m. and my lawyer was only informed about my whereabouts at about 5:30 p.m., after I pleaded with the investigating officer to inform him for my safety.

At a "peace and reconciliation" dinner meeting requested by Cele and held on 22 June 2012 in Durban, the former police commissioner admitted that he had been duped.

The meeting was attended by me, my colleague Hofstatter, Cele and his spokesperson Vuyo Mkhize.

Cele apologised. "I am sorry I was misled and I caused you harm. It wasn't my intention," he said.

We shook hands, smoked the peace pipe and had a delicious dinner.

My investigating officer Colonel Christopher Mabasa was forced to leave the SAPS and join the department of home affairs after his life was made unbearable in Mpumalanga.

Mabasa's office at Kabokweni police station was set alight after he had failed to deliver me on a platter, and one night there were AK-47 gunshots fired at his house. He was forced to leave Mpumalanga for his own safety.

Mabasa also called a meeting and apologised for the role he played. We met at a hotel near OR Tambo International Airport and he gave me a blow-by-blow account of what really happened behind the scenes.

He still maintained my life had been in jeopardy. "You were supposed to be killed while in police custody," he told me. "They wanted to kill me too because I know too much. I had no choice but to leave Mpumalanga."

Chapter 2

BAYETE: Son of the soil

"A people without the knowledge of their past history, origin and culture is like a tree without roots." – Marcus Garvey

I was born in Sibambayani, a village in the heart of Bushbuckridge, Mpumalanga, one of the nine provinces of South Africa, to parents who had no formal education and would later divorce when I was about four years old.

My village had neither running water nor electricity. To this day, the village still has dusty streets that zigzag across a dry landscape like a Zebra's stripes. They have no names nor do they show any signs of life.

Bushbuckridge, one of the biggest regions in Mpumalanga with more than two million inhabitants, is a place whose beauty has been ravaged by poverty and political myopia. It is sandwiched between Hazyview, the gateway town to the famous animal kingdom, Kruger National Park, and Hoedspruit, a popular game-farming town with its head lying peacefully on the feet of the great Drakensberg Mountains.

Mpumalanga, with its beautiful escarpment and tropical temperature, is the fruit basket of South Africa. It serves the world with a buffet of bananas, avocados, oranges and other exotic fruits.

There is an African proverb that says, "A family is like a forest: when you are outside, it seems dense, but when you are inside you see that each tree has its place." My family history is rich with poverty and decorated with pain.

My mother, Deyiwe Ilina Nxumalo, was one tough cookie. She did not give chase to lizards when the crocodiles were against her. She was an iron lady who pulled no punches and a disciplinarian who took no prisoners.

She did not spare the rod and spoil her children, neither did she take any excuses nor tolerate disobedience. She wanted everything done by the book.

No teacher had caned me as hard as my mother. I must confess I was not an angel but rather a naughty child, a rebel without a cause and a menace to society. I was often involved in fist fights. At times I would disappear for the whole day hanging around with my "friends", only to come home for supper and to sleep. I would take hours just to go to the shop around the corner to buy bread. However, I was never involved in any larceny, and was never a criminal.

My mother was my confidant, bosom friend and worst critic. Slender, regal and as tall as a supermodel, my mother was a natural beauty. Her black skin was soft like silk and her doe eyes twinkled like stars. She used to tease me saying if I brought home a girl less elegant and natty than her, she would chase her away.

"A chick that will grow into a cock can be spotted the very day it hatches," my mother would say. "No amount of rain can wash the spots off a leopard."

And true to her words, my mother chased away two of my girlfriends – some of those embarrassing moments of life.

One girl was accused of being a potential gold-digger, while the other was called a nerd.

"What makes a good woman, my son? It's not the thing between her legs but the things she does as a person. If she talks like her mother and behaves like her mother, then you are going to marry her mother and not her. But if she thinks like a woman, dresses like a woman and conducts herself like a woman even though she is still a girl, then she has the potential to be a good woman and a great mother to your children," she explained.

My mother was a princess of sorts. Her father, Dibane Wickard Nxumalo, affectionately known as Mdibaniso (the one who unites people), was a direct descendant of Mpisane Nxumalo, a Nguni tribal prince. Mpisane was appointed to act as a regent when the Portuguese in Mozambique captured his brother's son, King Nghunghunyane Nxumalo, in 1895.

Mpisane then acted as regent from 1897 to 1910, as one of Nghunghunyane's sons, Thulamahashe, who was the heir to the throne, was still a minor.

Facing a belligerent and ruthless Portuguese administration that was a threat to his subjects and having been defeated on the battlefield, Mpisane relocated almost his entire Shangaan tribe, based mainly around Gaza Province in Mozambique, and settled them in Bushbuckridge, a place in the far Eastern Transvaal. Today, this area is known as Thulamahashe.

In 1910, he resigned to make way for Thulamahashe. At the time King

Nghunghunyane and his two other sons, Godide and Buyisonto, were still in exile.

Reports claim that Nghunghunyane "was the last dynastic emperor of the Empire of Gaza", a territory that is now part of Mozambique. His nickname was the Lion of Gaza. On 28 December 1895 he was captured by Joaquim Mouzinho de Albuquerque at a village in Beleni, ending a reign that began in 1884. Already known to the European press, the Portuguese colonial administration exiled him rather than send him to face a firing squad. He was then shipped to Lisbon, accompanied by his sons, Godide and Buyisonto, as well as 17 senior military officers, before being transferred to the Island of Terceira in the Portuguese Azores, where he would die 11 years later.

In recent years, the Limpopo provincial government decided to honour the Shangaan king with an annual event called Nghunghunyane Day, every September, South Africa's heritage month.

My grandfather had two kids: a boy, the first born, and a girl, who happened to be my mother. She was given the Nguni name Deyiwe, affectionately known as Deliwe in Zulu which simply means "one has had enough".

My uncle, my mother's elder brother, Simon Buku Nxumalo, is a well-known businessman in Giyani, Limpopo Province, and he serves on the royal council for Eric Mpisane Nxumalo, the reigning Amashangane Tribal Authority king, who is his cousin.

Though my mother had never been to school, she was an intelligent woman and very streetwise. And she had cognizance of politics.

One day when I questioned my grandfather on how an educated man like him only managed to send my uncle to school and university but did not do the same for my mother, he said it was not a common practice at the time. He prevaricated when I probed further.

Alone I wondered whether my grandfather had ever heard of an African proverb that says, "If you educate a man you educate an individual, but if you educate a woman, you educate a nation".

In turn, my mother was passionate about education, particularly when it came to her children. You could never miss a day at school, even if you had a "headache".

N'wa-Dibane, as my mother was commonly known, was a social butterfly and a social commentator. As a teenager, I never got along well with my mother. I was obstinate, abrasive and opinionated. We used to argue about everything: my loud music, my choice of friends and even my dress code.

"I don't like that boy; he looks like a thug," she would say. Or, "I don't like that shirt; it makes you look like a punk."

However, our relationship improved as I grew older. We reached a cease-fire, and she would say I had begun to behave like a human being.

Even when I was over 30 years of age, my mother was still expecting me to be home by seven every evening when I visited her back at Sibambayani, where she still lived.

Strangely enough, she never did the same to my siblings. It was not because of age: two of my younger siblings were allowed to come home even after midnight.

To this day, I still do not know why she was so protective of me. Towards the end of her life, however, it seemed some truth of that slipped through: I was her pride and joy. And our mother-and-son fights had since come to an end.

My father, Simon Mashapule Ndzhukula, on the other hand, was the direct opposite of my mother. In contrast to her commanding height, he was small. Her liveliness was juxtaposed by his soft-spoken and reserved nature. Nobody heard my father sing or whistle, shout or scream, not even at us, his children. My father never raised his voice nor punished us. I sometimes think that my mother used to punish us on his behalf, because he could not.

My mother would say to my dad, "Simon, please whip this boy; he is lazy and doesn't listen."

"But he listens to me," my dad would protest.

"Are you scared of your children?"

"You are beating these children every day and turning them into monsters. *Nhonga a yi a ki muti* – beating doesn't solve a problem."

"*Nhonga yi goviwa ya ha tsakama* – if you want a tree to bend in a certain direction, you do it while it is still young – and I will show you how it is done."

My father, like my mother, had never been inside a classroom. A gentleman to those he interacted with and to his family, my father taught me a different, truer form of manhood.

My mother told me I was born just before the crack of dawn on 26 November 1971, which makes my zodiac sign Sagittarius.

Although she and my dad were hoping for a girl as they already had a son they were over the moon to have another boy. I was born exactly four years and one day after my elder brother, Thulani Mishack.

I was named Vusi, short for Vusimuzi – "the one who will raise the family from the ashes".

21

At the end we would be four boys: my two younger brothers were born from my mother's second marriage. We had no sister and sometimes I wish I had one. And sometimes I feel it was a good omen because if I did, I might not have learnt how to cook, wash my clothes and iron them as I do today.

My family's origins can be traced to a small village called Zucula in Gaza Province in northern Mozambique, where my great-grandfather, Gobani Zucula, was born and raised.

Gobani and his family are the traditional rulers of Zucula village, situated about 150 kilometres from the capital Maputo. Today there are still thousands of Zuculas living in that village.

According to oral history there were four Zucula brothers: Rivange, Xigovo, Xirindze and Ntekele, well known as great hunters in their time. They were also witchdoctors. One day they arrived at the Messano (originally Msani) area and found the region barren and facing a severe drought. The land once beautiful and lush was stripped bare and death was everywhere from the lack of rain.

The local chief, Riondo (sometimes pronounced as Liondo) Mkhabela was impressed when their muti (traditional herbs and African magic) produced a heavy rain that created two lakes, now named Rivange and Xirindze. The beautiful lakes can still be seen when you visit the area today.

Happy with the rain that saved his subjects from starving to death, Chief Mkhabela gave the four brothers a huge piece of land and convinced them to settle. The land would be named after their surname, Zucula, and it still uses the name to this day.

The four brothers went home and returned with their elders and relatives to establish their own kingdom. They installed their father, Xipapa Zucula, as their king. After Xipapa passed on, his first-born son, Virrikanhe, became the new chief. Chief Virrikanhe Zucula married Mpetassi Machel, who was one of the grandmothers of the first democratically elected president of Mozambique, Samora Machel.

My clan name is Somungca, also known as Ntekele, Tshevani or Rivange. These were clan names of the early ancestors of the Zucula family.

As they spread, the surname took on the dressing of several pronunciations and spellings. These include Ndzhukula, Ndzukula, Nzukula, Zukula, Zukule and Ndukuya, among others.

Most Zuculas still use the same praise poem for their surname, although some have made additions. The original one is Ntekele, Tshevani, Rivange,

Somungca and Ndzhukula. These were clan names of the early ancestors of the Zucula family.

Now that, I would say, makes me a prince.

After Nghunghunyane was captured by the Portuguese on 28 December 1895, my great-grandfather, Gobani, who was a member of the disposed king's battalion, took his two wives, who were siblings, Mothasi and N'wa-Pfalani, and fled Mozambique. They walked through the bushes for days, evading dangerous animals before they arrived at an unknown village in an area that later came to be known as the Eastern Transvaal, settling there in January 1896.

That village is today known as Sibambayani, where my grandfather, my dad and I were born years later.

Govani's first wife, N'wa-Pfalani, gave birth to their first-born child, a boy he named Nambureti (sometimes written as Namuneti, a Xitsonga word for a soft drink). Nambureti's wife, Hluphasi "N'wa-Nduna" Mbiza, gave birth to their fifth child, Simon, who happened to be my father.

Life at home was all moonlight and roses. We were one of the first families in the village to own a gramophone. There was always music at home as visitors came to admire our prized possession and listen to music. From an early age, music was my life.

At some point in July 1975 my mother decided to visit her mother, Linha Nyankwabo Nhubunga, who was residing at Ngodini near White River. The trip was supposed to be a regular social visit and to collect seeds before the ploughing season began.

I remember my father walking with us to the bus station, carrying me on his shoulders from time to time. Little did he know that my mother was walking out of their marriage for good, without any hint or any reason given to any of us.

That was my mother: an enigma and sometimes stubborn.

That is how my parents "divorced" when I was about four years old. It was a bloodless coup that my mother planned and executed with her radiant smile against my defenceless father.

For some strange reason, I still do not know whether it was anger or pride, but my father never came for us even though he knew where to find us.

We began a new life with my granny, my mother and her two siblings, Racy and the youngest, Amos, who was almost the same age as me.

My grandfather was working at Kwa-Ndabazabantu for Spoornet, now known as Transnet, and was based in Pretoria where he had taken a second wife. She was a city woman and he lived with her in Mamelodi township, East of Pretoria.

My mother and dad never got back together officially, but used to see each other casually. She passed away on 28 August 2006 after a short illness.

It was one of the saddest days of my life. I remember receiving the phone call from my brother just before 6:00 a.m., saying my mother had collapsed just after 5:00 a.m. I feared for the worst but I kept my hopes high. When she passed away, my brother was too devastated even to call me. I received the bad news first from my sister-in-law and later, from my uncle.

It would be my turn to pass the news on to my two younger siblings, Norman and Marvin. Norman, who was 19 years old at the time and the last born, was living with me in my house in Johannesburg. Marvin, born just after me, worked in Secunda where he was a mining engineer for the petrochemical giant Sasol. Marvin broke down in tears and cried over the phone while Norman locked himself in his room crying hysterically.

Regardless of the dark and painful cloud hovering over our heads, we had to gather the courage to drive from Johannesburg and Secunda to Bushbuckridge and make the necessary funeral arrangements.

The lowest point was when my family and friends gathered at my granny's house at Saselani Village near Dwarsloop to pay their last respects to my mother on Saturday, 2 September 2006. It finally dawned on me that day that the woman I called my mother was no more.

I was chosen by my brothers to be one of the speakers at the funeral. To this day I still do not know how I managed to finish my eulogy or what I really said. I spoke from the heart.

My father had remarried after my mother "divorced" him. He and his three brothers attended the funeral, and he announced that he was still her husband. He never demanded his *ilobolo* back and "never stopped loving her". He subjected himself to all the necessary mourning rituals without hesitation.

Years before my mother passed on I asked her why she walked away from what I thought was a perfect marriage. Her explanation shocked me, and seemed childish and immature. She decided to walk out of her marriage, she said, because of "peer pressure": all her friends' husbands were working in *eJoni* (Johannesburg) while her husband was local, a small-town man.

Back then, for reasons unknown to us, my dad returned from Johannesburg to take a job as a plumber with the department of water affairs at Thulamahashe office, under the former Gazankulu homeland administration.

The reason for his sudden return from the city of gold remained a mystery, varying from one person to the next. My father never spoke about this subject to the very end of his journey.

Some of his friends alleged that he *moered* (beat up) his boss back in Johannesburg and ran home to hide from the police. It is alleged that his boss took advantage of my father's natural quietness, verbally abusing him until one day my father had had enough, taking him out with a flurry of punches.

In those days it was a very serious offence to assault a white person. So my father, I was told, sneaked back to Bushbuckridge before he could be arrested for his crimes.

Over the years, he kept his lips sealed.

In those days, working in Johannesburg carried a certain amount of status. After my father lost that status, his beloved wife walked away.

He would return to work in Johannesburg in 1981.

For her part, my mother got remarried to Samuel Mbudzu, and the man treated us like his own blood every time we paid them a visit during school holidays.

When my older brother, Thulani, was sent to Msogwaba Primary School in January 1979, I used to wake up every morning, bathed and ready myself for "school". I cried when I was told I must remain behind, as I was too young.

In those days, you could find a ten or 15 year old in Grade 1. Some of the school beginners were fathers, who had left their children with their wives to come to school.

One day, around February 1979, after my mother was suitably worn down by my requests, she took me to Msogwaba Primary School in Pienaar near Kanyamazane township outside Nelspruit. I was admitted to Grade 1 when I was eight years old. Even though I was in a different class from my brother, I was the happiest boy on earth to be at school.

When I passed at the end of the year, my mother rewarded me with 20 cents for my hard work. At that time it was a lot of money.

As a child I was passionate about music and singing. I sang along to anything, annoying everyone in our home: it seemed I was not gifted in the voice department. My brother used to tease me, saying that I sang worse than any drunkard.

I would be a one-man band, playing an imaginary guitar and using empty tins as my drums – the neighbourhood's most annoying noisemaker.

One day, tired of my irritating voice, my stepdad bought me a spacegram, a vinyl record player, as a present. After this, the neighbourhood was never the same. Each day after school, I would showcase my music with the one 45 vinyl that I would play repeatedly. During the weekends my friends would come and visit, and we would dance as if possessed by evil spirits.

In early December 1980 my mother became ill and was admitted to Themba Hospital in Ngodini, near White River.

My brother Thulani and I were sent back to Bushbuckridge to stay with my granny from our mother's paternal side, Mathambose Nxumalo.

We arrived in the wild and bushy Bushbuckridge on 24 December 1980, and I realised I had no recollection of my birthplace.

Arriving at that village in the middle of nowhere with children of my age running around barefoot, dirty and half naked, I knew that we had been sent to hell. My brother did not have a happy face either. For the first time in my life, I felt rich even though I was poor. The poverty there was palpable and wretched.

I had left Bushbuckridge when I was too young to remember it, but to me the place now looked like a jungle.

Some days after Christmas, my father showed up, unannounced. He had heard that we were around.

We were happy to be re-united with our dad after more than five years and we spent the New Year's Day with my father and his new wife, as well as some of our relatives.

I was enrolled at Sibambayani Primary School in Standard 1, Grade 3, in 1981. My first day was to be marked by drama.

I had a fist fight with a boy, Sipho Khosa, who was three years older than me, over space in our classroom. I had not been allocated a desk. Many pupils, including myself, spent half the day standing against the wall.

Later in the day when Sipho went to use the bathroom (nearby bushes), I moved in, taking his space and refusing to vacate it.

After school he followed me outside and slapped me across the face in front of everyone. Little did he know that I had been doing karate.

I beat him to a pulp, leaving him sore and swollen with a couple of missing teeth. His father brought him to our house the following morning and demanded that my dad take his son to hospital and pay for the damages.

In the process, I had earned the respect of boys at the school: they knew better not to mess with the new kid after they saw what happened to poor Sipho. I also made a couple of enemies, most of them Sipho's friends and allies, but they backed off, as they did not want what happened to their friend Sipho to repeat itself.

I did have another problem, however, living there in Bushbuckridge: language. After five years away I could not speak Xitsonga any more, as SiSwati had become my tongue. I could not write in Xitsonga, nor speak the language. The other children laughed at me.

The school principal at the time, Louisa Mashego née Chabangu, stayed in a school cottage. I made a deal with her that I would water her vegetable garden after school, and in exchange, she would teach me how to read and write Xitsonga and English as my "salary".

Whatever she taught me, I would then go and teach my brother as we were in the same grade and same class this time around.

After six months under principal Mashego's mentorship, I could read and write Xitsonga perfectly. I became one of the principal's favourite pupils. Principal Mashego paraded me as an example of anything good happening at the school.

"If you studied like Vusi, you would be a top achiever just like him," she would say. "If you behaved like Vusi, you would be a better child just like him."

It was all Vusi this, and Vusi that and soon a rumour started doing the rounds that principal Mashego was my distant relative.

My brother and I were always competing for the top positions in class.

In 1983, on the day the Standard 4 (Grade 6) pupils started their final examinations, principal Mashego walked into our classroom to announce that she was promoting my brother to sit for Standard 4 final examinations. As she was walking through the door, she turned around and looked at me and said, "And why are you staying behind?"

My brother and I wrote the examination and passed through to Standard 5 (Grade 7) with flying colours.

In 1984, I was involved in another fist fight at the school with one Reckson Nghonyama, who was more than five years older than me, because he thought he could step on my toes and get away with it.

The following day, I received a whipping in front of the class from teacher Freddy Ngomane, with his infamous green sjambok.

I was one of the Standard 5 pupils in Gazankulu who passed their examinations, which were externally moderated, with flying colours, obtaining a distinction in 1984.

When my brother and I arrived in Bushbuckridge, my family owned a soccer team called Orinocco Sundowns: every boy in the family played for the team.

As I was younger and agile from my karate lessons I was chosen to be the team's goalkeeper. The soccer field was within the school premises and one day during a soccer session in 1982, while standing behind the poles, I heard the Sunday school choir rehearsing. The music was great and the singing was glorious. But the choir leader was a *ximatsatsa*, a "pretty girl".

That night, as soon as I got home, I composed my first song ever for the choir. I would give it to them the following day, during rehearsals.

Truth be told, I composed the song to impress the choir's lead vocalist, whom I had a crush on, and the song was simply titled "Holy Spirit".

> Now the time has come
> Time for Holy Spirit
> Because Jesus has made a promise
> Promise of Holy Spirit
> Chorus: Holy Spirit must come – to me
> Holy Spirit must come – to you
> *Tana tana Moya wo Kwetsima* (come come Holy Spirit)
> *Tana ka mina* (come to me)
> Because Jesus has made a promise
> Promise of Holy Spirit

Everybody in the choir loved the song and encouraged me to write more. At a tender age of 11, I became a "music legend" in the village. And I fell in love with music all over again.

Chapter 3

BOFU: Tears of a blind man

"If you think you are too small to make a difference, you haven't spent a night with a mosquito." – African proverb

I was just thirteen years and one month old when I enrolled at Qokiso High School, a junior secondary, to pursue my Grade 8 in January 1985.

Qokiso is one of many schools built by villagers who believed in the value of education for their children. The modest school built from bricks, with a corrugated-iron roof, was cold in winter and a sauna in summer, and was situated about two kilometres from Sibambayani Primary School.

At the time barbaric initiation practices for young boys and girls coming into high school were rampant. If a concise account of events were to become known, the perpetrators might be hauled before The Hague, the International Criminal Court (ICC), and tried for gross human rights abuse.

We knew we could expect no help from the teachers, who acted as both eyewitnesses and catalysts for much of the savagery that took place. The teachers made us feel like unwanted stepchildren who could not do anything right: if hands were not washed, we were dirty; if hands were washed, water was wasted.

As the saying goes, the best trees grow on the steepest hills. In those days, high school was like a lion's den for young boys and girls. Making it through in one piece, with sanity and humour intact, was not just survival of the fittest, but required the presence of both courage and bravery.

Out of more than 40 pupils in our class, fewer than ten of us were younger than 15. The rest of our classmates were "golden oldies", as we used to call them.

The oldest person in our classroom was a 28-year-old who went by the name of Violet Mnisi. She was a stout woman with a baritone voice, not dissimilar from a man's. She was also a first-grade bully. Some of us could not even take a pee without her permission. I was one of the victims of this corpulent woman. I seemed to become one of her servants, writing her homework and doing whatever else she deemed fit to demand. I had my fair share of fights with men, but she had the power to make me wet my pants. In the Bible, David took his chances with Goliath and defeated the Philistine warrior with just a stone and a sling, but at the time, I did not consider myself to have the heart of a lion nor did I have any wish to give up the ghost.

I used to curse her silently, telling myself hopefully that maybe if she escaped the jaws of a crocodile while bathing in the river one day, she would meet a leopard on her way back from the river.

As part of my initiation I was forced to kick around a *sala* – a green, wild fruit (yellow and delicious when ripe) as hard as a rock and round as a ball. I remember damaging my brand-new shoes beyond repair, the only pair I had. My right foot was swollen for more than a week and I hobbled for days.

Since my shoes were damaged, I had to brave attending school barefoot for the whole year, come winter or summer. Now, there was one golden rule about school initiations: nobody must know about the initiation ritual – *ingoma*.

Consequently, I could not tell anybody about my broken shoes and I would repeatedly lie to my grandfather, Dibane Nxumalo, with whom I was living at the time. When asked why I was not wearing them, the best lie I could conjure up was that I had been playing soccer after school and my feet were dirty.

I was not the only barefoot boy in the village – everyone was used to poverty. In fact, most of us embraced it as a way of life. We were poor, but very rich with love. Nobody would laugh at your rags of clothes or make fun of the hunger dancing in your stomach.

Poverty was a deodorant we wore with pride.

One classmate who caught my attention was Nathaniel "Nat" Makanete. The 13-year-old was from Diepkloof, that part of the world as renowned as Soweto, a black township outside Johannesburg.

Nathaniel was born at Chris Hani Baragwanath Hospital, Soweto, the biggest hospital in Africa, on 29 July 1971. He grew up in the house at 1963 Ritavi Street, Diepkloof, Zone 2, with his mother, Elizabeth Makanete, and his siblings. His father, who owned an amateur soccer team, the Young Tigers, passed away in 1979. Nathaniel was the last born in a family of seven.

Nathaniel began his schooling at Khomanani Primary School in Diep-kloof in 1978. Following the continual disruption of schooling in Soweto after the student uprising in 1976, he was sent to Bushbuckridge, where his sister was married, to continue with his education.

Upon his arrival in Bushbuckridge in 1984, he enrolled at Mpisane Primary School, a school named after my great-grandfather, Mpisane Nxumalo, and I never knew him until we met at Qokiso High School the following year.

Now, we had been told that schooling was fundamental because when we graduated, we would then be able to find better jobs in Johannesburg. So I did not understand why on earth a boy from the city of gold would come and study in the villages with no lights or running water.

Nathaniel was a jovial fellow, humble and down to earth. He was the only person in the class, if not the whole grade, with a dictionary. His sister was married to a local school headmaster, Andries Mathumba, who took over at Sibambayani Primary School.

One of the things I admired about Nathaniel was his soccer wizardry. He was one of the most feared strikers and was admired and idolised by most boys at school. I was a soccer fanatic but did not possess half the skills he had.

Nathaniel and two other classmates, Samuel Mashale and Josiah Masina, would become my best friends. Together, we formed a wolf pack. We were the youngest boys in the class and told ourselves that where the cattle stand together, the lion lies down hungry.

Before I came to Qokiso High School my only friend had been Robert Khosa, who was a grade ahead of me and from my village. Robert and I met after he heard my song, "Holy Spirit". Unlike me, he was a brilliant vocalist and an aspiring songwriter. We became like bread and butter, and have been best friends ever since.

Soccer was the initial bond between Nathaniel and me. We were playing for different teams. He was a striker and I was a goalkeeper but occasionally played as a striker.

One day, after a soccer game and out of curiosity, I asked Nathaniel the million-dollar question on everybody's lips: why did a city boy, affluent as he was, decide to move to a village with virtually nothing to offer?

Nathaniel looked me straight in the eye and said, "My friend, politics forced me out of Soweto, to this place. My family sent me here to be away from politics, to salvage something for my life."

And I asked, "Who is this politics and why are you so afraid of him?"

Truth be told, that day was the first time in my life to hear the word politics. I did not even know its meaning. Instead of laughing at me, Nathaniel explained to me the history of our country. I was not even aware of what was happening out there, beyond the bounds of our village.

Nathaniel asked, "Do you know who Nelson Mandela is?"

"No," I replied.

"Do you know who Hector Pieterson was?" he continued.

"No."

"Do you know what the ANC is?"

"No."

"Do you know anything about Winnie Mandela or Walter Sisulu?"

"No."

"Do you know who Steve Biko or Robert Sobukwe were?"

"No."

"Do you know why there are no white people living in this village?"

"No."

"Do you know what apartheid is?"

"No."

"Do you know anything about 16 June 1976?"

"No."

"Then, my friend you are not living but stealing the oxygen from those who really deserve it," he said mockingly.

This is how I lost my virginity to politics. From that day I was hooked, my appetite was huge and my desire for more was out of control.

Besides the accusation of being an oxygen thief, I was astonished that I knew almost nothing about life. Before this day, I thought I knew everything. I thought I was clever – certainly, I had always been at the top of my class. But I guess I knew nothing of substance.

Nathaniel told me about this man Nelson Mandela who was arrested and jailed for fighting for black people's freedom. He explained that I was a slave without freedom: freedom of association, freedom of speech, freedom of the right to vote, freedom to choose who I wanted to represent me in government.

He added that Nelson Mandela and his "comrades" were languishing in jail, in a place called Robben Island, after the apartheid regime accused them of "terrorism" – this terror being the fight for our freedom. He said

32

those who managed to evade jail had skipped the country and gone into exile, while many others were in hiding or working underground.

He told me about political organisations such as the ANC, PAC and AZAPO, pointing out that they were banned by the apartheid regime.

He told me a mouthful: about the Soweto student uprising on 16 June 1976, about Teboho "Tsietsi" MacDonald Mashinini, Abram Onkgopotse Tiro, Solomon Kalushi Mahlangu and about Steve Biko's death and many others.

"You know what Solomon Mahlangu said before he was hanged at Pretoria Central Prison in 1979?" Nathaniel asked. "He said, 'My blood will nourish the tree that will bear the fruits of freedom. Tell my people that I love them. They must continue the fight.' The man was brave, a soldier of Umkhonto we Sizwe and he looked death in the face and spat on it."

The information Nathaniel gave me was mind-blowing. I was scared and confused. It made me realise that for the past 13 years of my existence, I had been blind. But like the blind man from Jericho, healed by Jesus Christ, my sight would be restored by this young man from Soweto.

Nathaniel made me realise that for hundreds of years, we, as black people, had been lied to and told a distorted history about our beautiful continent, our struggle and our true leaders until African scholars decided to correct the misinformation by dispelling the lies with hard evidence and facts. To this day, nobody has apologised for feeding us propaganda during those days at school.

Throughout those dark years our ancestors were either deleted from the pages of history or described as an uncivilised bunch. We were taught that Jan van Riebeeck was the best thing ever to happen to our country. No teacher told us about Steve Biko, Robert Sobukwe, Nelson Mandela, Walter Sisulu, Winnie Mandela and many others.

Nobody was teaching us that we, as Africans, played a significant role in shaping the culture, politics and history of the world, and nobody taught us that Africa is the cradle of humankind.

One weekend after a soccer game, Nathaniel gave me a neatly wrapped piece of paper and instructed me to read it when I got home but to ensure that I was alone when doing so.

It was the speech that Abram Tiro, a leader of the South African Students' Organisation (SASO), delivered at Turfloop University (now known as Limpopo University) in 1972. Tiro was expelled from the university shortly afterwards.

Nathaniel explained that Tiro was forced into exile in Botswana where he was later killed by the apartheid government's security branch with a parcel bomb in 1974.

As soon as I got home, I locked myself in my room and read it. I still remember the conclusion of the speech. "Let the Lord be praised, for the day shall come, when all shall be free to breathe the air of freedom which is theirs to breathe and when the day shall have come, no man, no matter how many tanks he has, will reverse the course of events. God Bless you all."

Nathaniel kept this supply of information flowing like a river. He became my political commissar and I was his recruit, his protégé.

One day, Nathaniel gave me another package: a copy of the speech Nelson Mandela gave during the Rivonia trial. I read the banned speech several times before I burnt it as per Nat's instructions.

The speech was powerful, filling me with anger and rage, and moving me to tears. Mandela said, "During my lifetime I have dedicated myself to this struggle of the African people. I have fought against white domination, and I have fought against black domination. I have cherished the ideal of a democratic and free society in which all persons live together in harmony and with equal opportunities. It is an ideal which I hope to live for and to achieve. But if needs be, it is an ideal for which I am prepared to die."

And these words echoed in my head over and over again.

When Nathaniel returned from Soweto after the winter school holidays, he gave me a couple of newspapers. These were the first newspapers I had ever read in my life. Even though some of them were old, the information was new and fascinating to me.

Some time later, Nathaniel told me that he had a surprise for me: a tear gas canister wrapped in a plastic bag. He explained how police would use them to shoot at defenceless black people protesting against unjust policies around the country or wherever there was a march.

From the information Nat gave me and the material I was reading, the speeches and the newspapers, I was inspired in 1986 to write my first ever poem titled "Tears of a blind man".

The blind man looks through the window with fear
He tries very hard to hold back his tears
Outside bullets fly like butterflies
His pain and agony nobody wants to hear

34

The air outside is poisoned with death
He thinks about his son in exile
And his daughter in jail
His wife is on the run, she is the most wanted criminal
They say she is an interloper, asking wrong questions to the right people

The blind man looks up to the sky
He tries to find answers beneath the clouds
He hopes God will send him a sign
All he wants is peace and harmony
His rights have been violated so many times
He is tired of shedding so many tears
He has become a prisoner in his own house
A foreigner in his own country
And a stranger to his own brother
Out there is a bullet with his name on it
It is just a matter of time before he can get it

The blind man tries to sing a song of peace
Shut up! Your voice is too loud, they say
He swallows his words with a heavy heart
He steps on the blood flowing freely in his hut
Corpses piling up on the street like dirt
All killed in broad daylight by forces of darkness
From a distance a woman humming a song of sadness
Her husband shot dead for not being a good kaffir
The world has turned upside down
Did God forget we live down here?
The blind man asks himself so many times while trying to hold back his
tears.

I showed the poem to Nathaniel. After reading it, he told me that I had a
dangerous mind, and warned me to be cautious. But he also encouraged me
to write more.

I started then, writing songs and poems, working on a manuscript titled
Afrika my Bequest, Afrika my Patrimony.

The title was inspired by one of the poems I wrote, "Afrika".

Afrika, my bequest
Afrika, my patrimony
Afrika, my kingdom
Afrika, my royal palace
Afrika, my paradise
Afrika, you and I are one
Like fish and water
Like tea and sugar
Afrika, you are the home of the brave,
The home of courageous heroes
And the home of the children of the black Diaspora

Afrika, you are the rolling stone
Rolling from Cape to Cairo,
Rolling from Maputo to Morocco,
Afrika, you are my alpha,
And Afrika, you are my omega
Afrika, the world of chanting warriors
Afrika, the land of unbroken spears,
Afrika, the emporium of this world
Afrika, you are the adamant
Like a mountain, no one can move you
Like nature, no one can change you
Afrika, you are a legend
You stood and survived the test of time

People from Britain
People from Europe
Yes, people from America
The architects of bribery and malice
In my beloved continent
Did you loot our African pride and heritage,
In the name of Christianity?
Did you plunder from Afrika,
In the name of civilisation?
Did you sail slaves ashore?
Did you steal our gold and diamonds?

Afrika, the champion
Afrika, the emperor
Afrika, the martyr
Afrika, the rainbow
Sooner or later
Your sons and daughters shall sing in unison
Songs of liberation and victory
Afrika, sooner or later
You shall be free
Yes, Afrika shall be free, free, free, and free.

It was natural to share this awakening – my discussions with Nathaniel – with my other close friend, Robert.

We were so often in sync. For example, Robert and I played in the same positions for our team: if the team started with me as goalkeeper, Robert would start as the striker, and at half-time we would swap. Then I would be a striker and he would be the goalkeeper. Even though he was older, we got along very well.

My discussions with Robert inspired him to write his first protest song called "African heroes are born to suffer".

I was always a journalist, by instinct if not by training. In 1986, the tenth anniversary of the Soweto student uprising, Nathaniel and I decided to launch an underground "newspaper" aiming to introduce politics to our schoolmates.

We bought an A4 92-page book, popularly known as two quires. We pulled out four pages every week then cut and pasted relevant stories from real newspapers like the *Weekly Mail*, *New Nation*, *City Press* and *Sowetan* and later would circulate our "newspaper" around the schoolyard during breaks.

We used to meet every Sunday afternoon after our soccer game. Nathaniel would come with the newspapers and we would select the relevant stories before cutting and pasting them with tape or glue.

Our "newspaper", called *The Voice*, was circulated "underground" every Monday. At first, most of the students did not understand the stories as they were too political, I guess. We soon began to include editorials explaining the context of the content.

The Voice was soon in great demand: students started discussing and talking politics; debates and informal "rallies" during breaks or after school became normal.

Teachers tried to find out who the culprits behind *The Voice* were but all their efforts were in vain. Some of them even read it, if they could lay their hands on a copy.

One Sunday in June 1986, Nathaniel and I bought paint and wrote on the school wall, "*Siyayinyova*! Viva ANC!"

Location was important and we chose a maximum impact spot. The message was written on the wall where we normally had our morning assemblies: students were required to face the wall, with teachers standing against it. That Monday morning, there was a commotion during the school assembly.

After the assembly, the embarrassed teachers began the hunt for the culprits. All fingers were pointing at Nathaniel and me.

We were hauled into the headmaster's office where we were interrogated and threatened with expulsion. We denied every single allegation levelled against us. We denied vandalising the school wall. We even denied being the brains behind *The Voice*.

As they did not have any witnesses, the charges did not stick. Our cover had been blown, however, and that was the end of *The Voice*. Our mission, though not finished, was successful. We felt the receptiveness and hunger of other students. We knew we had an audience.

Some time later, a snitch told our history teacher, Vusi Bennet Mpangane, about my manuscript, which was always hidden in my school bag.

One day during a history test, Mpangane searched my school bag and pulled out my manuscript without saying a word.

He sat in front reading it, without uttering a word, while we were busy writing the test. I was nervous and sweating. I could see jail written all over me. But I told myself that every man, at one point in his life, must stand for what he believes in and be prepared to suffer the consequences of his beliefs, and if push comes to shove, he must also be prepared to lay down his life for it. That was, and still is, my belief and I was ready for anything.

After we were done with our test and Mpangane was done reading, he asked me to walk with him to the staffroom. Outside he warned me not to bring the manuscript to school ever again, but encouraged me to keep writing.

He said, "One day you are going to be the Nelson Mandela of your generation. Remember, if you ever get caught, I don't know anything about this. I never saw it and never read it."

He gave me back my manuscript with a big smile and said, "Good luck, my comrade."

Mpangane and I became close from that day and we are still friends today. We used to discuss politics outside the classroom. From time to time Nathaniel would be part of the discussion.

Our discussions remained "classified" and "confidential" among the three of us. The struggle at the time was in need of heroes and heroines like Vusi Bennet Mpangane and Nathaniel Makanete. You see, there were many cowards, and very few heroes.

Our alliance came to an end when schools closed at the end of 1987. Nathaniel went to Orhovelani High School, Mpangane remained at Qokiso Junior Secondary School, Robert had gone to Hluvukani High School a year before and I went to Mzwangedwa High School. But we touched base from time to time and kept the flames of freedom burning.

As I was writing this book, Robert was back at Qokiso High School, this time as headmaster.

Commenting on the book, Robert said, "After going through your autobiography I feel as if you have also written mine. It reminded me of a saying by Muhammad Ali which goes like this: 'Friendship is the hardest thing in the world to explain. It's not something you learn at school and if you haven't learnt the meaning of friendship, you really haven't learnt anything.'"

He added, "The way you have articulated the past is an indication of the fact that you are still that kind of person who believes that obstacles don't keep a champion down but make them fight harder. As your friend for many years, I know the mountains you climbed and the hurdles you jumped. It is so exciting and gives me a thrill to know that the end result will be rewarding. Good friendship, good books, and black consciousness – it's the ideal life we worked hard for and struggled for."

Sadly Nathaniel passed away on 9 October 2011 from cancer. At the time of his death, he was a teacher at Nqubela Primary School in Thokoza, east of Johannesburg. He was buried at Avalon Cemetery in Soweto. He was survived by his wife, Ntombi, and three children, Rhulani, Karabo and Musa.

Approached for comment about this book, Mpangane commended my bravery during my school days "for using your brains to put pen on paper on constructive matters, like those dark days where there was no freedom of expression".

He added, "You used your mighty sword to express your views knowing exactly the consequences you were going to suffer when getting caught. Your defiance really contributed as an eye-opener to those who wanted to see things happening without their involvement."

Mpangane said it was hard for him to be seen actively involved because of "fear of the regime" and "sell-outs". He explained, "Even amongst my own colleagues there were sell-outs and, being a coward, I did not want to openly associate myself with freedom fighters, while deep in my heart I was with you and the late Nathaniel in those trying times."

Mpangane, who was once labelled a communist by a senior police officer, added that he "wished to withhold the name of the informant who told me about your manuscript to spare them the embarrassment".

My former teacher said he had secretly encouraged me "to continue writing because it is a legacy that would be left for our great-grandchildren".

His last words of advice were, "My former student, keep up the good work without any fear of victimisation, as you are immune to any."

Chapter 4

MUBHOHIWA: From classroom to prison

"The things that will destroy us are: politics without principle; pleasure without conscience; wealth without work; knowledge without character; business without morality; science without humanity; and worship without sacrifice."
– Mahatma Ghandi

In January 1988, when I walked through the gates of Mzwangedwa High School, a brand-new government school built in Sibambayani, to pursue my Standard 9 (Grade 11), I was looking forward to a new beginning in my life and to meeting new friends.

Nathaniel, Samuel, Robert and Josiah, all friends from Qokiso High School, went to different high schools. I felt like a lone wolf outside the pack.

Mzwangedwa High School, built with a modern style of light brown face bricks and red roof tiles, was a stone's throw from my home. As we were the first group of students, there were no initiation activities for freshmen.

Unlike all the previous schools I had attended, Mzwangedwa High School had electricity, bathrooms and a laboratory.

It also had a library, one that was filled with the Heinemann African Writers Series. I read almost every title that triggered my fancy in one year. It was at this library that I was introduced to the renowned Kenyan author, Ngũgĩ wa Thiong'o, one of my favourite writers, when I read his novel *Weep Not, Child*. I have since collected all of Ngũgĩ's titles for my library at home.

One of my first friends at Mzwangedwa High School was Peter Mbetse – a short and skinny boy full of humour. Hilarious, crazy and outrageous, he could even make a corpse laugh.

He hailed from a neighbouring village called Rainbow, which was part

41

of Lebowa homeland. We became best friends although he could not kick a football even if his soul depended on it.

My second friend at the school was Rooi Vasco Manzini. A well-built young man who was something of a joker – even the way he walked would have you laughing before he even opened his mouth. He was the king of comedy and could make Chris Rock (and my friend, Peter) look like amateurs.

Rooi heard about my poetry writing and political activism. In time, he became my poetry protégé. Rooi and I started attending night vigils, especially those of our comrades from surrounding villages, reciting poetry.

Our English teacher, Ronny Ronald Mkhari, a graduate from the University of Venda, was the fuel that Rooi and I needed for our political tanks. He liked our poems and encouraged us to write more. He coached and mentored us behind the scenes. It is common knowledge that when the leopard has a toothache, then the goat can go and collect a debt.

Ronny studied in Venda, which unlike Gazankulu was an "independent" homeland where political activism was tolerated, to a certain degree at least. Ronny became exposed to politics while studying there.

One of the first assignments that Ronnie gave our class was to study Robert Frost's poem "Mending Wall" and have an open debate about it.

The debate created a great platform to engage one another in a political dialogue and education.

In my debate I argued and expressed how the stone wall of apartheid divided peace-loving South Africans: blacks on one side and whites on the other. Even though most of our neighbours did not want to keep the wall, the system forced us to keep on mending it. Most of our people were afraid to question the continuous existence of this wall, I added. They kept on replacing stones that had been chipped away from the wall, or that had fallen, lest they be labelled as terrorists and be sent to jail.

I explained that most white people were hoodwinked to believe that black and white South Africans living separately would make good neighbours.

I received a standing ovation after I finished with my debate. The word spread through the school. People were surprised that I had the courage to say what I said without any fear of going to jail.

Again, Ronny, behind the scenes, encouraged us to form a Student Representative Council (SRC). When the principal, Henry Siwela, was approached he said he could only accept SRC members handpicked by him and his teachers. Naturally, we told him to go to hell.

Siwela and some of the teachers approached their favourite students and promised them SRC positions. At the same time, we formed a united front and opposed the new SRC, even threatening those students who would accept the nominations from the principal. Just like any election, there were a lot of smear campaigns and malicious propaganda against the election candidates and the election process itself.

It turned out that Siwela and his teachers were scared of one particular individual, our candidate for the SRC presidency, Stanley Mokoena, a well-known comrade with links to the ANC underground structures.

One day, during a break in the raging SRC debate while I was having lunch with my friend, Peter, I was summoned to a meeting that was taking place under a marula tree outside the schoolyard.

As soon as I arrived everybody started clapping and whistling, and I was told by Stanley, who was at the podium, that I had been voted as the secretary-general of the SRC.

I was instructed on the spot to write a letter to the principal informing him that we, as students, had elected our own SRC members and provided him with the list of the elected members – and further that Stanley Mokoena unequivocally was the SRC president.

Siwela and his teachers had no choice but to accept us as the duly elected SRC members after I personally handed him the letter.

Before leaving his office, Siwela warned me that should there be any damage to school property I would be held liable and responsible for it.

"We know you are the leader. I have my eyes and ears on the ground," he said with lot of irritation in his voice. "If you keep going like this, you will be in jail soon. Mark my words."

Stanley and I became close and spent more time together. He used to take me on several trips into the Venda homeland to attend United Democratic Front (UDF) rallies where I would recite my poems. Ronny sponsored some of the trips.

After months of working together as SRC president and secretary-general respectively, Stanley told me that he wanted to introduce me to someone. We took a taxi to Acornhoek and got off along the way near a village called Ka Josefa.

After walking for a few minutes through the bushes, we waited under a tree for about 30 minutes. Then there was a soft whistle and a well-built young man with a clean-shaven head wearing a brown T-shirt and camouflage pants emerged from the bush. He was alone. He walked slowly towards us like he was counting his steps and his eyes were everywhere.

He was carrying a bag, held like a prized possession.

This young man did not even greet me. He took Stanley by the hand and walked a few metres away from me where they began chatting in whispers. I could see it was a friendly chat from the smiles and constant shaking of hands. The young man disappeared into the bush without acknowledging me.

Stanley and I walked back the same way we had come, taking different taxis – he was from Acornhoek. I went home, which was in a different direction.

Before Stanley left, he said the young man's name was BA and that he liked me. I was puzzled as BA had looked at me with suspicious and probing eyes and had not uttered a word to me.

Weeks later Stanley took me on another trip to see BA: same directions but different stop sign. Same modus operandi: we took a taxi, got off somewhere seemingly random then walked through the bush before waiting under another tree.

As usual, BA appeared from nowhere, wearing the same clothes.

This time he was cheerful and greeted me, addressing me as "comrade". He even introduced me to his "girlfriend" – a Makarov semi-automatic pistol in his bag – the same one he was carrying when we first met. BA was never without his girlfriend in almost all the encounters I had with him.

He interrogated me about my knowledge of the struggle: the ANC leadership in exile and in jail. He was taken aback that I knew more than he thought. He seemed impressed.

Again he confirmed that his name was BA, which I believed was taken from a television series macho man, Sergeant Bosco "BA" Baracus, better known as Mr T from *The A Team*.

He encouraged me to remain at school because, he said, "Oliver Tambo [then ANC president who was in exile] wants educated cadres.

"When some of our comrades skipped the country to exile, some of us decided to stay behind and fight. And we need young men and women who can read and write when we take over this government one day. Even a soldier must know how to count his bullets. The regime must be fought from all directions. From this village to all the townships, from Lusaka to Maputo, they must feel the heat," he said without a smile while brushing his bushy goatee.

He requested me to recruit more youths under the auspices of the South African Youth Congress and advised me to form underground cells for my troops.

He enquired about my reason for staying alone in a two-bedroom house while most African family homes are filled to the brim with many family members. I told him that it was by choice to be alone.

He asked me to bring my *josaka*, a school bag that was popular at the time, to our next meeting as he had an assignment for me.

"Our comrades on the other side are starving and I want you to carry some groceries for them," he said.

The next meeting came a few weeks later – same modus operandi, but different location. BA loaded my school bag with groceries – 9-mm pistols. I was given strict instructions: walk back home, no taxi ride and no hitchhiking.

I was also told to keep the bag at home. The comrades would come to collect during school hours and I must not lock the doors.

Two days later when I returned from school the groceries had been collected. There was a sign, on the table, that the right person(s), as per our agreement, had collected them: a copy of *New Nation* had been left behind.

Stanley and I undertook several more of those trips to "collect the groceries and feed the hungry nation" from BA.

The groceries changed from time to time, from pistols to assault rifles such as AK-47s: the *josaka* was for pistols while the *Shangaan* bag was for assault rifles.

BA and I became closer the more we met, but I hardly knew anything about him: his real name, where he lived or his position within the ANC or Umkhonto we Sizwe. I was just happy that I was part of our people's struggle against apartheid. All our meetings were brief and all instructions were given to Stanley.

To this day, I do not even know the person(s) collecting "the groceries" from my house, but the one thing I do know is that the guns were coming from Mozambique.

I later interviewed ANC stalwart Jacques Modipane, who was BA's handler and his mentor at the time, while writing this book.

He said, "I gave Ripho the name BA because he was our Mr T, a man of action: a militant genius and very aggressive. Most of the guns that you used to carry around were coming from Mozambique. We had other comrades smuggling them across the border. Then it was you and other recruits, mainly the youth who wouldn't draw any suspicion from the public and police, to move them around from village to village. It was the only way to arm our people."

He explained that after they heard about my arrest, they did not have sleepless nights as they knew even if I was tortured I could not reveal anybody's identity as I did not know the entire network except for BA, and of him I knew very little.

"Our strategy was simple: you didn't know who was collecting the guns from your house and you also didn't know the supplier. Nobody knew who was who in the zoo except the top leadership."

One man who was the catalyst of the gun suppliers from Mozambique was Nakedi Mathews Phosa, an ANC member who was in exile in the former Portuguese colony with the blessing of the Mozambican president, Samora Machel and his party, Frelimo. Phosa, a Mbombela Nelspruit-born politician, is a lawyer by profession who later became the first premier of the Mpumalanga province. He attended Maripe High School in Bushbuckridge – the school later changed the name to Orhovelani High School – before his family moved from there.

In fact it was the whole Bushbuckridge region, led by Modipane, that pushed for Phosa to be the first chairperson of the ANC in Mpumalanga after the liberation movement's unbanning. Phosa took over from Ntombi Shope, who was a caretaker chairperson deployed by Luthuli House, the ANC head office.

Phosa was one of the first four ANC members who entered South Africa from exile in 1990 to start the process of negotiations with the National Party government that led to our first democratic election in 1994.

He was also legal adviser to the ANC and served as a member of the party's National Executive Committee (NEC), as well as the treasurer-general.

It was after the unbanning of the ANC that I later learnt that BA was born Ripho Machate in Brooklyn, outside Acornhoek in Bushbuckridge, on 3 February 1965. Modipane recruited Ripho to join the ANC underground structures in 1986.

That year Bushbuckridge was burning: the youth were up in arms and burning businessmen who were making a killing. Some of these businessmen became millionaires, literally from killing local residents and selling their body parts to so-called witches. The businessmen and the witches were rounded up and burnt to death one afternoon. And Ripho was at the forefront of those youth.

When the ANC heard about this chaos, the burning and looting happening in Bushbuckridge, they summoned Modipane to Swaziland where he was instructed to put an end to it and recruit the youngsters into the ANC and join the real struggle.

Upon his return from Swaziland, Modipane and local ANC members formed the Bushbuckridge Crisis Committee. Ripho was one of the youth recruited.

"I told Ripho that there was a bigger struggle to pursue than to kill and burn so-called witches and business people," Modipane said.

Modipane organised for Ripho to get a crash course in military training at Swalala village outside Hazyview.

"We used different houses for those courses and the youth we identified as future leaders were taken in. Ripho was later sent to Mozambique for advanced military training late in 1987. He was a polished diamond, a born soldier. He played a very important role, not just in Bushbuckridge but in the whole of Mpumalanga," Modipane explained.

Businessmen implicated in the human body-parts killings, and those who were benefiting from the apartheid regime, formed a vigilant group called Sofasonke Civic Union in Bushbuckridge. Sofasonke was sponsored by the apartheid government, in particular the Lebowa government, and protected by the police and South African Defence Force.

A school headmaster, Chocket Nelson Mashile, who was the first cousin to the local chief, Nkotobona Chiloane, became the leader of this group. With the help of the police, they went around hunting the youth who were involved in the burning of the businessmen and so-called witches. They then proceeded to murder some of them and burn their houses.

Anybody on Sofasonke's list of "most wanted criminals" would be arrested by police and tortured by both police and soldiers.

Ripho was arrested, on Sofasonke's instructions, along with a group of other "comrades" on 24 October 1989. But when the group appeared in court three days later, Ripho was missing.

It later transpired that police had brutally assaulted Ripho and pushed him into a hole when they wrongly assumed him dead. He had lost consciousness. The police were surprised when he came round but they refused to take him to the hospital. One of the officers is reported to have said, "The dog was not dead," and Ripho was taken back to the police station where he was assaulted again.

Ripho's lawyer had to convince the police that they had wrongfully arrested his client and were compelled to bring him before the court. The police were forced to bring a badly bruised Ripho to court on 30 October 1989, although he was only released on bail the following day.

After Sofasonke realised that police arrests and brutal assaults did not break the spirit of the "comrades" they decided to burn seven houses on 26 November 1989 – my eighteenth birthday – belonging to some of the families of these youth. Modipane's and Ripho's family houses were gutted and the families left homeless.

To this day, Ripho's family has not been compensated for their loss. The new government "rewarded" them with an RDP house – paper walls that blow over whenever there are strong winds.

On the same night of 26 November, Modipane collected 22 youths who were on Sofasonke's most wanted list and smuggled them to Swaziland. Ripho was one of them.

Just weeks after former president FW de Klerk unbanned the ANC and other liberation movements, Ripho, who was still on the police list of "most wanted criminals", managed to sneak back into South Africa.

He addressed a low-key rally on 4 March 1990 where a decision was taken to deal with Sofasonke members responsible for the burning of the seven houses in 1989, including his family home. The following morning, on 5 March 1990, a sedan vehicle whose official registration number was BFB 035 T, parked at German Chiloane High School at Moloro Village outside Acornhoek where Chocket Mashile, the leader of Sofasonke, was a headmaster. A local businessman and "comrade", Edward "Boy Boy" Hlongwane, drove the car and he arrived at school that morning around 7:30 a.m. Its number plate read: "MANDELA".

One of the passengers was Ripho Machate.

Chocket Mashile, smelling trouble, pulled out his gun and tried to shoot at the overloaded vehicle but he was pelted with stones, disarmed and set alight in front of the shocked school children. His bakkie, which was parked within the school premises, was also torched. Unconfirmed reports claim it was Ripho who crushed Mashile's head with a rock before he was burnt.

The crowd, now joined by some of the school children whose relatives and friends had been victims of Sofasonke, proceeded to Mashile's house and burnt it as well. Three other members of Sofasonke managed to escape

EXCLUSIVE BOOKS

MORNINGSIDE

Tel: (011) 798-0210/1

Shop B37, Morningside Shopping Center

VAT Reg # 4710258628

TAX INVOICE

49259 Reg 2 ID 91 10:05 am 02/11/14

Sales for Fanatic Member

000 783 446

E NOTHING LEFT TO S 1 @ 246.00 246.00

E 9780143538929

SUBTOTAL	246.00
V	0.00
TOTAL	246.00
DASH PAYMENT	250.00
CHANGE	4.00

Receipt Amount Includes VAT @ 14%

death. One of them, Donald Father Dilebo, was attacked with a panga and had his car set alight.

Bushbuckridge was burning again, an eerie resemblance of 1986.

Ripho was back on the "most wanted criminal" list. He skipped the country, heading back to Swaziland but continued to sneak in and out of the country from time to time. He would address us at Maripe High School, outside Greenvalley, in full disguise. He was convicted in absentia for the murder of Mashile.

Ripho received full military training as an Umkhonto we Sizwe cadre in Tanzania. He returned to South Africa officially in 1991 at the time the ANC and the apartheid regime were locked in negotiations for a transition to a democratic society. It was at this point that Ripho and I got to know each other better. He first became a bodyguard to Modipane, who was then finance MEC, before being seconded to be Mathews Phosa's bodyguard. Phosa was Mpumalanga premier at the time.

As a bodyguard, Ripho later saved Phosa's life during a freak car accident on 25 June 1998. He was the last man standing after the accident but later fainted as the ambulance was rushing everyone to hospital.

Phosa was travelling to Johannesburg from Nelspruit, after arriving from Germany where he attended a meeting with investors, when his brand-new Mercedes Benz 280E collided with a 22-metre long truck on the N4 freeway in Wonderfontein near Belfast. The car had been bought a week before the accident. Ripho managed to pull Phosa out of the car seconds before it burst into flames.

Phosa broke his left leg and was admitted to Middelburg Med Hospital for a week. Ripho and his colleague, Patrick Mathebula, as well as the driver, Theli Magagula, sustained minor injuries. When Phosa was discharged from hospital, he hosted a party where he thanked the trio, especially Ripho, for saving his life.

Ripho died mysteriously on 19 November 1998. His death has raised more questions than answers. Officially we were told that Ripho committed suicide by shooting himself in the head but circumstances surrounding his death suggest otherwise.

A few days before his death, Ripho had a verbal clash with one of Phosa's bodyguards and he decided to take a few days off to cool down. While he was home in Brooklyn, he received a phone call informing him that his leave days had been revoked and he should report to work the following day.

Hours after he returned to a room he was renting at Pienaar in Msogwa-ba on the outskirts of Nelspruit, he allegedly shot himself in the head after an argument with a "woman from Swaziland".

The Ripho who most of us knew and loved was not suicidal. He went through a lot in his life and had a promising career. Never once did he, to our knowledge, even consider it.

It later emerged that Ripho's leave days were in fact not revoked and that he was not expected at work the following day. The person who made the call was not even questioned. The case was closed as a suicide.

During an interview for this book, Phosa, who also spoke at Ripho's funeral, said, "I have never understood Ripho's death; it's one of the most mysterious deaths that couldn't be explained. The killings in Mpumalanga started earlier and Ripho's death is one of them. As usual, just like most of the killings in Mpumalanga, nobody was arrested or prosecuted for that."

Phosa said Ripho was a loyal and disciplined man who was a committed member of the ANC. "He was a very intelligent person," he explained.

When asked for comment about being my mentor and funder, my high school English teacher, Ronny Mkhari said, "No one expected that a young man from the dusty streets of Bushbuckridge could one day rise up and be counted amongst some of the thinkers of this country. I believed in you from the first day I met you as your teacher because you were sedulous, not just as a student, but also to the struggle, and became your mentor, financing some of your clandestine trips to Venda to be schooled politically. You were a rough diamond that needed to be polished and a very brave young man who refused to shout in silence. I feel proud, humbled and honoured to have been a catalyst in your life, but most of all, I am elated that you turned out to be more than what we expected of you and made all of us proud."

Sometime in 1989 a man who looked like the former Ugandan dictator Idi Amin appeared overnight in our village with his coloured-looking wife, their son and a herd of cattle. Rumours started flying that the man was one of the "witches" involved in the human body-parts saga. It was also reported that he had escaped from another village after his homestead had been burnt to ashes.

The elders in the village approached me as the local leader of the youth and asked if I could arrange a general meeting with the local *induna* (head-man), Sherman Qhibi, to address the matter of this man's appearance in the village.

The *induna* agreed to the public meeting and as instructed by the elders

I addressed him as the representative of his subjects. I said this uninvited guest was not welcome as he had a bad track record. I requested the *induna* to inform the man, his wife and son that they should find refuge at another village, as we were not willing to have them in our midst. The *induna* washed his hands of the matter and said we must do as we wished.

At home we had a two-ton truck since we owned a brick-making factory. We loaded the man, his family and all their belongings into the truck and ferried him to another village of his choice. When I returned from the trip I discovered that one of the man's houses, a rondavel with a thatched roof, had been burnt to ashes and his other house had also been vandalised.

All was well, we believed, but we had attracted the vultures – the police.

A week later I was invited to recite a poem at a UDF rally in Venda and on my return I found that police had arrested some members of the executive committee from our underground cell.

My cousin, Charles Ndzhukula, and I had become wanted criminals. I rounded up everyone from our underground cell who had managed to escape the arrest and we spent the next two days hiding in the caves and bushes while strategising our next move. Nobody was going to school. Police cars were patrolling our villages and harassing our parents, searching for us.

One morning on 9 October 1989, as I was returning from the cave to collect food and clean clothes at my home, I was arrested by a policeman who was hiding in the outside toilet. I had walked into the toilet, ready to do my business and there was a gun pointed straight at my forehead. I was told that I was under arrest.

I was then handcuffed and assaulted. The officer made a call to his colleagues via the two-way radio and reported that he had just caught the "big fish". When the other police officers arrived, I became a punching bag. I was assaulted with the butt of a gun, stomped with police boots and beaten.

All the time the officers kept asking me where the guns were. They said they had a sworn statement from a police informer who confirmed that I had a stash of all sorts of guns in my house, that I was a terrorist and an ANC member.

They ransacked my house looking for guns and ammunition, taking any documents they found, including collections of my newspapers and books such as *By Any Means Necessary* (Malcolm X's speeches and writings).

After the police failed to find any arms cache, they took me to Mhala police station in Thulamahashe where the interrogation and torture continued.

Little did they know that the guns were hidden inside the coal stove in the kitchen. The stove had not been used for months and the pots on top were placed there as a disguise. That simple trick saved me from possible treason charges and life imprisonment.

At the police station, my explanation that I was just a student who knew nothing about guns fell on deaf ears. One of the officers angrily said in Xitsonga, "*Namuntlha u ta baba ka nharhu, u ta wu nya ntiyiso.* [Today you will shit three times, you are going to shit the truth.]"

The officer asked me, "Tell us how many times you have been to Mozambique and Swaziland?"

"I can't go to Mozambique or Swaziland as I don't have a passport or know anybody there."

Clap! Kick! Punch!

"Who is supplying you with all these guns?"

"I don't know anything about guns, you've searched my house and you didn't find a single gun or a bullet."

Clap! Kick! Punch!

"Who is your commander?"

"I don't have any commander. I told you I am a student."

Clap! Kick! Punch!

"Give us the names of your handlers and we will let you go home."

"I don't have handlers."

Clap! Kick! Punch!

"Where did you get these books?"

"I bought them in Johannesburg."

Clap! Kick! Punch!

"Do you know Stanley Mokoena?"

"Yes, I know him."

"And do you know he is a comrade?"

"I know him as my schoolmate at Mzwangedwa. I don't know what he does after school as he stays at Acornhoek and I am staying at Sibambayani."

Clap! Kick! Punch!

"Do you know Ripho Machate?"

"I have never heard that name before."

Clap! Kick! Punch!

"I swear to God."

Clap! Kick! Punch!

"What were you doing in Venda?"

"I went to the University of Venda to submit our applications for next year. I want to study as a dietician there."

Clap! Kick! Punch!

One officer screamed, "Stop lying, you piece of shit!"

The officer shoved a gun into my mouth and threatened to blow my "shit brains all over the place".

I was assaulted until I passed out. When I regained consciousness I was inside a police cell with other inmates.

I was officially facing 16 charges including burning a police car, being found in possession of an AK-47 and being a gun smuggler.

The same afternoon after my arrest, half if not all of my villagers arrived at Mhala police station in trucks and handed themselves to the station commander at the time, one Isaac Mnisi, in solidarity.

Mnisi's biggest headache was that he could not lock up everybody in his police station: there were hundreds and hundreds of villagers. In the end, Mnisi decided to lock up every villager who was at the meeting with the *induna*. He suspected that those were the comrades and sent everybody else home.

All the men, young and old, were locked up in one cell and the women in another. I was one of the 45 men crammed into cell number two. The cell had an invasive stench, disgusting and inhuman: it was not even fit to hold suspects, whether criminals or not.

It was tiny, filthy, suffocating and smelt like a urine and faeces brewery. The stinking came from what used to be a stainless-steel toilet bowl but now looked like it would eat your bum if you sat on it. To make matters worse, the drinking-water fountain was next to the filthy bowl.

The cell wall was like a notice board: it seemed to me that everybody who had been there left some kind of writing on it. I did too. I simply wrote, "Mzilikazi: the warrior was here. Aluta Continua!"

Most of us were arrested just weeks before we could sit for our end of year examinations, including the matriculants, and we were strictly told that no books were allowed inside the police cells.

I then received a message, smuggled through by one of the police officers, that Francis Legodi, who is now judge of the North Gauteng High Court, Pretoria, had been hired as our lawyer. Mathews Phosa told me that he was instrumental in getting Legodi as our lawyer.

"After I received the message that you were arrested, I made the call to Francis requesting him to take care of the situation," Phosa said.

He added that they had police informers who were notifying them whenever one of the "comrades" was arrested. "We armed people not only in Bushbuckridge but as far as Polokwane. We had a lot of young men like you distributing guns to the right people. Locally not everybody knew who was who in the zoo but outside we knew what was going on and everyone.

"We had an arrangement that whenever one of the gun runners is arrested for political activism we should defend them. The young men and women were risking their lives for a good cause and we had to show that we care."

Legodi had been Phosa's second articled clerk at the politician-turned-businessman's former legal firm Phosa, Mojapelo and Partners, the first black-owned law firm in Nelspruit. Phosa was a partner at the firm before he went into exile.

I had no previous criminal record and had a fixed address. Most of all, I was a student who was about to write his matric examination. Legodi did not need major convincing to secure bail for all of us. I was released on R1 000 bail while the rest were released with a warning.

After writing my last examination paper, Stanley informed me that he had been instructed to "take me on vacation" as members of the notorious Security Branch were circling us like vultures. That night I said goodbye to my comrades. I was smuggled out of Bushbuckridge at 1:00 a.m. after making sure "the chickens had gone to sleep".

They took me on "holiday" to Embalenhle township in Secunda, about 300 kilometres away, for the festive season, where I stayed with my uncle, my father's younger brother, Edwin Ndzhukula.

Magistrate Hanyani Mnisi postponed our case several times while waiting for the police to produce their evidence: a burnt police vehicle, an AK-47 found in my possession and witnesses to come forward linking me to gun smuggling or supplying arms to comrades. But as the police failed to produce any evidence or any witnesses, Magistrate Mnisi was left with no choice but to strike the case from the roll in April 1990. The ANC had been unbanned by then and was no longer referred to as a "terrorist organisation".

We were free to carry on with our lives with no monkey on our backs.

After reading this chapter, Judge Legodi commented, "When most people read your memoir, some of them might think it's a work of fiction because they don't know what you guys in Bushbuckridge went through. The history and the struggle of the people of Bushbuckridge has not been told to the nation. You guys went through hell and survived. As a lawyer working in that community, I witnessed your struggle, trials and turbulences, and I have seen it all."

Legodi promised that in his biography, which he plans to write soon, he will tell more stories about the tears, pain and joy the people of Bushbuck-ridge went through during the struggle.

Chapter 5

WA AFRIKA: Watering the roots

"Tigers die and leave their skins; people die and leave their names."
– Japanese Proverb

My friend Robert Khosa went to the University of the North (now known as the University of Limpopo) to study towards his Bachelor of Science degree in 1989 while I was doing matric.

We managed to sell two of his granny's cattle to the local butcher to pay for his tuition fees. The beasts were sold with *gogo's* blessing.

After a few months at "Turfloop", as the university was affectionately known, Robert sent me two books. One was Archbishop Desmond Tutu's biography, *Voice of the Voiceless* by Shirley Du Boulay and the other Chief Albert Luthuli's autobiography, *Let My People Go*.

Besides being the former president of the ANC, Luthuli in 1969 became the first black South African to be awarded a Nobel Peace Prize. He was a former school teacher who inherited his chieftaincy after his grandfather died. This was long before threats and insults started ruling this country's political platforms.

The two books inspired my thirst for knowledge about our struggle for freedom and fighting for our rights. The books became like a force of nature, pushing me to new heights.

During the winter school holiday, Robert told me about a film he had watched at the university called *Roots*. It was based on a book by American writer Alex Haley, who is also the co-author of *The Autobiography of Malcolm X*. Robert explained that *Roots* was about an African teenager from the Mandingo tribe named Kunta Kinte, who was kidnapped from a village called Juffure in The Gambia in 1767 and taken to America where he was sold as a slave.

The slave master, John Waller, who bought Kunta Kinte at the slave market, tried to give him the slave name "Toby", but Kunta Kinte refused to accept a foreign name. He chose to remain true to his African roots and kept his African tribal name.

Robert emphasised that Kunta Kinte was repeatedly beaten and forced to accept his slave name but refused. After frequently trying to escape he had his right foot chopped off.

Nathaniel managed to get a copy of *Roots* on VHS after I told him about it. Though the movie is long, I watched it over and over again. I was touched, moved, motivated and inspired. I thanked God a million times that I was an African. I was, and still am, proud to be black and African.

I began to search for my own roots and I decided to drop my English name, Leonard, which is a slave name. I wanted something representative, a name that would identify me as a true son of the soil. A name that would speak for itself, identifying who I am and what I believe in as a person and what I stand for as an individual.

A true African name must carry some weight and identify the person either by tribe or rank in the society. Most African names described, and some of them still do, events that were happening at the time of your birth or what inspired your father at the time. Fathers have to name their children first before the mothers give them second names.

An African proverb says a good name is better than riches. Even the Bible endorses it in Proverb 22:1 where it says, "A good name is more desirable than great riches; to be esteemed is better than silver or gold".

Tokunbo Adelekan in his book *African Wisdom: 101 Proverbs from the Motherland*, explores the basis of this proverb. "Abraham is known for his faith, not his finances. Job is regarded for his patience and not his pecuniary fortune. Solomon had the world's wealth, yet he prayed for wisdom, not wealth," wrote Adelekan and he concludes, "Be a person of integrity, peace, and justice, and your name will provide you access to places that money cannot."

I didn't want to be a Toby in *Roots* or to be known as Leonard any more. If having an African name was too much for my slave master and his brainwashed servants, I too was prepared to be sjamboked with harsh words and whatever venom would come my way. *Roots* changed my way of thinking, how I looked at myself and my way of life.

After weeks of soul-searching and toying around with different names and researching in the library, I announced to my friends and shocked class-mates in the spring of 1989 that my new name would be "Mzilikazi wa Af-rika", which simply means "Mzilikazi from Afrika". Mzilikazi means "a little path", and this would be the road of my journey in life.

I was also inspired by the history of King Mzilikazi, a fearless warrior and one of the great Shaka Zulu's advisers. He freed himself from Shaka Zulu and defied the great king after he had been sent to attack Chief Ranisi. After defeating the Sotho chief, Mzilikazi took the spoils and rounded up everyone to start his Ndebele Empire. He settled across Limpopo River, conquering the small tribes along the way. He died in Ingama, Matabele-land, in Zimbabwe near a place today known as Bulawayo on 9 September 1868.

Mzilikazi kaMashobane was a rebel against King Shaka Zulu and I saw myself as a rebel against the apartheid regime. My new name, Mzilikazi wa Afrika, made me feel completely new. Not like an old wine in a new bottle or rotten bread buttered on both sides. I felt like a man who has just embraced a new religion, a man who has recently fallen in love with the woman of his dreams. Like a house that has just been painted, I could smell the fresh paint dripping on my soul. After all, I didn't want to be a South African living in Africa; I wanted to be an African residing in South Africa. God created me an African but politics, tribalism and geography made me a South African.

A month or so after selecting my new name, I received an invitation to the Congress of South African Writers' Annual General Meeting in Johan-nesburg. The letter was addressed to me as Mzilikazi wa Afrika. Nathaniel had sent them my manuscript, *Afrika my Bequest, Afrika my Patrimony*.

I was 18 years old and had never been to Johannesburg. I had heard conflicting stories about the city. But I was excited to be recognised by the Congress of South African Writers and to be invited to such an occasion.

Friends, comrades and classmates raised the money for my transport, enough to take me to Johannesburg and back. I arrived at the busy Noord taxi rank and asked around for the directions to the Congress of South African Writers' offices in Braamfontein as specified in my invitation letter.

The Annual General Meeting was held at a Protea Hotel on the corner of O'Reilly and Tudhope in Berea. My accommodation was booked at the Moulin Rouge Hotel in Hillbrow, one of the best hotels at the time though it would eventually become a haven for prostitutes and drug dealers. It was my first time sleeping in a hotel.

My friend Robert had bought Mzwakhe Mbuli's first two albums *Change is Pain* and *Unbroken Spirit* and he made me listen to them for inspiration. I was blown away and hooked on his poetry. His poems were like "fuel for the feet and food for the brain". Like a drug that I needed every day to get myself going, it inspired me. Mzwakhe Mbuli's art of romancing with words left me mesmerised, and influenced me to change my way of writing poems. He seduced me with his passion.

I had shots of "Mbulism injections" as I walked into the Council of South African Writers' AGM to rub shoulders with some of the country's best writers and poets. Even though I was the youngest kid at the conference with no writing credit to my name, everybody treated me with great respect.

It so happened that after being inspired by Mzwakhe Mbuli, I had written a poem titled "We March" for this special occasion. Coincidentally, acclaimed playwright and poet Maishe Maponya also wrote a poem with the same title. We had never met but we both recited our different versions of our poems on the same platform.

The incident brought Maishe and me closer and we became friends. Maishe also played a part in the early stages of editing this book.

We march
From Thulamahashe to Thabazimbi
From Thokoza to Thohoyandou
From Soweto to Soshanguve
From Khayelitsha to Kwa-Mashu
We march
Embracing the spirits of our forefathers
Paying the instalments for our freedom
A spear in one hand
And a shield on the other
We march
From dawn to sunset
Singing and chanting
Lizobuya izwe lethu
Ziyojabula izizwe
We march
From Tugela River to *intaba zokhahlamba*
From Phelandaba to Pretoria

From Mdantsane to Mtubatuba
We march
Facing guns and bullets
Without fear or compromise
With blood oozing from our wounds
We march
It's death or glory
No pain, no gain
No retreat, no surrender
Hand in hand
We march
Forward we go
And backwards never
United against tyranny
Black and white
We march
From Umtata to Umlazi
From Sebokeng to Seshego
From Mmabatho to Mamelodi
We march
Like great warriors
Hunting for our freedom
And advocating for our birth rights
We march
To the left
We march
To the right
We march
To the centre
No John Vorster Prison
Nor Robben Island Prison will stop this march
The people shall march against racism
We shall march against antagonism
The people shall march against police brutality
We shall march against Bantustan citizenship
We march
Against all odds

And pushed against the wall
Full of hope
And boiling with anger
Full of energy
And no will to surrender
We march
We shall march
We will march
Until freedom is won
Until justice is served
We march
We will march
And we shall march
Until those who pretend to be deaf listen
Until those who pretend to be blind see
We march
Until prison doors fling wide open
Our leaders walking free
Until chickens come home to roost
We march
We will march
We shall march
Until South Africa belongs to all those who live in it
The march will never stop
The march will never be postponed
And the march will never be derailed
We will march
We shall march
Until democracy is resorted
And this march will continue
From this generation to the next
We march
They will march
And the march shall never stop
Until South Africa is free

The past haunts us and the future is rejecting us. We have been described as "the lost generation"; a generation of sex maniacs and alcohol abusers, who contribute almost nothing to the universe except polluting the ozone with our loud music, whose lyrics are explicit and overloaded with vulgarities and whose luxury cars are damaging the environment. Our contribution to global warming is horrific and alarming.

Our elders believe that we are out of touch with reality and that we can't be tamed or grounded.

My high school English teachers will swear with their hands on the Bible that I was a bookworm and my friends will testify that I was a vigorous reader but I beg to differ. I was just a young man hungry for knowledge and got my exuberance from reading.

Just like any other teenager, I was a rascal but my vices were books and music rather than alcohol and women.

Ever since Nathaniel Makanete had opened my blind eyes when I was oblivious and had given me an affinity to politics that inspired me, and since Robert Khosa had fixed me up with books to keep me high, I was sedulous about reading; a glutton, eating any book on sight, chewing it and grinding its bones, gnawing every last morsel of meat from the pages.

There was narcissism in my writing, but my peers venerated me and my poetry had resonance. It was at this point in time that I realised that the pen could be a dangerous weapon. If used correctly, it can disrobe lies, expose the truth and paint an aesthetic picture. A pen talks directly to the man in the mirror and often shames the devils.

Coming from a country with a turbulent political history whose echoes of the past can still be heard today, the truth can bring a smile and laughter to your face. But once the laughter has faded, the truth creeps in and floods your eyes with tears.

Every man at some point in his life must have the courage to stand up for what he believes in and be prepared to suffer the consequences of that belief. If push comes to shove, he must be prepared to lay down his life for it.

It was at that point I decided to be a cultural activist using my pen as a machine gun. I started writing protest plays and launched a cultural group called *Amaqabane*, which performed in my village.

The cultural group was faddish and didn't go far after the first play: parents stopped their kids from attending rehearsals because they were afraid they'd be arrested and end up in jail.

My community's silence against apartheid gnawed at me: their silence was so loud even the deaf could hear it. I refused to be pushed into a drowsy silence or into a corner. I have been a fighter all my life, and a brave one.

After *Amaqabane* was canned, my spirit was broken and wounded but it didn't stop me from reading and writing as my ideas and passion had not been castrated. I began writing more poetry and short stories. My friends encouraged me, my comrades gave me the gumption to keep on, but my family was mortified. I was the black sheep and a loose cannon.

My father was solicitous, disregarding his brothers' encouragement to knock some sense into my head before I ruined the family's good name and dragged it into the mud. I was grubby and uncouth, they argued.

"This boy will end up in a grave or jail sooner than later unless you do something," they told my father.

I took no notice and I cared less for their ranting: I was not one of the generation of cowards.

Just when I thought my world was falling apart and my family was vilifying me, I met a young man who became my writing mentor and a bosom friend.

One day, in December 1987, as I was walking on the dusty village road, reading a book as usual, I met a young man, a stranger, walking in the opposite direction and also reading a book. Behold it was the same book I was reading, from the James Hadley Chase series.

The young man and I paused, smiled at each other without saying a word, and looked at each other's books before we exchanged greetings. It was a funny, serendipitous moment.

The young man, who was a few years older than myself and a little bit shorter, introduced himself as Ephraim Christmas Hlatshwayo and he informed me that he and his family has just moved into our village.

We talked about books around the fireplace at his home, and I am not exaggerating when I say we went from 5:00 p.m. that day until 6:00 a.m. the following morning.

I thought I was a reader and a collector of books until I met Ephraim, who made me look like an amateur. The man was a walking encyclopaedia and brilliant raconteur; his knowledge was seemingly limitless and his writing was superb. He let me read some of his manuscripts and I was more inspired than ever.

This was the first man I had met who enjoyed reading and writing as I did; he was the first man to criticise my writing, constructively, while everyone was showering me with praise.

He was what Frank A Clark was referring to when he said, "Criticism, like rain, should be gentle enough to nourish a man's growth without destroying his roots."

Everything I knew about writing then I had taught myself, and Ephraim had an immediate empathy with my work and extended his hand in helping to sharpen my skills. He also made it his task to speak to my parents, especially my granny with whom I was staying at the time, not to discourage me from writing and to respect my political ambition.

Ephraim had had his own experience of police brutality while he was a student at Orhovelani High School in Thulamahashe in 1986.

Commenting on this book, Ephraim said, "The world must get to see what Sibambayani has produced when your book hits the shelves. The peoples of the world are yet to discover what men of valour have emerged from Bushbuckridge."

It wasn't a surprise then that after I finished writing this memoir, I asked Ephraim to have a look at it.

Chapter 6

NTSHUXEKO: Long walk to freedom

"Let the Lord be praised, for the day shall come, when all men shall be free to breathe the air of freedom and when that day shall come, no man, no matter how many tanks he has, will reverse the course of freedom."
– Onkgopotse Abram Tiro

The late American author Maya Angelou, a source of inspiration for me, once said, "No man can know where he is going unless he knows exactly where he has been and exactly how he arrived at his present place."

My journey of a thousand miles did begin with one step, but has required a lot of perseverance, determination and zeal. Each twist and turn did not mean the end of the road but simply other roads, another chance to continue forward, to take an alternative route.

After my arrival at Embalenhle township in Secunda I was reunited with Petro Malaza, an old friend of a former classmate of mine, from Qokiso High School.

Petro was of mixed race – a black mother and an Indian father – and slender and light in complexion. At school we used to call him Mahatma Ghandi. On the outside, Petro's style was neat and smart; on the inside he was a carefree fellow who had little interest in politics, poetry or football. Nonetheless, he was my good friend and my homeboy from Bushbuckridge.

Petro and I found a way of making some pocket money – not a lot – by pushing trolleys at OK and Pick n Pay at Secunda Mall.

I was staying with my uncle Edwin, my father's younger brother, who is the last-born in the family. He was working at Sasol at the time.

Secunda had a different political vibe, unlike Bushbuckridge. In Secunda you could have a decent political debate with comrades whose minds were as sharp as razors and who had oceans of experience. It was a golden opportunity for me to grow politically. Here, my poems would be recited as often as I was offered the platform.

My matric results came: I passed but my granny could not afford to pay for my fees at a tertiary institution from her social grant. She was already feeding four mouths at the time.

As a sole breadwinner, my granny would not let us go to bed with empty stomachs. At times there would be contributions from her sons, that is, my father and his brothers, but she would always make sure that we were well fed.

When Frederik Willem de Klerk, the seventh and last apartheid state president, announced the unbanning of the ANC and other political parties on 2 February 1990, the people of eMbalenhle, like those in the rest of the country, were electrified. There were celebrations on every corner and every street. Finally, we could smell the aroma of freedom in the air and I was free to return to Bushbuckridge any time I pleased, without the fear of being followed by members of the Security Branch.

Shortly after Nelson Mandela's release from prison on 11 February 1990, I returned to Bushbuckridge as a card-carrying member of the ANC to rejoin my comrades.

I used to travel between Bushbuckridge and Secunda, looking for jobs and engaging in political activities.

I used the money I had saved from pushing trolleys and other donations to register for a marketing course, which I studied part-time.

That year, 1990, was the year of mobilising the youth to join the ANC and the youth league. The year of building structures, giving our people a free political education and building a strong foundation for the elections. It was a busy year and we were all over the show. There were no salaries, no tender rewards, no luxury cars to drive around or posh hotel accommodation, but we were prepared to sweat and toil for free, for our beloved country and our people.

There were times when we were bussed, many other times when we walked and hitchhiked to attend rallies and listen to our leaders. For the first time, they would be talking to us, singing with us, seeing us, and we were seeing them live. It was also a year to prepare for the forthcoming provincial congresses when provincial leaders would be elected in 1991.

Following the formation of the National Youth Organisation [NYO] in 1987 during the State of Emergency and under the nose of the security branch and former intelligence mafia, young lions such as Peter Mokaba, David Abrahamse, Cassel Mathale, Obed Bapela, Frans Mohlala and Dan Motsitsi, who were the founding members, became our new struggle heroes for the youth of this country. Peter Mokaba led the South African Youth Congress (SAYCO) at that time.

After the unbanning of the liberation movements, there was a need to mobilise the youth around the country in preparation for the re-launch of the African National Congress Youth League (ANCYL) and to prepare the youth for the elections.

The years between 1990 and 1994 were crucial times when the youth of the country were needed more than ever before to revive the unbroken spirit of 16 June 1976. This was the second phase of our struggle – the first one being to defeat and dismantle apartheid. Some of the leaders of today were made and groomed around this period. This was the time to stand up and be counted.

A message was sent that I should return to Bushbuckridge full-time, as my skills and presence were needed. We were preparing for the first provincial conference of the ANC following its unbanning. It was to be held at Mgwenya College of Education, outside Nelspruit. It was here that Mathews Phosa was appointed as the provincial leader in Mpumalanga.

It was an honour for me to be called on stage after Phosa was elected to recite my poem "We March".

After the congress, I was one of the comrades chosen to attend the historic occasion to launch the African National Congress Youth League in South Africa after its unbanning at the seventeenth Congress, held at Kwandebele College of Education in Siyabuswa in December 1991.

We arrived exhausted in the middle of the night, straight from the provincial ANC conference, only to be forced to evacuate the area immediately because of several bomb threats.

The following morning after the place was cleared, we were graced by the presence of the ANC national leadership including the late president Oliver Tambo, Walter Sisulu, the ANC deputy president who addressed the congress, and Jacob Zuma, among other leaders who were present.

It was at this congress that Peter Mokaba, the fiery leader from Limpopo, was elected as the president of the ANCYL, a position he held, regardless of his age, until 1994 when he was appointed as the deputy minister of environmental affairs and tourism.

In January 1992, the village elders intervened to keep me in the village when they heard that I was moving to Phalaborwa where I had been offered a full-time job. Freddy Ngomane, my former primary school teacher, who was then a principal at Mathambo Primary School, offered to employ me as one of the teachers.

Mathambo Primary School is a modern-style government school built at the same time as Mzwangedwa High School. The two schools are opposite each other, separated by a dusty main road in the village of Sibambayane.

While I continued with my own studies, I taught environmental studies and religious studies at Mathambo Primary School for two years, and received the nickname *Mfundisi* (Reverend) for my devotional and spiritual lessons. My grandfather had wanted me to be a pastor but I chose politics and journalism instead.

Teaching I believed would give me a great opportunity to help shape and build a foundation for our future leaders, but after one year I was both bored to death and frustrated. It was then that I realised that teaching was a calling but it was not mine. The principal, realising my frustration, appointed me as the school sports organiser but that did not help the situation. I wanted out.

In January 1993 I joined a multinational company as a sales representative and moved to Witbank to be stationed at its regional office. As soon as I was in Witbank, I joined the local ANC branch where I met the likes of Jackson Mthembu and Lassy Chiwayo, who later became MECs within the Mpumalanga government. Mthembu ended up being the national spokesperson for the ANC while Chiwayo, the former executive mayor of Mbombela, was deployed as the ambassador to China. I had known, met and interacted with Mthembu and Chiwayo on a number of occasions at rallies and conferences before moving to Witbank.

On 27 April 1994 I stood in a long queue outside Zacheus Malaza Secondary School in Witbank to cast my vote for the first time along with 19.7 million other South Africans across the country; it was a fulfilling moment indeed. A moment our struggle heroes and heroines died for. The moment our grandparents, fathers and mothers were denied for such a long time. The moment we struggled for, the moment we shed blood for and our defining moment. This was not just a historic moment but it marked the end of over three hundred years of colonialism, segregation and white minority rule. It was the birth of our democracy.

It was the day that gave birth to our new constitution, hailed as one of the best in the world.

The ANC won the elections with 62.65 per cent of the vote, followed by the National Party (NP), which received 20.39 per cent, Inkatha Freedom Party (IFP) 10.54 per cent, Freedom Front (FF) 2.2 per cent, Democratic Party (DP) 1.7 per cent, Pan Africanist Congress (PAC) 1.2 per cent and the African Christian Democratic Party (ACDP) 0.5 per cent.

Speaking at the first democratic anniversary, Nelson Mandela, the first democratically elected president of South Africa said, "As dawn ushered in this day, the 27th of April 1995, few of us could suppress the welling of emotion, as we were reminded of the terrible past from which we come as a nation; the great possibilities that we now have; and the bright future that beckons us. Wherever South Africans are, across the globe, our hearts beat as one, as we renew our common loyalty to our country and our commitment to its future. The birth of our South African nation has, like any other, passed through a long and often painful process. The ultimate goal of a better life has yet to be realised. On this day, you, the people, took your destiny into your own hands. You decided that nothing would prevent you from exercising your hard-won right to elect a government of your choice. Your patience, your discipline, your single-minded purposefulness have become a legend throughout the world."

At that point in time, looking at our long walk to freedom, it reminded me of the American civil rights leader Jesse Jackson who once said, "Both tears and sweat are salty, but they render a different result. Tears will get you sympathy; sweat will get you change."

Chapter 7

N'WAMAHUNGU: A pen is mightier than a sword

"The world is a dangerous place to live; not because of the people who are evil, but because of the people who don't do anything about it." – Albert Einstein

On our beautiful continent of Africa there are two kinds of journalists: those who write about missing cats and those who write about missing money. If you write about missing cats, then you are safe but if you write about the missing money there are two scenarios: expect a bullet in your head or to spend your life looking over your shoulder.

If you have a bullet in your head, you are dead and safe but when you have to spend your life looking over your shoulder there are two scenarios: you could either be neutralised or be labelled as an enemy of the state. If you are neutralised, you are safe because they would offer you a government job with good packages, where you would become a praise singer and defender of maladministration and corruption. Most former journalists, though not all, become hypocrites once they join the government. But when you are labelled an enemy of the state there are two scenarios: if you are white, you are isolated; and if you are black, you and your next of kin are victimised.

If you are white, you are safe: they will call you a racist and you may be left alone. But if you are black, you are called a traitor, a sell-out, a coconut or, the worst, a bloody agent. These are some of the derogative names I have had to live with since the day I chose to be a patriot, defending my country's democracy by fighting corruption and exposing those who think joining the government is like winning the jackpot. As some of my former comrades informed me, they "didn't join the struggle and fight against apartheid to end up poor".

Some of my former comrades want us to turn a blind eye, to ignore the fact that they are looting from our government coffers and robbing blind the citizens of this country.

Desiderius Erasmus Roterodamus wrote, "In the country of the blind, the one-eyed man is king." As a blind man, I decided to use my pen as my walking stick, to help me find my way to his Majesty's palace where I would tell "the man" that I would be watching him like a hawk.

Addressing the International Press Institute Congress in Cape Town in February 1994, the former South African president Nelson Mandela said, "A critical, independent and investigative press is the lifeblood of any democracy. The press must be free from state interference. It must have the economic strength to stand up to the blandishments of government officials. It must have sufficient independence from vested interests to be bold and inquiring without fear or favour. It must enjoy the protection of the Constitution, so that it can protect our rights as citizens.

"It is only such a free press that can temper with the appetite of any government to amass power at the expense of the citizens. It is only such a free press that can be the vigilant watchdog of the public interest against the temptation on the part of those who wield it to abuse that power. It is only such a free press that can have the capacity to relentlessly expose excesses and corruption on the part of government, state officials and other institutions that hold power in society.

"I have often said that the media are a mirror through which we can see ourselves as others perceive us, warts, blemishes and all. The African National Congress has nothing to fear from criticism. I can promise you, we will not wilt under close scrutiny. It is our considered view that such criticism can only help us to grow, by calling attention to those of our actions and omissions which do not measure up to our people's expectations and the democratic values to which we subscribe."

Around June 1995 I decided I wanted to be of better service to my country than an award-winning sales representative. I was a good sales person, but I was tired of being on the road every week, sleeping in different hotels or guest houses every night, living like a rock star. The money was good but it did not mean anything to me – my heart was in writing. Marketing bored me. I made a decision that changed my life: I walked into the offices of *Witbank News*, a Caxton-owned community newspaper, and asked to speak to the editor, Amanda Botha. There was no post advertised.

After all, I was a salesman and I believed I would be able to sell myself to Amanda and convince her that *Witbank News* was not covering the news from the local townships. More than a year after our democracy, they did not have a black reporter. I asked her if she could give me a chance to do just that.

Amanda did not hesitate: it was a brilliant initiative that would pay off very well for the newspaper. That is how my journey as a professional journalist began: as a freelance reporter for the *Witbank News*. Amanda asked me to start the following day and I had my byline on the front page of the newspaper in my first week.

Two of my colleagues at *Witbank News*, Suzette van der Merwe and Braam Hartzenbert, made me feel welcome, mentored me and showed me the ropes. It was a great learning curve as I was doing something I really loved and it was the beginning of a new road for me. That road led me to become a multi-award-winning investigative journalist, recognised as one of the best in South Africa.

I was living my dreams and doing what I really wanted to do: being a member of the Fourth Estate. But I was also made aware that with great power comes great responsibility and that a pen is mightier than a sword.

I chose to become a journalist because I wanted to stand for something, something worth living for and something worth dying for. Steve Biko once said, "It is better to die for an idea that will live, than to live for an idea that will die."

Since the days of our infamous class newspaper, *The Voice*, at Qokiso High School, I was inspired by some of the torchbearers of investigative journalism in South Africa: *DRUM*, *Weekly Mail*, *Rand Daily Mail* and *New Nation*; journalists like Nat Nakasa, Henry Nxumalo, Zwelakhe Sisulu, Eddie Koch, Enock Sithole, Janet Wilhelm, Jacques Pauw, Shaun Johnson and Benjamin Pogrund to mention just a few. These scribes had had the courage and had risked their lives walking where angels feared to tread.

After a year at *Witbank News*, I managed to convince my brother, Thulani Mishack, who was still enjoying his marketing career, that we should start our own newspaper. His job would be to handle the marketing and advertising side of the business while I would take care of the newsroom.

After doing some research and producing a convincing business plan, we managed to raise enough money to start our own newspaper. We also knocked on other people's doors looking for potential investors. We had to speak to different companies and managed to get enough support including a giveaway car as part of promoting the newspaper. I recruited a small team of four reporters.

My brother and I launched our newspaper in September 1996. We called it the *Mpumalanga Mirror* and it was one of the first 100 per cent black-owned newspapers in Mpumalanga – and the only newspaper circulating in the province. The newspaper's head office was in Witbank and we rented a house just a stone's throw from the *Witbank News*. We did not regard ourselves as competitors, however. We had regional offices in Kwaggafontein, in the former Kwa-Ndebele homeland, and Bethal. In Nelspruit, we used *African Eye News Service* (AENS), a news agency owned by Justin Arenstein and Sharon Hammond, as our news supplier.

I also made a deal with the late former SABC news boss in Nelspruit, Steve Nkosi, to feed the national broadcaster with breaking news from our newsroom. As part of the deal I became the SABC freelancer for the Highveld region.

Mpumalanga Mirror, with the help of AENS, broke a number of stories including the exposé on the IFP hitman Romeo Mbambo, and the confession about his killings and the story of the selling of degrees at the University of Zululand.

The business was good from the news side but the printing cost was too much. We were paying a fortune to print the newspaper. To a certain extent, the money had also gone to my brother's head: he was enjoying overseas holidays while I was labouring in the newsroom.

On April 1998, after more than a year of running *Mpumalanga Mirror*, my brother and I decided to part ways. I was not happy with the way he was running the company. I moved to Nelspruit and joined AENS as a senior crime reporter.

Chapter 8

NDZALAMA: If a child washes his hands he could eat with kings

"You can fool some of the people all the time, and all of the people some of the time, but you cannot fool all of the people all the time." – Abraham Lincoln

What happens when you put five hungry journalists in a small office the size of someone's bathroom, with just two computers, a fax line and one telephone?

What happens when you put a bunch of hungry politicians in positions of power, with access to billions of taxpayers' money and tenders worth millions of rands?

What happens when you give a microphone to someone with verbal diarrhoea to address a crowd of hungry and unemployed people looking for jobs and a better life?

And what happens when you lock a hungry dog, cat and mouse in a dairy where all the cheese and fresh milk is kept?

When I joined AENS after the Easter holidays in 1997, the agency was a small axe trying to chop down a big tree. We were five hungry journalists: Justin Arenstein, Sharon Hammond, Sylvester Lukhele, Eric Mashaba and me, sharing a small office along Bester Street in the Nelspruit CBD with two computers, a fax line and one telephone. But the energy, the enthusiasm and the drive was bigger than the room.

Besides our different backgrounds and personalities, we were like one big family, eating from the same plate while cracking some of the biggest stories in South Africa.

AENS was fast becoming one of South Africa's leading investigative powerhouses exposing corrupt politicians and their dodgy deals. It was supplying some of the country's big newspapers like *Sunday Times, City Press, Mail & Guardian* and *The Star* with news, most of it breaking and investigative stories.

The agency was becoming a brand and an institution where young journalists from rural areas were trained, mentored and given a platform to shine.

It was an AENS exposé that got ANC senator and Member of Parliament Patrick Mogale fired from the National Assembly. Mogale was the first Member of Parliament to be axed since the new government in 1994 after he was exposed and convicted for statutory rape.

Mogale, a former school principal from Bushbuckridge, had impregnated a 14-year-old schoolgirl in 1991, and failed to pay a monthly R300 child maintenance fee for a baby he knew was his. He ignored several court orders for more than two years to pay for his child. He was arrested in August 1995 after he had managed to avoid the police for almost 11 months.

Mogale was expelled from the ruling party for behaving "in a disgraceful manner that brought the ANC into disrepute" and was later sentenced to seven months in prison, suspended for five years.

After Mogale's sex scandal, AENS delivered another blow when it exposed ANC chairperson Baleka Mbete-Kgotsisile, the speaker of Parliament at the time, for having a fake driver's licence.

Former Mpumalanga safety and security MEC, the late Steve Mabona, had arranged for his driver and bodyguard to fetch the deputy speaker from the OR Tambo International Airport and take her to Delmas, a small town east of Johannesburg, where she was "tested" for her licence.

But our investigation established that there was no record of her testing in Delmas and that instead her licence was issued at Kabokweni, more than 350 kilometres away. To make matters worse, the licence was issued a day before she was supposedly "tested". Mabona resigned before he was fired and Mbete-Kgotsisile's licence was ruled to be invalid. The ruling was made by the Moldenhauer Commission of 1997. Months later, Mbete-Kgotsisile apologised and committed herself to returning the licence.

Months later, former ANC spokesperson Jackson Mthembu was exposed for ordering ten BMWs as "Christmas presents" for his fellow colleagues at a cost of R2.3 million while he was transport MEC in Mpumalanga. The deal was cancelled after the exposé and the intervention of former transport minister Mac Maharaj, as well as the public outcry that followed.

Following the *WaBenzi* scandal, the agency nailed former Mpumalanga environmental affairs MEC David Mkhwanazi, who employed his wife, daughter, sister-in-law and cousin in his department. He also employed more than 300 other people, believed to be his supporters, and spent R20 million from a slush fund on their salaries. Mkhwanazi would also become embroiled in the controversial R12.5 billion deal between the Mpumalanga Parks Board and the Dubai-based Dolphin Group. Eventually, he was forced to resign and was suspended from the ANC.

Then came another story when former housing minister Sankie Mthembu-Mahanyele and the local government and housing MEC in Mpumalanga Graig Padayachee lost their jobs. A R198 million housing deal was awarded to a company called Motheo Construction owned by Dr Thandi Ndlovu, a family friend of the minister.

In October 1997, AENS editor Justin Arenstein and Thomas Kwenaite of the *Sunday Times* were named as the joint winners of the South African Award for Courageous Journalism. The award was sponsored by the Ruth First Memorial Trust.

Accepting the award at the ceremony at Rhodes University in Grahamstown in the Eastern Cape, Arenstein said, "Death threats are a routine in our business, but are, in my experience, the weakest and most unsophisticated weapons used against probing reporters."

Rhodes University and the Ruth First Memorial Trust paid my very first flight, ever, to the awards event and it was a wonderful experience. I remember vividly when the South African Airways airhostess served us drinks, and I told her, "I don't have money to pay." I was surprised when she told me the food was for free and gobbled everything on my tray.

Flying to Port Elizabeth airport was amazing but it was far more satisfying flying back with the award on my lap.

AENS also exposed a conman masquerading as a political analyst calling himself Dr Eugene Nyathi. This Zimbabwean national, whose real name was Albert Nana, was a genius of note and an eloquent orator. He managed to pull the wool over our eyes every day, gracing our television sets and having us adjust our radio sets to hear him telling us what we wanted to hear.

"Dr Nyathi", a high-school dropout, and the lawyer Ntsoaki Mohapi, were employed as consultants to restructure the Mpumalanga Development Corporation (MDC) and Nyathi rode the gravy train by paying himself a salary of R15 000 per hour as an "expert".

After the exposé, "Dr Nyathi" admitted to receiving irregular payments, repaid R700 000 and confessed to having falsified his academic qualifications. He was also forced to pay some of the money back and conceded that he overcharged for his services. That was the last time most of us ever heard of him.

Then there was the speaker of Mpumalanga legislature, Elias Ginindza, who was forced to resign from his powerful position after another AENS exposé revealed how he turned a blind eye when his deputy, Cynthia Maropeng, embezzled more than R1.1 million from the legislature to enrich herself and her friend, Jomo Siboza, a finance director in the Mpumalanga legislature. Maropeng and Siboza were sentenced to seven years in jail while Ginindza merely got a slap on the wrist.

The agency was giving former Mpumalanga premier Mathews Phosa sleepless nights. We kept him on his toes and gave him some grey hairs. We were all over these MECs and officials, making them accountable for deals they were brokering on behalf of the provincial government. We became a thorn in their flesh; we were the eyes and ears of the people in the province, and the voice of the voiceless. We tackled the issues head on and set an agenda for the people. We exposed corruption and maladministration without fear or favour. We made a name for ourselves as a collective and as individual reporters.

The Media Institute of Southern Africa (MISA) bestowed AENS with the Press Freedom Award in 1998 for "courage, professionalism, consistency and defence of media freedoms against all odds". It was the first time in the history of MISA that this prestigious award was given "to a courageous and outstanding media institute rather than an individual".

In its press statement, MISA stated that AENS's "bold and extremely courageous reporting has earned it several enemies in both public and private sectors of the South African community. The agency has attracted numerous multi-million-rand defamation suits, and to date it has won every case. Its journalists, especially Arenstein, have also been targets of physical and verbal harassment, including death threats and threats of assault, while also being physically marginalised. Despite this harassment and hostility, the AENS team has carried its mission with excellence, exhibiting mature and professional journalism with depth and carefully verified detail."

Chapter 9

RIFU: When bullets fly like butterflies

"When the people fear the government there is tyranny, when the government fears the people there is liberty." – Thomas Jefferson

One of the main purposes of journalism in a democratic society is to provide citizens with news that is accurate and reliable, and the information that is needed to function in a free society. For this purpose, every journalist needs a source for that information, indeed not just one, but as many as possible.

Without a source, a journalist is like a tree without roots, an empty river or a toothless lion. If needs be, a journalist must protect his source by any means necessary and be prepared even to go to jail for that.

Section 6 of the South African Press Code states, "The press has an obligation to protect confidential source of information." Almost all media houses and journalists abide by this code, which is a universal golden rule for all journalists. A number of journalists have been imprisoned to protect a source, including:

- *Los Angeles Times* reporter William Farr was sent to jail in 1972 for 46 days for refusing to reveal his confidential sources in the case regarding the murderer Charles Manson;

- Vanessa Leggett, an American freelance reporter, was sentenced to 168 days in jail in 2001 for refusing to disclose information obtained during her research for a book about a murder in Houston;

- Pulitzer Prize-winning *New York Times* reporter, Judith Miller, spent 85 days behind bars in 2005 after refusing to reveal her source in connection with a government investigation into the wrongdoings of the Bush administration;

- Her colleague Matthew Cooper escaped jail after he agreed to testify, claiming his confidential source encouraged him to do so;

- There was a public outcry in Australia in 2012 after investigative reporters, Nick McKenzie and Richard Baker, of *The Age* newspaper, were subpoenaed to give evidence and reveal a confidential "senior government source" in court after they exposed the country's Reserve Bank for corruption;

- SAPS minister Nathi Mthethwa tried to subpoena *eNews* news editor Ben Said and reporter Mpho Lakaje in a bid to force them to reveal the identity of the two criminals who were interviewed by the television station wearing masks. The men had openly admitted to planning to rob visitors during the FIFA World Cup in South Africa in 2010.

The above are some of the many examples of journalists who were either prepared to go to jail or face prosecution in their bid to protect their source.

Tess Lawrence, former president of the Australian Journalists Association once wrote, "Shooting the messenger is still a favourite pastime of despotic regimes and corporate institutions and their lawyers, who use various types of silencers on their weaponry, aimed at those who light even a candle to disturb the dark of corruption."

South African media lawyer and media freedom champion Dario Milo said that although there had been many attempts in South Africa since 1994 to subpoena journalists and force them to reveal their sources, so far the needs of democracy have been upheld and the pressure has been in vain.

In Professor Franz Kruger's journalism handbook, *Black, White and Grey Ethics in South African Journalism*, as a contributor I stated, "A friend of mine, also a journalist, once said that a reliable source of information is like having an affair outside your marriage – you don't want anybody to know about it."

Around May 1998 I received a call from a source who informed me that I "will get a scoop of a lifetime" if I could go and interview a woman who was lying in a sickbed in a specific ward in a Nelspruit private hospital.

I went to the hospital and visited the ward and the specific bed that I had been told to go to. Indeed there was a woman in the bed but she was sleeping, and even though I am not a doctor, I could tell that she was in pain. As I stood nearby my eyes scanned the room and fell on a medical aid card on top of a small table next to her bed.

The medical aid card stated that its main member was Luckson Mathebula. I knew Luckson Mathebula: he was the safety and security MEC in Mpumalanga at the time, and a former comrade of mine from Bushbuckridge. This woman in the bed was unknown to me.

I pulled out a chair next to her bed and sat reading a magazine that I had found next to the table, and waited for her to wake up. She was taken aback to see a stranger sitting next to her bed when she eventually came to. I introduced myself and apologised for invading her space and privacy.

Politely she told me that her name was Aletta Rose Mnisi, a common-law wife to Mathebula. She accepted my apologies. Aletta told me, off the record, that her husband had assaulted her and that she was not prepared to air their dirty laundry in public.

"One day when you get married, you would also do the same, to protect the one you love," she said. She humbly requested me to leave, as she did not want to get into any trouble should her husband find me there.

Before I left, I gave her my business card in case she decided to talk about what happened in future. I promised her that our discussion was completely off the record. A few weeks later, Aletta called me and requested that I meet her at a restaurant in Hazyview, a small town about 50 kilometres outside Nelspruit.

When we met that weekend, Aletta poured her heart out, with tears running down her face. She told me of her "abusive husband", the recent alleged assault when he had beaten her with a wooden giraffe curio that led her to being admitted to hospital.

Aletta spent six weeks in hospital and sustained permanent damage to her jaws. She also gave me explosive information that I cannot repeat, as my probe into those matters would be hindered by circumstances beyond my control.

I asked her to think carefully about the information she had and to speak to her lawyer. Two days later Aletta called to inform me that her lawyer had advised she open a case of assault against her husband. She also said she had moved out of the marital home.

After I obtained a copy of her affidavit submitted at the local police station, I broke the story on how a safety and security MEC assaulted his wife. The story made national headlines even though Mathebula refused to comment on it.

A few days after the story was published, I received a phone call from Mpumalanga premier Mathews Phosa, informing me that Mathebula had officially complained to him that Aletta and I were having an affair even though she was 18 years my senior. He also alleged we were plotting to destroy him.

I advised Phosa to lodge an official complaint with my boss Justin Arenstein, which he did, only to be surprised when the evidence was produced that proved beyond doubt that when I met with Aletta in Hazyview, I was accompanied by my girlfriend. The only place where I met Aletta alone was at the hospital.

After seven months of police investigation, Mathebula was arrested and charged with assault with intent to do grievous bodily harm. The police were also investigating some of the serious allegations that Aletta made in her statement that I could not repeat.

The story was not over yet. One Sunday morning in June 1999, I received a frantic phone call from Aletta who informed me that Mathebula was threatening her life and had been making death threats over the phone.

She said, "My only crime is that I know a lot of things I should not have known. I was supposed to be a good wife and keep my mouth shut and eyes closed." I encouraged Aletta to report the matter to the police but she dismissed my suggestion as "a waste of time".

"I reported the first death threats I received from him last year but this culprit has not been questioned about it so far. When the car I was driving was sprayed with bullets near Acornhoek, another attempt on my life, and told police that Luckson was the main suspect, they didn't do anything," she explained.

Three days later as I was driving from Sun City on 9 June 1999 the four o'clock news headlines came on that Aletta Rose Mnisi, a school teacher, had been shot dead in broad daylight while walking from school with her colleague.

When I asked the police spokesperson, senior superintendent Phuti Setati, about the murder, he said, "Mnisi's killing was well-planned. Information at our disposal indicates that the gunman followed the two teachers on foot and shot Mnisi. A getaway car then appeared from nowhere and the suspects sped away from the scene."

Mathebula, who was out on bail at the time for the assault case, was supposed to appear at Thulamahashe Regional Court on 15 June. He was never convicted. Aletta was killed before she could testify and offer any evidence against him. A few days later Mathebula was arrested for ordering a hit on his wife.

The arrest came after a local sangoma Jimmy Chauke went to the bank to deposit a large amount of cash. When the bank manager asked Chauke, as required by the Financial Intelligence Centre Act, where he had obtained that much money from, the unsuspecting and honest old man explained that it was his payment for the muti he had supplied to the guys who had killed a teacher recently. The bank manager phoned the police immediately after Chauke left the bank. The sangoma was arrested and he disclosed the names of the people he had supplied the muti to and, bingo, Mathebula was one of them.

Mathebula's lover at the time, Pretty Thembi Gama, was also arrested and she made a confession to the effect that she had supplied the murder weapon, a 7.65-millimetre pistol as well as her car, a Volkswagen Polo Classic, which was used as a getaway vehicle. Gama entered the state witness protection programme.

Gama later retracted her statement after alleging that she and her extended family were getting death threats. She then walked out of the witness protection programme and fled the province to an unknown destination before she could provide any testimony.

Moses Sambo, the man who pulled the trigger, was sentenced to life imprisonment for the murder of Aletta. Mathebula was acquitted. Mathebula's nephew, Moshe Mathebula, who drove the getaway car also walked free.

Judge Tjibe Spoelstra told the court he could not find any evidence to link Mathebula and his nephew to the murder as the state witness had vanished without a trace. After hearing the judgement, Aletta's disappointed father, Kelias Mnisi said, "The justice system seems to defend criminals more than victims."

Police closed the other investigations on Mathebula, which were more serious, because their star witness, Aletta, was no more. The death of Aletta haunts me from time to time. I still do not know what I could have done, if anything at all, to save her life.

Mathebula was fired as MEC and suspended from the ANC and he has since joined another political party, Congress of the People (COPE). He remains a senior member of the party in Mpumalanga.

Chapter 10

MAKHOMBA NDLELA: Time to say goodbye

"If your actions inspire others to dream more, learn more, do more and become more, you are a leader." – John Quincy Adams

AENS was on a roll and the hyenas around Mpumalanga were running scared and feeling the heat. The agency was making money. We moved to bigger and more luxurious offices on Brown Street, still in Nelspruit. Individually we were making names for ourselves, being called by various national radio stations to comment and provide analysis on a constant basis.

A new crop of young and fresh-from-school journalists had joined AENS, including Dumisane Lubisi, Phillip Nkosi and Landiwe Dlamini.

In June 1997, former president Nelson Mandela visited Amersfoort in Mpumalanga to hand over the title deed for the Daggakraal farm as part of the government's land restitution programme. I attended the ceremony. The farm was managed by the Lephatsoana II Trust and was the only source of employment and income in the entire village.

This little-known village is rich with history and is very close to the ANC's heart. ANC stalwart Dr Pixley Ka Isaka Seme and his friends used to buy farms and sell them to Africans through an entity called African Native Farmers Association of Africa LTD. One of the farms they bought in 1912 was Daggakraal, located on the outskirts of Amersfoort, purchased from farmer Willem Gouws. Since Seme was an attorney involved with the landowners in Daggakraal area, he was obliged to finally settle on that particular farm.

Seme took over the home of Gouws as the farmer had already left the area. The house was also used as the company's office, doubling as the South African Native National Congress before it became known as the African National Congress. Seme is one of the ANC's founders and served as president of it.

When addressing the crowd of about 4 000 rural villagers, Mandela said, "For many generations the land has been at the heart of division and conflict in our country. Daggakraal is a community that knows that history only too well.

"When Pixley Seme organised African farmers to purchase Daggakraal, he was seeking a way of realising the right of all our people to use the land to sustain themselves and contribute to the wealth of the country. It was not to be. The area did not find fame as a centre of agricultural production. Instead it became known for its fierce resistance to forced removal.

"This is a history which can be told across our land, in our towns and cities and every corner of the rural areas."

I was busy enjoying Mandela's speech and taking notes along with other scribes when I noticed a teenager shadowing me. To make sure that he was indeed following me, I started walking around in a circle, speaking to the local people while keeping an eye on him. Unaware he was being watched, the boy was there, following me like a vulture.

When I was satisfied that I had a tail, I confronted him and asked, "*Mfanawam*', why *ungilandelela kanje*? [My boy, why are you following me around like this?]" To my surprise, the young man, full of shyness and speaking with his right hand on his mouth, said, "I want to be a journalist like you." I spoke to the teenager for about 15 minutes and I realised that although he was just 18 years old he had an extraordinary agility of mind and passion for journalism. He was a local Daggakraal boy.

I handed him my business card and told him that whenever he was ready to go into the big jungle, infested with dangerous lions and mambas, to hunt for news he must call me. Three weeks later, while I was at the office in Nelspruit, I received a phone call from the young man and he simply said, "I am at your local taxi rank, please come and fetch me. I will wait near the public phones."

I rushed to the taxi rank like a headless chicken, found him by the public phones and brought him to the office. My boss, Justin Arenstein, said the teenager could only join AENS on the condition that I was prepared to train him and be his mentor. Jokingly I told Justin that once I was done training this teenager, he would be forced to vacate his position as the editor because I was training the future editor of AENS. I also told Justin that the teenager was going to be one of the most influential men alive.

The young man is today an award-winning journalist, known as Sizwe sama Yende, a fearless and courageous journalist in South Africa and the Mpumalanga bureau chief for *City Press*, a leading Sunday weekly newspaper.

I took Sizwe under my wing and housed him in the townhouse I was renting in Nelspruit where he stayed for two weeks. When I was sure that he was ready for my gruelling training, I sent him back to Daggakraal to fetch his clothes and belongings because he had a long journey ahead of him.

He returned in September to tell me he was ready to go to the jungle and hunt. In his own words, Sizwe said: "I arrived at [AENS]'s Nelspruit offices back in 1997. A scrawny 18-year-old boy then, I had no diploma or degree in my hands except my clothing bag and a burning desire to be a journalist.

"It was never easy, but soon enough I realised that I was pursuing the right career and was at the right place that opened possibilities for me to be the kind of journalist I wanted to be.

"[AENS] was building up prestige as an investigative news agency, breaking big stories and causing waves with its exposés.

"I found my role models right there in [AENS]'s charismatic owners, Justin Arenstein and Sharon Hammond, and senior journalists, Mzilikazi wa Afrika and Dumisane Lubisi."

"During the early 2000s, AENS was at its peak, and that was when it dawned on me that I had a very big and important role to play to give a voice to the down-trodden and, more importantly, protect their rights against the scourges of corruption and abuse of power by those in leadership positions.

"That seed of activism planted in me during those years has grown eternally inside me. I found myself writing for most national newspapers and magazines, which opened doors for me to move up and work in the national media, win awards and get a writing fellowship at Wits University."

I asked Sizwe why, out of all the journalists who were gathered there at Daggakraal that day, he chose to follow me and he said, "I hesitated a lot on who to follow but my heart told me to follow you."

Similarly, Dumisane Lubisi, speaking about his experience at AENS, said, "Armed with a one-year journalism diploma, I thought I had my career made until I stepped into the offices of [AENS] in 1997 – although it wasn't my first visit, since I had been in and out of those offices the year before.

"What was to follow for the next five years was learning the craft of the trade and mastering it. This included the courts, the municipality, legislature, provincial politics, and investigations up to a level where I was made news editor.

"Were the five years a waste? Absolutely not – AENS provided the platform that one required to do well in journalism. Perseverance, asking the right questions, investigating, paying attention to details and being the first one with ground-breaking news were the skills one gained at the agency."

It paid off. Dumisane Lubisi is now the executive editor at *City Press*.

Landiwe Dlamini, who is current affairs executive producer for SABC radio in Nelspruit, said: "[AENS] broke very important stories particularly about corruption in the Mpumalanga province. Names such as that of Justin Arenstein, Mzilikazi wa Afrika, Dumisani Lubisi, Sizwe sama Yende were names that were mostly talked about around the Nelspruit area and today they are journalists known nationally. So as the new kid on the block at that time, I am proud to say, I learnt from these guys and I can safely say I learnt from the best."

Philip Sibusiso Nkosi, who is now a senior manager of communication and marketing at Pan South African Language Board (PanSalb), said, "When I joined [AENS] in 1998 as a freelance journalist, I had been without formal work for a year after completing my studies. Although we were remunerated on a commission basis, the work experience I gained there is incomparable, second to none and solid gold.

"Working life presents many challenges and you need to show employers that you're the kind of person who will find a way through and remain cheerful even when the going gets tough. That's what defines me today and it's all because of AENS."

Around November 1998, I received a phone call from veteran journalist Styles Lucas Ledwaba, who was working for the *Sunday Times*, telling me that the company was starting another publication called *Sunday World* that was to be launched in February the following year.

Lucas said both he and *Sunday World* editor at the time, Fred Khumalo, had identified me as one of the journalists they wanted to bring onto their team and that my contract was ready for collection at their office in Johannesburg, if I was interested.

So two days before my birthday on 24 November 1998, I decided to go to Johannesburg and collect the said contract as my birthday treat.

Fred Khumalo was based on the fourth floor at 4 Biermann Avenue in Rosebank, which served as a makeshift *Sunday World* office, while the *Sunday Times* was on the second floor of the same building. It so happened that I had to drop off some photos at the *Sunday Times* desk for a story I was doing for them that week, enabling me to quickly head to Fred's office afterwards.

Sunday Times office manager Sandra Hattingh asked what I was doing in the building since I did not have to come all the way from Nelspruit just to drop off some photos. I told her that I was going to see Fred upstairs and collect my *Sunday World* contract.

I had a short meeting with Fred before he gave me the contract for the *Sunday World* and I told him that I needed time to read it before signing it. He welcomed me to the *Sunday World* in advance.

As I was walking out of his office, I found Sandra Hattingh and Jocelyn Maker, who was *Sunday Times* news editor at the time, waiting for me by the door. Jocelyn, without even greeting me, said, "Whatever Fred promised you, I will pay you R2000 more. Please come and work with me at the *Sunday Times* because that's where you belong." I asked Jocelyn to email me her *Sunday Times* contract as I needed time to read the two contracts before I could decide which of the two newspapers to join.

I had known Jocelyn for some time and she had often assigned me to do stories for the *Sunday Times* from AENS. She would make all the necessary arrangements, hiring me cars and booking accommodation. She also paid me handsomely.

One of the assignments I did for *Sunday Times* at her request was a story about a sangoma from Venda, Nalendzani Mabuda, who "slaughtered his 23-month-old baby as a sacrifice to his ancestors". I broke the story and wrote it exclusively for the *Sunday Times*.

Jocelyn assigned me to go to Mutale Magistrate's Court in Venda to cover the bail application. I remember Mabuda, saying in court without shame or thinking twice, "I have a right to kill my son if my gods demand it from me. My ancestors made me who I am today, so who am I to refuse them?"

The story was covered prominently by the *Sunday Times* and made international headlines. By the time I got to the AENS offices in Nelspruit the following day there was a *Sunday Times* contract waiting for me on email.

I consulted with my friends and family about the two offers. Everybody said the *Sunday Times* had history, a reputation and was the biggest newspaper in South Africa, while *Sunday World* might not be there in six months and people may not even buy it.

I decided to join the *Sunday Times* and my contract stated that I should report to work on 1 January 1999.

It was time to bid my friends and colleagues at AENS a goodbye and take my career to another level.

THE SECOND TESTAMENT

"The grace of our Lord Jesus Christ be with you all. Amen."
– Revelation 22:21

Revelation is the revealing of truth or knowledge
through communication with a deity.

Chapter 11

EMZINI WENSIZWA: A graduate from the University of Wisdom

"A child educated only at school is an uneducated child." – George Santayana

There is a Moroccan proverb that says, "Some will learn through pain and sorrow, others through joy and laughter." Adding his words of wisdom, the American writer and philosopher Elbert Hubbard said, "God will not look you over for medals, degrees or diplomas but for scars."

I do not want to be known just as a multi-award-winning investigative journalist. Instead, I would like to be remembered for the pain and the scars I have collected as my ultimate price in my endeavours to pursue the truth and seek justice.

I want to be celebrated for the ground-breaking stories I have written and the impact they have made as well as the agenda they have set for the nation.

I don't want my journey to evoke pathos but to be a lesson to others as well as a litany of hope for many.

New Year's Day 1999 fell on a Friday. I did not report for work, as it was a public holiday. The following day, I was still on holiday, still celebrating the New Year when I received a phone call at around 11:00 a.m. from Mike Robertson, the *Sunday Times* editor at the time.

"Good morning, Mzilikazi," he said, "and Happy New Year. Where are you?"

I was excited to receive his call and proudly I replied, "I am on holiday, sir, celebrating the New Year."

"Are you not supposed to be at work today instead of being on holiday?" Robertson queried.

"I thought since it's a Saturday I will start on Tuesday, the beginning of the week," I protested.

"Some of us are at work as you can tell, and not celebrating the New Year and our readers are expecting the *Sunday Times* on the street tomorrow. And I am expecting you to be here too."

My exuberance was short lived, as I understood Robertson's seriousness. With my tail between my legs, I apologised and tried to explain to my new boss my ignorance and promised to behave in future as well as follow all the rules.

I then phoned Justin Arenstein to tell him about Robertson's call. Arenstein promised to speak to him and plead my ignorance and vouch for my good behaviour as an employee on condition that I spend a week at AENS training Sibusiso Philip Nkosi, a reporter who was going to take over from me.

A gentlemen's agreement was reached between Arenstein and Robertson and I was loaned to AENS for a week, a move that later proved to be detrimental to me.

While I was in Nelspruit for that week, my landlord at the block of flats in Rosebank decided that since I had not moved into her flat on 1 January as we agreed, I was no longer interested. Without even calling to check, she rented out the place to a new tenant. This was regardless of the fact that I had paid her a deposit and one month's rent in advance.

When I arrived in Johannesburg on 10 January 1999, I faced a grim situation. Johannesburg welcomed me with a kick between the legs and a punch to the face: I did not have a place to stay; I couldn't afford a hotel; I was homeless on my first day in the City of Gold and I knew very few people.

My cousins, Piet and Charles Ndzhukula, after receiving a frantic phone call from me, invited me to come and stay with them. Their place of abode was the Johannesburg City Power men's hostel in Orlando East, better known as Orlando Compound, near those two colourful towers that have become the global symbol of Soweto.

A hostel is a migrant compound, mainly single-sex dwellings, designed by the apartheid government in its effort to keep black people away from their "whites only" cities and towns, and they were always built on the outskirts of the cities or towns.

There I was, a *Sunday Times* journalist wearing a tie every morning and staying in room 23 at the noisy hostel with my two cousins and five other tawdry men.

I had never set foot in a hostel before, but I had read and heard horrible stories about hostel life, especially during the struggle days. Now I was forced to experience it first-hand.

A hostel might not be a prison on paper, but it is like a modern-day prison without wardens. Unlike a prison cell, one has a bigger and open space at the hostel, but like a jail cell, there is no privacy, no tranquillity and no order. It is like a jungle where only the strongest survive.

An illiterate man can go to jail and come back with a degree as a prisoner, but I can tell you it would be difficult for anybody to reach the same academic achievements in a hostel as a free man.

Of my three roommates at the hostel, one was from Lesotho, and spoke Sotho; one was from Eastern Cape and spoke Xhosa, and the last was from Limpopo, speaking Tshivenda. And then there were my two cousins and I, speaking Xitsonga.

Each of these men had his own radio set and everyone was trying to make sure that his radio was louder than the rest. Anyone could switch his radio on or off at any time, and it could be as loud as its owner would like it to be at any time of day or night depending on the owner's mood at any given point in time.

In the morning, you had to wake up early to queue for a shower, and if you were early enough you would be lucky to get hot water. In the evening you had to join another queue for cooking in the open space kitchen.

I am a very private and neat person: my mother would not come to my room because she knew I would polish the floor after she left. My room was always spotless and clean. I always prefer and feel comfortable to sleep in the nude, whether it is winter or summer. To start with, it was difficult for me to sleep in pyjamas and I also did not have any. I was forced to buy some the following day.

My consolation prize was the saying that "beggars can't be choosers". I love movies, and I watch almost three to four films every week. I read and write almost every night. These are my personal routines and rituals.

Some might call me a snob or a spoilt village brat, but these are my daily routines. I do not drink or smoke; three of my roommates were smokers and all of them were consumers of alcoholic beverages. One of them was a serious alcoholic who was drunk every night.

There was nothing I could do: that is the way of life at the hostel. I was like a prisoner and for a moment my life was "stolen" from me. I was just breathing and not living.

I could not bring my work "home" as there were no tables in our room, just five three-quarter beds and steel lockers. There was no peace of mind, just chaos and confusion. I could not even call my sources or accept their calls once I was in there; the noise was unbearable at times. My creativity was caged in bondage.

I stayed at the hostel for three weeks but never spent a single weekend there. I used to travel to Nelspruit every Saturday afternoon to spend the weekend with my sweetheart.

But it was at this hostel where I got my degree in life and learnt about the other side of the coin – about the continual struggle of the black men who want a better life for their families. The men who were making an urgent call to the government to come and see the people and the way they were living.

At this hostel, I learnt about exploitation and unemployment and how men are reduced to modern-day slaves, forced and caged in hostel dwellings as the only alternative to being on the streets or homeless.

Men are forced into being widowers while their wives are alive and they are denied their conjugal rights. They are cut off from their families. Their beloved children grow up without a father figure or a role model. It must be noted that any man can make a baby but it takes a real man to be the father. There is a Ghanaian proverb that says when you follow in the path of your father, you learn to walk like him, but these men were away from their children, some of them only managing to see their offspring twice a year.

The Bible, in the Book of Ephesians 5:25, says, "Husbands, love your wives, just as Christ also loved the church and gave Himself up for it."

In Timothy 5:8 the Bible says, "But if any man does not provide for his own, and especially for those of his household, he has denied the faith and is worse than an unbeliever."

For these men, in order to provide for their families as God expects them to do, had to live like prisoners for most of their lives. They were being denied their basic rights to raise their children and be there for their families. That is how most women in South Africa have become fathers and mothers to their children – raising their children on their own while their husbands are living in hostels far away from home. Hostel life is better for students but not for family men.

One observer once wrote, "Hostel life is very interesting. It is the combination of sadness and pleasure. It is not very easy to live far from our family but we have to live there for making our future bright."

Dr Mamphela Ramphele, in her PhD thesis in social anthropology, "The Politics of Space" (later turned into a book titled, *A Bed Called Home: Life in the Migrant Labour Hostels of Cape Town*) wrote, "In my view, poverty is partly a matter of income and partly a matter of human dignity. It is one thing to have a very low income, but to be treated with respect by your compatriots; it is quite another matter to have a very low income and to be harshly depreciated by more powerful compatriots. Let us speak then of human impoverishment: low income plus harsh disrespect."

There were no tears but a sense of relief and joy when I said goodbye to my cousins and roommates at the hostel and moved into a cottage in Brixton, near Auckland Park, in February 1999.

Hostel life could be hell and it was a traumatic experience. It was also a learning curve and an experience of a lifetime. It was at the hostel where I was educated about life and became a graduate from the University of Wisdom.

I did not let the hostel situation dampen my spirits. Against all odds I announced my arrival at the *Sunday Times* with a bang: a front-page story on 17 January 1999, not an investigative story but it was a marvellous piece to write.

It was my first week with the biggest newspaper in South Africa. Ask any journalist working for any newspaper in the world, getting a front-page story, especially in your first week, is a record and an achievement any journalist should be proud of. In my case, I did not only have one front-page story but a double whammy.

The *Sunday Times* had a news section called *Metro* that carried news from Mpumalanga, Limpopo and Gauteng. I had a front-page story in the *Metro* as well.

For the *Metro* I led with a story about the self-confessed child rapist and killer Dan Mabote's plot to escape from jail. Mabote was arrested for killing seven-year-old Mammokgethi Malebane the day before she was to testify against him. He had been arrested for raping her and two other girls in July 1997.

The court heard evidence on how Mabote used his nephew to lure young girls, including Mammokgethi, from school before taking them to an open veld where he raped them. Mabote strangled Mammokgethi after raping her and buried her body in a shallow grave where she was discovered after a four-month search.

My story exposed a plot by Mabote's 15-member gang who were planning to help him escape from Germiston Magistrate's Court where he was appearing on three other rape charges. Their cunning plan was to have Mabote's brother, Johannes, faint in court and, while the police and other officials were attending to his "sick" brother, they would spring the child molester. But the police foiled their plan. Even doctors confirmed that Johannes was not sick. Mabote and Johannes were charged with attempt to escape from court and found guilty.

Mabote had escaped from custody before and was later sentenced to life imprisonment for the brutal murder, kidnapping and rape of Mammokgethi and other girls.

In the main newspaper front page, under the headline, "I begged him not to shoot his teachers" was a shocking story about a 29-year-old student at Tompi Seleka Agricultural College, David Malebane, who went on a shooting spree, killing three of the lecturers after he failed his practical exams in January 1999.

I was the only journalist who had an exclusive interview with Malebane's girlfriend, Lindi Sedibe. I had just returned to the office from the Germiston Magistrate's Court where I was covering Mabote's case when my news editor, Jocelyn Maker, told me to go to Tompi Seleka Agricultural College to find out what had happened.

After writing the Mabote story, I left the office with my colleague Michael Schmidt and arrived in Groblersdal late at night. The following morning, we went to Tompi Seleka to find a couple of other journalists already sniffing around for a scoop. My exclusive interview with Sedibe was not pure luck, but came about because of good journalistic instincts and good timing.

When we arrived at the college, most of the journalists were hanging around the administration office trying to speak to some of the lecturers and students. Seeing that we were already "scooped" by the journalists who had arrived before us, I decided to cast my net away from the administration office and walk around the school looking for different voices and witnesses.

As I was walking around the yard, I saw a young woman standing alone inside one of the classrooms crying. We had eye contact for about a minute, and then I realised that she might know something or be a victim of the tragedy. I walked inside the room and introduced myself, asking her why she was crying. As it turned out, she was Malebana's girlfriend.

This was the story:

I BEGGED HIM NOT TO KILL HIS TEACHERS

Girlfriend went down on her knees to try and stop student and his deadly mission to "finish off" lecturers

By Mzilikazi wa Afrika and Michael Schmidt

A young agricultural student told *Sunday Times* yesterday how she fell on her knees and begged her lover of two years not to kill his lecturers. But minutes later, David Malebana, 29, armed with a 9-millimetre pistol gunned down the lecturers on Friday in an incident which shattered the close-knit community at Tompi Seleka Agricultural College in Northern Province.

Lindi Sedibe, 25, of Kabokweni near Nelspruit, described yesterday how she battled to stop Malebana after he told her his plan to kill the lecturers he blamed for extending his studies.

Sedibe said she sprinted about one hundred metres to the house of lecturer Mmabana Moshoeshoe, Malebana's best friend, to raise the alarm.

But Moshoeshoe was showering and by the time he had wrapped a towel around himself, dressed and listened to Sedibe's story, a crucial 12 minutes had elapsed. These were the minutes during which Malebana calmly shot dead Anton Wittwer, 52, of Marble Hall, Petros Mashilo, 34, of Ga-Malaka, and Vincent Selepe, 30, of Bochum.

In a dramatic twist, Malebana was on his way to confess his crimes to his mother when he met a police patrol and blew his brains out.

"On Friday morning, David drove up and told me he was on a mission to kill three lecturers," said Sedibe.

Malebana had failed to complete his practical year, so Wittwer, Mashilo and Selepe told him to do six more months.

"I begged him not to kill them," said Sedibe, "but he was wild and aggressive and insisted on finishing them off, so I went down on my knees and held him tight around his legs.

"I cried and pleaded with him not to do it. But he broke loose, jumped into his car and drove off."

Malebana's best friend, Joel Moremi, 25, was in a field with 12 classmates when Malebana drove up.

"David parked the car and sat inside it for a few minutes," he said. "Then he climbed out. Our mentor, Petros Mashilo, was standing about six metres away from the car, writing in his diary. David sat on the bonnet for a moment, then walked over to him, pulled a gun out of his pants and shot him in the head.

"We were all terrified and ran away. I looked back to see my friend walk up to Mr Mashilo, lean over to him and shoot him again in the right temple."

Malebana then drove towards the office block, where he calmly shot Selepe, who was in a staff meeting, and Wittwer, who was walking down the corridor.

Malebana then found Moshoeshoe and handed him a list of his siblings to call to inform them of the incident and that he was going to commit suicide.

Malebana then drove to his home near Pietersburg, where his father, Piet, 84, demanded that he tell his mother, who was working in a field, of the shooting.

"David drove ahead in his car and my father and his brother followed him in another," Malebana's brother, Simon, said. "But en route they saw two police vans with flashing lights heading towards them. David just stopped and shot himself in the head."

The following Sunday, 24 January 1999, I cemented my stay at the *Sunday Times* with my exposé of a modern-day slave trader.

The story had started when I was a crime reporter at AENS in 1998 and had received a police press release about a minibus taxi that had overturned near the Komatipoort border at 4:00 a.m. killing all 21 passengers on board.

The police, in their statement, reported that all passengers except for the driver were foreign nationals. As an aspiring investigative reporter I asked myself a thousand questions: where on earth did the driver get 20 foreign nationals at 4:00 a.m.? Where was he rushing to at that time of the morning?

Out of journalistic curiosity, I took a taxi to Komatipoort police station where the taxi wreck was kept and took down the registration number and used it to trace its owner.

I discovered it was owned by a John "Sols" Nkuna. I started building a profile on this man by asking questions from my sources. One source told me that Nkuna was a wealthy businessman who was making a killing by trading in human beings, cross-border slavery, selling them for cheap labour in South Africa. Most of his slaves were sold as labourers to builders of the infamous RDP houses that were collapsing within months of being built, while others were sold as farm labourers.

Police arrested Nkuna several times with his human cargo, but each time he would pay an admission of guilt fine and would be let off the hook to continue with his dirty business.

I researched the story for more than a year in my spare time and when I joined the *Sunday Times*, I told Jocelyn Maker about it and she was keen that I take my investigation to another level.

This was my story:

THE MAN WHO TRADES IN HUMAN BEINGS
Reporter Mzilikazi wa Afrika describes his ordeal at the hands of a slave trader

This is the man who smuggled scores of illegal immigrants into South Africa, selling them to businesses and farmers in Mpumalanga and Gauteng.

John "Sols" Nkuna is also the man who beat me up after holding a gun to my head when I was flushed out of a slavery ring I had infiltrated during an investigation into the massive slave-labour trade across South Africa's borders.

Nkuna runs his business in human cargo from Mozambique and Swaziland using safe houses in Boschfontein and Langeloop in Mpumalanga, about 20 kilometres from the Lebombo border post in Komatipoort.

Also a well-known taxi boss, Nkuna lives in the biggest house in the rural area of Nkomazi.

Police say he has been caught on numerous occasions for smuggling illegal aliens into South Africa. He has been given spot fines ranging from R1 500 to R2 500, which he has paid.

Nkuna makes his money by selling illegal labour to businesses and farmers who pay up to R600 per illegal immigrant.

The immigrants, who come looking for work, also pay him for finding them jobs – as much as R530 each.

He uses four vehicles to ferry people every day of the week. He owns a luxury car, three minibus taxis, a Toyota Cressida and a bakkie with the registration number BPR 509 MP, which is one of the vehicles he uses to ferry people from his safe houses to businesses.

This was the bakkie I was driven around in before he discovered who I was.

On Monday I went to the offices of the Border and Internal Tracing Unit in Nelspruit, where I discussed my undercover investigation with the unit's second in charge, Inspector Cornelius du Preez.

On Tuesday morning Du Preez drove me to the Lebombo border post and I crossed the border legally. Although I was wearing very old clothing as a cover, I had to keep my passport hidden so I could prove I was there legally.

At Ressano Garcia, a border village in Mozambique, I pretended I wanted a job in Johannesburg. A man came up to me and said I should take a taxi to Maputo, where I would meet with their "chief" at a park. When I got to the park, I met a man who said his name was Augosto Makwakwa. He said he would help me get into South Africa and find a good job – I would have to pay him R480 in return.

But nothing came of this and, on Wednesday morning, I took a taxi back to Ressano Garcia, where I made new contacts and was taken to a safe house in the village along with four other men.

At 10:00 p.m., after 17 young men had gathered at the house, we left on a seven-hour walk to the Komatipoort border. A man who said his name was Paulos Mboweni, a Mozambican citizen, led us to where we would cross the fence.

After illegally entering South Africa, all of us were arrested by three South African National Defence Force soldiers.

The soldiers demanded R50 from each of us and took anything else they wanted – including watches and a Bible – before letting us go.

We walked another 10 kilometres and then Mboweni ordered us to wait for him. He had arranged beforehand to sell six of us – including a crippled man – to a sugar-cane farmer near Komatipoort.

We walked another 300 metres and, as we turned a corner, there was Nkuna, sitting in his white bakkie with the registration number BPR 509 MP.

He drove us to a safe house at Block B near Tonga. In a windowless room, Nkuna told us to strip so he could see we were not hiding more money from him.

By this time, we had all already paid him for our trip to Gauteng. I had given him R70 and told him he would get the rest when we reached Gauteng.

But it was during this sudden search that Nkuna discovered my passport and ID book, which I had tucked away in my underwear.

The modern-day slave trader went crazy, held a gun to my head and told me he was going to blow my brains out.

I felt my life was about to end. It was my worst nightmare – the only thing I had feared when I first decided to infiltrate the trade in illegal labour.

Initially, I had told people my name was Carlos Bernard Bilankulu – now I had been caught out.

Nkuna was aggressive, punching me several times and screaming: "Who the hell are you and what do you want?"

Then Nkuna began hitting me with a thick wooden pole about a metre in length, but I could not scream for help – I was too terrified.

After a while, Mboweni grabbed the pole from him. By this time, Nkuna was in a rage. He ran outside and returned with his gun.

"I'm going to kill this dog. He wants to mess with my bread and butter – I'm going to kill him," he said repeatedly and put the gun to my head.

I pleaded with him, telling him I was an undercover policeman investigating the smuggling into South Africa of Mozambican women who were then used as prostitutes in Johannesburg.

He replied: "You're lying! First you said your name was Carlos and now it's Leonard. Who are you? You bastard!"

I insisted I was an undercover policeman and he threw me onto the back of his bakkie, with the other immigrants.

Nkuna drove around and then dropped the others off at the sugarcane farm. He told them there was a job there for each of them and that he would return later to collect his money.

I was still in the back of the bakkie, shaking with pain. Nkuna drove for more than 10 kilometres and suddenly stopped, dropping me off in the dark in the middle of nowhere.

I was lost and disorientated from the beating but walked for at least 12 hours before I found my way back to Nelspruit.

I then contacted Captain David Chilembe, head of the Border and Internal Tracing Unit, and told him I knew of at least ten illegal immigrants who had just been smuggled into South Africa – and where Nkuna had been holding them.

Police raided a number of houses in the area, arresting eight illegal immigrants on a property belonging to Nkuna. Five of them told the police that they had been with me and witnessed the beating I had received from Nkuna.

They told me they knew Nkuna well because some of them had been on the trip before, but Nkuna himself was nowhere to be found.

After evading police for more than a month following my exposé, Nkuna was later arrested at Embalenhle township in Secunda. He tried to sell a disabled boy back to his own father as nobody wanted to buy the boy from him. The teenager was described as "useless" by most of Nkuna's clients because of his physical disabilities.

The boy's father couldn't afford Nkuna's price for his own son and asked the businessman to return him at the end of the month when he is paid. The concerned father called the police as soon as the businessman had left with the boy in his car.

Police cornered Nkuna on the road and rescued the boy. The businessman was sentenced to more than ten years in jail.

I did not lay any criminal charges against him even though I was assaulted in the line of duty. Some of my nemeses said I got what I deserved. But for me, I got a good story and exposed a man who was making a living from selling other human beings.

Chapter 12

MINTIRHO YA VULAVULA: Aluta Continua

"Good people do not need laws to tell them to act responsibly, while bad people will find a way around the laws." – Plato

It was late on Friday night, 12 February 1999 when I received a call from a person asking to remain anonymous; I didn't know the caller from a bar of soap.

"A cellphone belonging to one of the members of Parliament was stolen at the assembly today. I can guarantee you the thief is not one of the cleaners or workers but one of us," the caller said.

The source suggested I call the crime victim, Member of Parliament Adrian Crewe, to get more information about the theft of his cellphone.

It is scandalous for members of Parliament to be stealing from each other. These are the people who are lawmakers in our country, people who should lead by example. It is a tragedy and a shame for the nation, I was thinking after the call.

I managed to speak to Crewe the following Tuesday, and he told me that he was not the first victim of cellphone theft in Parliament. "It is sad to think that some of our members are kleptomaniacs," Crewe said.

He explained that he didn't have a suspect in mind and had no idea how it was stolen.

"I left my phone on my desk during a short break, I thought it was safe to do so, after all I was in the company of distinguished and dignified members of Parliament, but when I came back it was gone."

I asked Crewe for the names of all the members of Parliament who were with him in the room on that day as well as all the details about his phone.

He told me it was a Nokia 5110 and he had bought it for R2 700. I then befriended someone working for the service provider. After intensive lobbying and begging, he agreed to locate the phone signal for me. A few hours later, he called to say that they were picking up the phone's signal around Hazyview in Mpumalanga.

From the list that Crewe had given me, I saw that one of the members was Steve Mbuyiswa, a former MEC for youth affairs in Mpumalanga, who was from Hazyview.

I drove to Mbuyiswa's house near Hazyview to try and speak to him, but his wife, Agnes Sambo, told me her husband was back in Parliament. Lo and behold! There she was holding a Nokia 5110 in her hand.

"You have a nice phone," I said.

"Thank you, my husband bought it for me as a Valentine's Day present," she said proudly, flaunting her special gift.

The 32-year-old Mbuyiswa, a former ANC youth league chairperson in Mpumalanga, who was also my leader and role model during my days as a political activist, was arrested for theft on 17 February 1999. This disgraced MP, who was earning R250 000 per annum, stole a cellphone from a colleague and gave it to his unsuspecting wife as a Valentine's Day present.

The investigating officer Detective Sergeant Anton Coetzee had also traced the phone to Sambo after getting information from the service provider.

Mbuyiswa was released on R500 bail after spending a few hours behind bars and he was suspended from Parliament.

In its 1999 annual report, the ANC stated, "Comrade Steve Mbuyiswa has been charged under Rule 26.3.3 of the ANC Constitution following his conviction on the serious charge of cellular phone theft. The hearing took place on 12 November 1999 and he was found guilty of this charge. His membership of the ANC is suspended for five years, with the proviso that the PDC can ask for a review after three years."

My story about Mbuyiswa's shenanigans made it to the front page of *Sunday Times* on 28 February 1999 under the headline. "The House of Shame: MP suspended for theft of cellphone and cop probed after Mandela's polony cutter disappears".

The story included a piece written by my colleague Henry Ludsk, about a police officer stationed at Tuynhuys in Cape Town, the official residence of Nelson Mandela, who was the president of the country at the time. The police officer was also facing an investigation after goods worth about R28 000 were stolen from Madiba's house.

The goods included four cellphones, a television set, a video machine, two printers and a polony-cutting machine. The story also highlighted how goods worth more than R700 000 were stolen from Parliament in three years.

One Saturday evening in February 1999, I was in a taxi travelling from Johannesburg to Nelspruit to spend another weekend there. It was the last taxi of the day with only seven passengers, most of them drunk.

The drinking continued on this four-hour trip and my fellow passengers, who I later discovered were Mozambican nationals, started talking about how they bought their South African identity documents from our home affairs office. They mentioned how they bribed officials and the different offices where one could buy these documents.

I listened with keen interest, posing a question or two while pretending to be a foreigner myself.

Back at the office the following week, I told Jocelyn Maker about the stories I had heard on my trip to Nelspruit. Even though they were half drunk I believed their gossip, I said.

Jocelyn thought this can't be true and suggested it was just the booze and ego-tripping from my fellow passengers. But I told her I would like to find out myself and test their gossip. Accompanied by a photographer, I went to the home affairs offices at Harrison Street in Johannesburg. I stood outside for a few minutes before I was approached by one of those cameramen who asked if I needed an ID or passport photo.

I said, "I don't want a photo but a South African ID, my brother."

He asked, "Are you a *kwerekwere* [an immigrant]?"

"Yes I am."

"Where are you from?"

"I am from Zimbabwe."

"The ID will cost you. Do you have money?"

"Yes, I have some cash."

"Just wait here and someone will come and sort you out."

After a few minutes, a tall man wearing a colourful striped T-shirt and a hat approached me. I explained to him that I was looking for a South African identity document.

"It will cost you R2 000," he said.

I told him that I had the money and we started doing the paperwork.

I explained to the man that I was a Zimbabwean national who just found a job in South Africa and that my boss, who believed that I was a South African, wanted to see a copy of my identity book or I was going to lose my job.

Photos were taken and I got my official temporary identity document on the same day after money exchanged hands in a public toilet. We exposed the ID book scam on the front page of the *Sunday Times* on 7 March 1999. We bust the fake ID racket.

SUNDAY TIMES SPECIAL INVESTIGATION

The head of South Africa's busiest home affairs office fled and locked himself in a parking basement yesterday when confronted with proof of wide-scale ID document fraud in his department.

A *Sunday Times* team presented Dumisani Buthelezi, acting regional representative for the department of home affairs in Johannesburg, with an ID document bought by a reporter posing as an illegal alien.

Buthelezi and his deputy, Ben Makgalemela, refused to answer questions and ran down a flight of stairs into the basement and locked the door.

In a telephone interview 15 minutes later, Buthelezi confessed that he was linked to the sale of ID documents, saying: "Yes, I am involved."

The dramatic confrontation followed a three-week investigation which found that new temporary and permanent ID documents were being sold illegally by officials in Harrison Street, Johannesburg.

The documents can be used for voter registration, undermining the government's huge drive for a fraud-free election.

Independent Electoral Commission officials at registration points were stunned when shown an ID document bought by the team. It bears a false ID number and the name of a fictitious man, Mfukuwa Joseph Mbowani.

The deputy minister of home affairs, Lindiwe Sisulu, said she was shocked by the findings. She thanked the team for exposing the alleged corruption, saying it would be fully investigated.

Sunday Times reporter Mzilikazi wa Afrika went undercover on 19 February in a bid to buy an ID book. Outside the Harrison Street office, he was approached by an "agent," who gave his name as Simile Reginald Ndiza. Ndiza said the price for a temporary ID was R300. The money was exchanged in a small room in the basement of an adjoining building. An hour later, Ndiza returned from the home affairs building with a receipt which falsely stated that the applicant had submitted a birth and baptismal certificate.

"If you want a barcoded ID book come with R2 000 – our boss will fix everything for you," Ndiza said.

On 25 February, the reporter paid the R2 000 in a nearby municipal toilet and supplied ID photos. Ndiza disappeared into the home affairs building and returned two hours later with an official temporary ID document – which has the status of a complete ID book. Besides registration, it can be used to open a bank account and buy property.

Ndiza said the barcoded ID book would be ready in three days – but later said they had problems getting the book as inspectors were monitoring the building. The book was to have been handed over on Friday, but officials involved in the scam disappeared after another customer stormed into the building, demanding a driver's license he had paid for.

However, the team pinpointed a number of officials involved in processing the documents. The middleman between the agent, who operates at street level, and home affairs officials is a man known as "Oupa".

During negotiations for the ID book, Ndiza and Oupa introduced the reporter to an official in enquiries booth 15, identified as Johan Victor. Meetings were arranged away from his desk – either on the street or in a quiet corner of the building.

On Friday, Victor said: "We are very busy with all these people coming here to get their temporary ID books to register to vote. I don't have time to get out your ID book. Please come back on Monday and it will be ready."

On Friday Wa Afrika met Buthelezi and showed him the documents purchased from his officials. Buthelezi said he was aware of a "major scam" among his officials and promised to meet our team yesterday morning in order to confront those implicated. However, yesterday the team was told he was not in the building.

They were introduced to Makgalemela, who said Buthelezi was not at work. But seconds later Buthelezi was seen in the main foyer. When confronted by the team, he shouted: "I don't want to speak to you – I don't like your tactics."

He walked to a nearby lift with Makgalemela. The team followed them and they ran down a flight of stairs into the basement, locking the door behind them.

The national director-general of home affairs, Albert Mokoena, said he had been told by Buthelezi that the *Sunday Times* had uncovered an ID racket at the Harrison Street office. But he could not explain why the man had run and locked himself away.

Sisulu said the department believed the barcoded ID had the least chance of being corrupted.

She said the IEC had discovered that a "sizeable number" of people registered were not South Africans. But once registration was complete, the voters' roll would be compared to the population register to weed out the corruption, he said.

The following morning, former home affairs director-general, Albert Mokoena, was on radio accusing me of being an irresponsible journalist who enticed his poorly paid officials with money to sell an ID book. I was shocked by Mokoena's accusations.

Mokoena was doing radio interviews to defend his corrupt officials and the corruption taking place at the home affairs offices. For a man holding his position and defending corruption, it made me wonder.

I started doing a profile on Mokoena, asking around for more information about this staunch defender of corruption. Someone told me that Mokoena was from Soweto and that he owned a professional basketball team, Mecer Soweto Panthers.

I went to the basketball league website and looked at the profile of his team. Listed, as contact details, were some Pretoria numbers. I dialled the numbers and a woman on the other side said, "Home affairs department, director-general's office; how can I help you?"

I told the lady that I was a professional basketball player and wanted to speak to Mokoena. She requested that I fax my CV to the same number listed on the team's profile and confirmed that it belonged to the home affairs department, to be more precise: Mokoena's office.

There and then it dawned on me that Mokoena was running his basketball team from a government office. Now I needed to find out from the then home affairs minister, Mangosuthu Buthelezi, whether he gave Mokoena such permission.

I called Buthelezi several times and left about a dozen messages. He returned my call at about 3:30 a.m. He told me he was busy with his election campaign as the president of IFP, one of the political parties in South Africa. The only time he could talk to me was later.

I explained to Buthelezi that Mokoena was running his basketball team from his government office and asked him whether the minister was aware or had given his permission. Buthelezi said he wasn't aware that Mokoena had a basketball team. It is a government policy that all senior government officials should declare their businesses or entities where they have interests, but his director-general never made such a declaration.

The worst was that he was running his team from his government office behind the minister's back.

"If you have all this evidence that you are telling me about, go ahead and expose him," said Buthelezi fuming.

Mokoena's exposé was on the front page of the *Sunday Times* on 21 March 1999 with the headline, "Expose him! Buthelezi confronts his DG after probe shows he runs a sports team from office".

Home Affairs Minister, Mangosuthu Buthelezi, this week urged the *Sunday Times* to expose his director-general, Albert Mokoena, after an investigation established he was running a baseball team from the department's head office in Pretoria.

Mokoena owns and manages a professional basketball team, Mecer Soweto Panthers, in direct contravention of the Public Service Act. Buthelezi said he found the information that Mokoena had a basketball team disturbing.

"He did not ask permission from me to own the team. I will confront him," he said.

Yesterday Mokoena denied he was violating the Act, which forbids government employees from using office equipment for private business without permission. It also forbids public servants from doing any private work connected with any official duties without permission.

But it has been established that:

- Mokoena used his official home affairs telephone and fax in his Pretoria office to do his basketball business. The numbers also appear on the basketball team website;

- As the director-general of home affairs, he dealt with the final work permit applications for foreign players he recruited for his team;

- He requested a R543 000 sponsorship for the Panthers from a computer company, Cenit, at a time when it had a three-year service contract with the department. The company turned down his request; and

- His basketball team later received a R250 000 sponsorship from Mecer Computers.

Dr Sandi Baai, director of ethics at the Public Service Commission, said the public protector should investigate the case. "If there is proof that Mokoena is violating the code and there is a case for conflict of interest then the necessary steps should be taken against him," he said.

The *Sunday Times* three weeks ago exposed a major illegal ID racket in the Harrison Street offices of home affairs. At the time Mokoena slammed the *Sunday Times* investigation as irresponsible.

But yesterday he promised to apologise for what he said in a newspaper and on radio.

Buthelezi, meanwhile, applauded the *Sunday Times* investigation into his department. "We need this kind of co-operation between civil society and government if we are to uproot corruption."

Mokoena said he did not believe he needed to ask permission, as required by the Act, from Buthelezi to own the Panthers, because he had put his details in his CV. "I have had the Panthers for a number of years. Buthelezi saw my CV – he employed me."

He admitted his private office telephone and fax numbers were used to conduct the team's business. But he said he did not think this conflicted with his job as director-general.

Mokoena said he did not believe that using the telephone and fax at taxpayer's expense to run his privately owned basketball team was a problem.

Mokoena admitted he had checked the final applications for foreign players who applied for work permits but denied requesting sponsorship from Cenit.

But a former director of Cenit, Johan Smook, confirmed that a request had been received from Mokoena in February last year.

While writing the story, I went back to the team's profile on the website and scrutinised all Makoena's players. Three of them caught my attention – Boniface Kabongo, Humphrey Mapulango and Billy Banda – all registered as South African-born players but I smelt a fat big rat.

I started going to basketball games and training sessions, asking more questions about the three players until one day, one of the players whispered to me that the three were foreign nationals from Zambia and that Mokoena had illegally given them South African identity documents and citizenships.

The Zambian Basketball Association also confirmed the nationality of the three players and explained that they had already written a letter to their South African counterpart addressing their official grievances about them. They were even willing to share the letter with the *Sunday Times*.

I managed to trace one of the players, Boniface Kabongo, with the information and the letter. I brought him to the office where he burst into tears while trying to explain how Mokoena had lured them into South Africa and given them citizenships under illegal circumstances.

Another Mokoena exposé made the front page of the *Sunday Times* on 11 April 1999 under the headline, "The game's up, Mr Mokoena":

Home affairs director-general registered three Zambians in his basketball team as born and bred South Africans.

The director-general of the department of home affairs, Albert Mokoena, has three foreign players in his basketball team who are illegally registered as South African citizens.

Mokoena runs the team, Mecer Soweto Panthers, from his home affairs office.

All three players come from Zambia, but have all illegally acquired South African ID books. In the application for the books, they claim they were born in this country.

Mokoena used the ID books to register the players as South African with the Premier Basketball League.

They were brought to South Africa to play for Mokoena's team.

At the time they applied for the ID books in 1994, Mokoena was not director-general, but two of the players got their South African citizenship after he was appointed to the position.

All three still play professional basketball for Mokoena's team.

Billy Banda, a former Zambian national player, entered the country on a Zambian passport.

Boniface Kabongo told how the Zambians had acquired the false ID books: "Banda told me he had spoken to Mokoena, asking him to get ID books for us.

"He told us we should all go to the home affairs office in Market Street – Mokoena had given us a letter and someone would be waiting for us.

"We didn't stand in a queue. We had no documents such as birth certificates with us. I do not know the people who are claimed to be my parents in my application for late registration of birth.

"We did not pay a cent. Banda went inside while we waited outside. We were called in once to sign papers. We did not know what these papers were about – all we knew was that we would all get South African ID books."

Kabongo admitted that he lied about his place of birth. He was actually born in Mandevu Compound in Lusaka, Zambia. He said he had lived in Johannesburg in a flat at Anchor Towers – opposite the Harrison Street home affairs office – for which Mokoena paid the rent.

He said Mokoena had also supplied the three with food and spent many weekends with them at the flat.

Mokoena this week refused to answer any questions relating to the players.

Documents handed to the *Sunday Times* show that the three players were not entitled to South African citizenship. As foreigners, they had to have lived in South Africa for five years before obtaining citizenship. None of them qualified and one got his citizenship after only one month in South Africa.

Captain Ernest Madzhie of the Organised Crime Unit said there was no doubt the players' applications were incomplete and illegal.

"The applications were purposefully filled incomplete, so no one could trace the people mentioned in them. I have seen many of these – someone in home affairs helped them to get ID documents illegally."

The general manager of the league, Al Feinstein, said: "It is true that Mokoena registered the three players as South African citizens. But I want to make it clear that the league accepted these players as South Africans only after Mokoena provided us with valid ID books and other documents required by home affairs."

An official letter, dated 8 September 1994 – about the time the players arrived in South Africa – to the Basketball Union of South Africa from the Zambian Basketball Association – stated that six players, including two of the three Zambians, had defected to South Africa without official clearance from the association.

A representative of the association said: "They are Zambians. When they started playing in South Africa, they did not have clearance from us. That is why the letter was written."

Here are the facts about Mokoena's "South African" players:

- Captain Billy Banda attended Munali Secondary School in Zambia, where he was a junior jump-champion. He played for a Zambian basketball team called Basketball Heroes and he was in the Zambian basketball team when they played against a US university team in 1991.

  He came to South Africa through Johannesburg International Airport using a Zambian passport – number 174750 – on 18 March 1994 and applied for citizenship six months later. On 5 August 1997 he was given a South African ID number – 681224 6294 088. His application said he was born in Johannesburg. That year, Mokoena registered him as a South African citizen with the league;

- Boniface Kabongo entered South Africa on 24 August 1994 through Beit Bridge using a Zambian passport. He was born in Mandevu Compound in Lusaka, Zambia, and educated at Metropolitan Secondary School. He played basketball for a Zambian club called Premium Hawks. In February 1995 – within six months of arriving in South Africa – he applied for citizenship. On 5 March 1994, he was a South African citizen in possession of an ID book – ID number 711015 5962 087. His application said he was born in Benoni. He too was registered with the league by Mokoena as a South African citizen in 1997. He was selected for the South African squad to play in the All Africa Games in Johannesburg in September;

- Humphrey Mapulango, the third Zambian in Mokoena's team, was born in Kabwe, Zambia. He entered South Africa using a Zambian passport through Johannesburg International Airport in December 1993. He played for a Zambian basketball team called the Lusaka City Council Looters and was a member of the Zambian national team. Mapulango applied for his late registration of birth and ID books at the home affairs office in Market Street, Johannesburg, on 2 August 1994. He got his South African ID book – which bears the number 730906 5963 082 – on 31 July 1997. His application said he was born in Soweto. Mokoena also registered him with the league as a South African citizen in 1997.

After a series of investigations on Mokoena, I opened a can of worms, rotten to the core. *Sunday Times* published a number of my exposés on him; most of them front page stories.

Mokoena tried to claim that I was an illegal immigrant in South Africa. He went through my personal file at home affairs, and because he was not convinced that I was a bona fide South African citizen, he and his team drove to my village at Sibambayani in Bushbuckridge to verify my records.

After interviewing dozens of villagers and checking my records at the local primary school, Mokoena realised that he had sent his team on a wild goose chase. And then he did the unthinkable: he went to my father and lied to him, declaring that I had claimed over R4 million from an unnamed insurance company by stating that my dad had passed away.

My angry dad phoned me that day demanding to know why I had declared him dead. After a brief discussion, my dad smelt the rat and asked one of my cousins to take down the registration number of the BMW this man was driving: it turned out to be Mokoena's personal vehicle.

Meanwhile, Mokoena was investigated by the Public Service Commission, which found him guilty of:

- Conflict of interest after seeking sponsorship for his team from a company with an existing contract with the department;

- Using work facilities for private interests by putting home affairs telephone and fax numbers on his team's website;

- For abusing his position as a home affairs director-general to obtain South African ID books for non-South African players on his basketball team;

- Improper use of state vehicles; and

- Directing that members of his basketball team be transported in state vehicles, causing two government officials to perform private work outside their official hours.

At a hastily arranged press conference at OR Tambo International Airport in September, the same minister Buthelezi was at pains to explain his director-general's conduct that led to the guilty verdict.

Buthelezi said, "The report indicated that Mokoena's conduct has been of such a nature that it constitutes a breach of truth and confidence which underpins his employment relationship with me. The report recommends that I direct Mr Mokoena to resign from public office."

Former South African president, Thabo Mbeki, accepted Mokoena's resignation.

And that was the end of the maverick Mokoena's career in the public service.

Mokoena resurfaced a few months later as the South African Football Association (SAFA) chief operating officer in January 2002 but was forced to resign from the organisation three years later after he was involved in a sex scandal with his personal assistant, Herbert Rasekhula.

Mokoena's relationship with Rasekhula, a married man, had raised a lot of eyebrows as the two men went on a number of international trips together at SAFA's expense. To make matters worse, it emerged that Mokoena allegedly fired Rasekhula's live-in lover, Faith Ramupi, from SAFA after she started questioning their closeness.

In a dramatic turn of events, Mokoena bounced back as the chairperson of the South African Basketball National League late in 2013. It looks like everyone, including sports minister Fikile Mbalula, who attended the league launch in Randburg, had forgotten about Mokoena's dodgy past, which messed up the original basketball league in South Africa.

Chapter 13

MAKOMBANDLELA: Let's start a revolution

"Critical, independent and investigative media is the lifeblood of any democracy." – Nelson Mandela

During my first year at the *Sunday Times* I managed to get slave trader John Nkuna arrested and convicted; Member of Parliament Steve Mbuyiswa arrested and convicted; and home affairs director-general Albert Mokoena exposed and resigned.

I started receiving journalism awards during my first year with the newspaper including the *Sunday Times* Journalist of the Year, the Ruth First Courageous Journalism Award, and the Nat Nakasa Media Integrity Award. I was also the runner up for a Foreign Correspondence Association Award.

There is an African proverb that says if you want to go fast, go alone; if you want to go far, go with others. My grandmother used to say that a river that swells from its tributaries does not need rain to survive.

At the end of 1999 I approached my boss, Jocelyn Maker, a woman who since became my second mother, and suggested that we should start a *Sunday Times* investigations unit.

After careful consideration and deliberation, Jocelyn indicated that I should approach Mike Robertson, who was the *Sunday Times* editor at the time, and try to convince him. I had her backing. Mike was happy with the initiative but he needed to convince top management, as well as source some funding as investigations require money.

Within days, the top management approved the plan. They gave Mike their blessings and provided a handsome budget for the unit. Mike suggested that we bring in two more people and that Jocelyn should be the unit boss as I had a good working relationship with her. She was one of the most experienced editors in the newsroom and a distinguished journalist herself.

The hunt for two additional members to join the unit started. I was still new. My year with the *Sunday Times* did not make me an expert for sourcing the best candidates. Since Jocelyn had spent years with the newspaper, she was the best person to choose the best of the best. The first person to be roped in was André Jurgens, based in our Port Elizabeth office. The other was Jessica Bezuidenhout, who was brought in from our Cape Town office.

The *Sunday Times* investigations unit was put together late in 2000 and accommodated in a secluded corner office, away from the newsroom, with a secret pin code to open the door known only to the four of us. Not even Mike Robertson, the editor, knew the code.

It also happened that in 2000, I was tasked to be one of the researchers helping Mark Gevisser who was writing a biography of former president Thabo Mbeki, the second head of state in a democratic South Africa.

Gevisser started working on his critically acclaimed biography, *The Dream Deferred*, in 1998. It was an eight-year project and I would spend more than a year working on it. My first assignment was to find out what happened to the then president's only child, Monwabisi Kwanda Mbeki.

Mbeki had Kwanda with his high school sweetheart, Nokwanda Olive Mphahlwa, out of wedlock when he was just 16 years old. Kwanda was born in Durban on 8 October 1959, and was working at a company called Everite in the Vaal Triangle when he disappeared around 1981.

Initially it was believed that he had joined his father in exile but Phumelelo Rulumeni claimed to have seen Kwanda in Tanzania and Zambia in 1983 and 1984 and, though he refused to be interviewed, he told Mphahlwa that he had seen her son in exile.

Testifying before the Truth and Reconciliation Commission (TRC) in Port Elizabeth on 23 May 1996, she said, "Monwabise last saw his father when he was two years old. Not knowing him hurt him very badly. He complained bitterly to me about this. In 1981 his letters suddenly stopped. I am certain that he was involved with the ANC because he idolised his father but we never spoke about politics."

There were also rumours that Kwanda was spotted in Cuba, but in my investigation I failed to trace Kwanda's whereabouts.

My second assignment for *The Dream Deferred* was to trace the former president's younger brother, Jama Mbeki, who had also disappeared during the struggle.

Jama studied law at Leeds University, England, on a scholarship arranged by this brother, Thabo. He and his brother, Moeletsi, were sent to Lesotho when he was ten years old to live with their aunt, Mphuma Moerane. Jama considered himself a Lesotho national rather than a South African. He would even join the Basutoland Congress Party (BCP), an arch rival of the ANC.

After he concluded his studies in England, he decided to join thousands of BCP supporters who were exiled. He opened his practice at Selebi-Phikwe, a vibrant mining town in the north-east of Botswana. He continued being an activist and frequently met his brother, Thabo, who was stationed in Botswana at the time.

Jama was arrested early in March 1982 after a fake truck business deal, a sting orchestrated by the notorious South African Security Branch. Shots were fired during the arrest. After being charged with attempted murder and denied his diabetes medication, Jama managed to escape from prison on 16 March 1982, the day before he was to appear in court. How he managed to escape or who helped him, nobody knows.

From Botswana, Jama headed for Soweto before he was smuggled to Lesotho. But it was in Lesotho where he met his fate, executed by a senior intelligence official from the Lesotho Defence Force who claimed to have had some vital information for him. At the time, the Lesotho Defence Force was working closely with Umkhonto we Sizwe, but Jama belonged to the rival political party of the ANC.

I managed to trace the man who is alleged to have killed Jama in Maseru, the capital of Lesotho, where he was running a security company. Within days, I was forced to escape Lesotho in the dead of night as the man wanted to kill me too.

The Mbeki family hired a Lesotho-based lawyer to investigate Jama's death and he came to the same conclusion as my research: namely that the gunman was the very same man who tried to kill me.

The Dream Deferred was well received by the South African and international reading public and critics alike. It would win the Alan Paton Award in 2008. Sponsored by the *Sunday Times*, the award is named after famed novelist, Alan Paton, the author of the critically acclaimed *Cry, The Beloved Country*.

While I was busy with my research for the book, Jocelyn was hard at work putting our investigations unit together, and dealing with the logistics.

My grandfather, Dibane Nxumalo.

My mother, Deyiye Nxumalo.

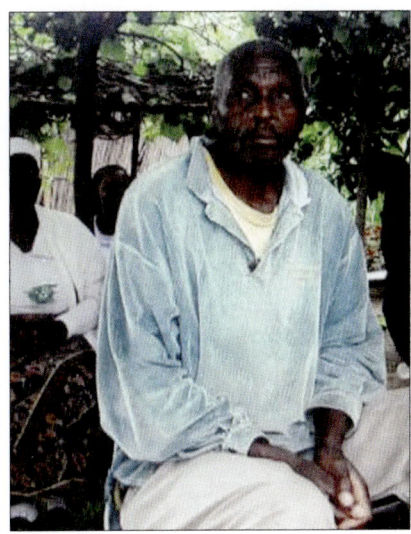

My father, Simon Ndzhukula.

Nathaniel Makanete, my high-school friend, who opened my eyes to the world of politics.

Ripho Machate, a former MK soldier and body-guard to Mathews Phosa. He used to supply me with guns for distribution to "comrades".

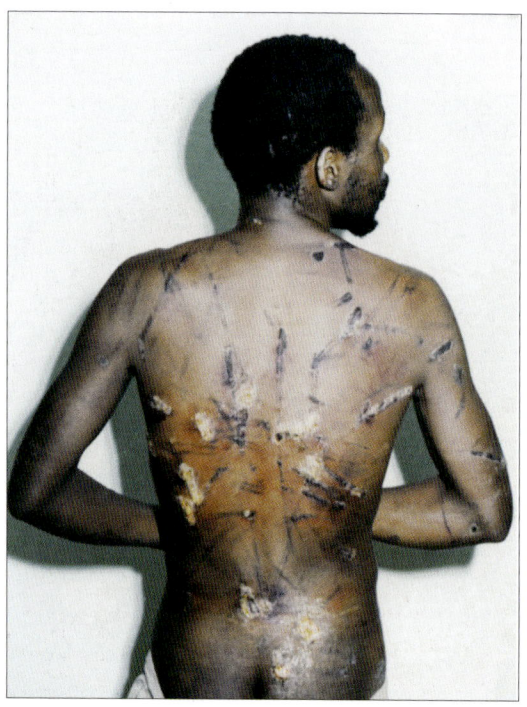

Ripho after he was brutally assaulted and left for dead. But he survived.

Man about town: on holiday in KwaZulu-Natal in 2013.

My friend from primary school, Robert Khoza, with whom I started a band at age 11. We shared a special bond through music, soccer, books and politics.

Sitting on a broken boat at Catembe overlooking Maputo in Mozambique.

A long walk to the lion's den: walking along with my lawyer, Eric van Den Berg, to Rosebank Police Station before I was bungled into an unmarked police car and whisked away without any explanation.

Having a chat with Public Protector Advocate, Thuli Madonsela, at her office in Pretoria.

Elizabeth Sejake @ Sunday Times

The original members of the *Sunday Times* Investigations Unit and myself, this time winning the Nat Nakasa Award for Courageous Journalism. Also in this photo is proud Unit editor, Jocelyn Maker, who is like a second mother to me.

With my colleagues from the new *Sunday Times* Investigations Unit: Stephan Hofstatter and Rob Rose. We won the Global Shining Light Award in Rio de Janeiro, Brazil, in 2013. Our story about the Cato Manor police unit was selected from 65 entries from 28 countries.

Me and Stephan Hofstatter after winning the Taco Kuiper Investigative Journalism Award in 2011.

With house music icons in 2009: Culoe de Song, G'Sparks, Boddhi Satva, Black Coffee, Silly-m.

In my recording studio making music in 2004.

At Capitol Hill in Washington DC, USA, in 2001.

Me and Milton Machel at the Global Investigative Journalism Conference in Rio de Janeiro in 2013.

Whenever I had a moment, if I was not travelling out of the country on my research, I would come to the office and work on a story or two, bonding with my new colleagues.

I had little free time that year. But one of the few stories that I did was an exposé of a former Mpumalanga director-general who, just like most people I write about, threatened to kill me.

The story started after I received an email from Knightsbridge University in England inviting me to study for a business administration degree.

"You can study through email or distance mail order," the email stated.

After a number of email exchanges, I began to suspect that the institution was either bogus or dodgy. In trying to get me on board and also trying to impress me, the university made the grave mistake of sending me a list of some of the "South African graduates" from the institution. Shadreck Coleman Nyathi was one of them.

I knew Dr Coleman Nyathi as a director-general in Mpumalanga, who was regarded as one of the "highly qualified civil servants in the province".

To make certain that Dr Nyathi had indeed "graduated" from a university – I suspected his qualifications were dodgy – I sourced his curriculum vitae from the Mpumalanga government. Indeed, he listed his "doctorate degree" in business administration from Knightsbridge University.

I wrote back to the university to ask how long it would take to finish my "business administration degree" and was told that if I had access to the Internet I could do it in 30 minutes or a month via long-distance learning.

Nyathi was known in Mpumalanga as a corruption buster and esteemed civil servant. As a matter of fact (and ironically), Nyathi had announced a commission to probe all senior public servants' academic qualifications in the province.

He even called on the *National Intelligence Agency (NIA)* to vet the qualifications of all senior public servants and none of them picked out that his qualification was bogus. He claimed, ironically, that the NIA would make sure that top public servants take an oath and pledge not to divulge sensitive documents to anyone outside government.

During my investigation, I established that Nyathi spent R23 387 of taxpayer's money for his "degree" without any government approval.

One day, I called a government official I had seen hanging around with Nyathi on several occasions, to ask him more about his friend. This official told me that he had known Nyathi from back home in Bulawayo, Zimbabwe. Trying to impress me, the official told me how the two met at primary school and even attended the same church, GutaRamwari Church, in Bulawayo. He said Nyathi had just left for Zimbabwe to check on one of his relatives who was reportedly sick.

Nyathi's CV, which I had sourced, claimed he was a South African.

I received an unexpected phone call from Nyathi the following week, rabidly curious about why I was asking his friend questions about him. I was frank and open: I told him that I was investigating his academic qualifications and citizenship. The man went ballistic over the phone, threatening to shoot and kill me if I dared write any story about him. He then slammed the phone down in anger.

The following day, after I had sent him the official questions, Nyathi telephoned once again to repeat his threats. Politely, I told him that I would only be happy if he could respond to my questions before my impending deadline.

Nyathi's story would be the front page of the *Sunday Times* on 21 May 2000 under the headline, "Expose me and you die".

One of Mpumalanga's most powerful civil servants has threatened to shoot a *Sunday Times* journalist if he exposes him.

Today we unmask the man as a fraud.

Director-general Shadreck Coleman Nyathi has spun a web of lies from Zimbabwe to South Africa about his academic qualifications and citizenship. It is alleged that he is an illegal immigrant from Zimbabwe. This week, a Department of Public Service and Administration investigation into the qualifications of 71 senior officials in the province found that ten of them have fake degrees.

The qualifications of ten others are being viewed as "highly suspicious".

Nyathi, who is the administrative head and accounting officer in Mpumalanga, denied lying on his CV and twice told the *Sunday Times* reporter that "if you expose me I will kill you. I will shoot you".

Nyathi claimed in his CV that:

- He was a "doctor of business administration" – but the *Sunday Times* has established that he only has a Standard 8 and a diploma;

- He was a marketing director designate with the Zimbabwe Tourism Development Corporation now called Zimbabwe Tourism Authority, but it denies he held a management position.

Zimbabwe Tourism Authority chief executive Etherton Mpisaunga said Nyathi used to work in their Bulawayo office, but he was never in management.

"He was never a marketing director. This is the biggest joke – Nyathi is a Zimbabwean from Bulawayo. I don't know why he had to lie about his nationality."

On Friday, Nyathi admitted that he did not hold the position of Zimbabwe Tourism Authority marketing director, but said he worked there as a regional manager. He refused to say why he had lied in his CV.

Nadina Coetzee, the head of Evaluation of Educational Qualifications with the South African Qualifications Authority, studied Nyathi's certificates and said his highest academic qualification was a diploma in management studies equivalent to a level four qualification at a local technikon.

Nyathi claims he obtained his Doctorate in business administration from Knightsbridge University in England. But Coetzee said the university was not officially recognised by major international organisations.

Nyathi claims he is a South African born in Port Elizabeth.

"I grew up in Zimbabwe. I went there as a child and attended school there."

But *Sunday Times* established that Nyathi's file at the department of home affairs is incomplete.

He only applied for a birth certificate on 16 September 1998, eight years after he received his ID book.

He said in his ID application that he was a labourer at a time when his CV said he held the position in tourism.

Nyathi joined Mpumalanga government as a director-general for the Department of Economic Affairs and Tourism. MEC Jacob Mabena said his qualifications were not checked when he was appointed.

Nyathi tendered his resignation with immediate effect the following day and he was arrested at Lebombo Border Post, between South Africa and Mozambique after he tried to escape with a state vehicle, a Mercedes-Benz, and he was later deported back to Zimbabwe.

This piece won me the *Sunday Times* Story of the Year Award for 2000.

An editorial published in the *Sunday Times* on 28 May 2000 titled, "Failing the nation by degrees", also highlighted how people with bogus qualifications were getting senior positions in government because of their connections and not skills, it stated:

> In what is increasingly becoming a national embarrassment, South Africans are regularly being subjected to revelations that high-ranking public servants faked their qualifications or lied in their CVs.
>
> Mpumalanga director-general Coleman Nyathi last week joined a gallery of rogues when this newspaper revealed that he had lied about his academic qualifications, management experience and citizenship.
>
> In this gallery are the likes of Eugene Nyathi, who, after being paid more than R1 million for consultancy work by the Mpumalanga government, was exposed as also having lied about his qualifications and – more critically – his identity.
>
> Then there's Frank Gondwe, who exaggerated his qualifications to secure a position as North West's chief tax man. And Zakes Ximba, who with a mere Standard 3 education, secured a senior position in Gauteng's local government department.
>
> There are hundreds of other such chancers on senior rungs of the civil service who managed to circumvent normal employment criteria, primarily because they had the right connections in high places.
>
> All this is happening in a country that aspires to become a role model of good governance for other African nations.
>
> We recognise the fact that high-flown tertiary qualifications cannot be the only criteria for judging an individual's ability to perform public service duties. South Africa's history is such that many were denied opportunities to study and garner experience in public service administration and private sector management.
>
> But it is also true that skills and experience gained by many in running organisations or development projects in the apartheid days and in negotiating the transition to democracy far outweigh those long-serving civil servants.
>
> Many highly competent managers who hold positions in the civil service today are people who never set foot in a university campus or studied subjects which had nothing to do with the areas they now very ably manage. Their life experiences equipped them with an understanding of South African society's complexities and their abilities to assess and respond to the needs, exceed conventional qualifications.

However, there has been over-exuberance in the recognition of the non-conventional qualifications, and this has resulted in a gradual break-down of hiring controls.

An assortment of chance-takers and shysters has been able to move into jobs for which they should never have made the shortlist.

This laissez-faire attitude to qualifications and employment procedures in the national and many provincial and municipal governments has also paved the way for nepotism at senior levels of the public service.

But it is not just in the area of ascertaining the qualifications of those they hired that South Africa's civil service chiefs have failed the nation.

There are many qualified and highly experienced managers who should never have been hired because of their less-than-savoury backgrounds.

The likes of Albert Mokoena and Khulekani Sitole, who both lost their positions for abusing them and state resources, are cases in point. [Neither had obtained the teams with permission or declared them when they had been employed in their positions.]

They may have had some management experience, but they had neither integrity nor ability to manage public funds. A simple background check would have revealed that much.

The decision by the Minister of Public Service and Administration Geraldine Fraser-Moleketi to institute an audit of senior public servants' qualifications is welcome but, unfortunately, not far reaching enough.

What is required is a thorough review of hiring procedures and the control throughout the public service.

If it is serious about instilling a culture of respectability in the public service, the government should conduct an appraisal of criteria, procedures and norms used in the different tiers.

Reminiscing about the good old days at the *Sunday Times* investigations unit, André Jurgens, who recently re-joined me at a new unit in January 2014, said, "All hell could be breaking loose but Mzilikazi always had a relaxed demeanour, even while pinning down the most slippery of characters. And plenty of them were unmasked by the investigations team, some for having their fingers in the corporate till, others for abusing powerful positions in government.

"The investigations team in its early days had a reputation for producing bulletproof stories, journalism that went the full monty. The stories had impact. They got the country talking and cost several high profile people, with their snouts in the trough, their jobs.

"While the team dropped several bombshells on the pages of the *Sunday Times*, many of the best stories were painstakingly researched over weeks or months and pieced together like a jigsaw puzzle. Fortunately, the team was given the time and resources to break some of the country's biggest stories."

Chapter 14

NGHUNYUPESI: Ruffling some feathers

"Patriotism is supporting your country all the time and your government when it deserves it." – Mark Twain

In Africa, more than a few of our politicians are enigmas, sly and inscrutable characters. For many citizens, such persons – well suited and corpulent – are often incomprehensible in their words and actions. It takes an investigative journalist, who is thick skinned, to unpack their baggage and put the dirty laundry on the washing line.

But as I have said, there is a heavy price to be paid for being a journalist of that calibre and sometimes the price is a double-edged sword.

When former *Sunday Times* editor Mike Robertson walked into the investigations unit office on 5 December 2000, we could see from his facial expression that we were in some kind of trouble. As soon as Robertson walked in, he demanded to know why his core investigations unit was ignoring one of the infamous and current stories at the time: the government's controversial arms deal.

"Every newspaper in this country is writing about the arms deal, but my own investigations unit is not even working on it. Come on, guys: give me an arms deal story," Robertson said before he walked out of the door.

Truth be told, we did not have any interest in the arms deal – tagged at R43 billion – due to the complexity of the story and the massive coverage accorded it by other papers. We wanted to break exclusive stories based on facts. We did not want to recycle coverage.

By the time Robertson left, we were all licking our wounds: our boss, Jocelyn Maker, my two colleagues, Jessica Bezuidenhout and André Jurgens and myself included.

We realised that we knew practically nothing that was exclusive or original about the arms deal except for the swipe that the former Pan African National Congress of Azania (PAC) Member of Parliament and now Independent Democrats (ID) leader, Patricia de Lille, took at the National Assembly on 9 September 1999 when she claimed that she had evidence that some members of the ruling party were implicated in the arms deal corruption.

The veteran politician supported her statement with a 29-page document, now famously known as The De Lille Dossier. Most journalists repeated De Lille's dossier, reported it widely, without taking it a step further by deepening the investigation.

We stopped everything we were doing and began right from the start, trying to analyse and understand the arms deal.

Like every journalist, our first point was to get The De Lille Dossier, scrutinise and interrogate it and then follow the leads.

The months that followed were devoted to collecting thousands of pages of documents about the arms deal, travelling across the country to interview people, suppliers, analysts as well as informants. Some of the people we spoke to, especially senior government officials, were too afraid to be identified or even to speak off the record.

Yet pieces of a very complex puzzle started falling into place. We no longer thought a corvette was a car and a frigate was a big war gun.

Dozens of allegations were analysed. Little did we know that one of them, about a 4x4 luxury car allegedly given to ANC chief whip in Parliament at the time, Tony Sithembiso Yengeni, would hit the headlines for months.

From all the allegations, we settled on Yengeni's car. Every car has a paper history and it is easy to prove it. We asked everyone about the registration number, but ironically, nobody – including the journalists who wrote about Yengeni's car – actually bothered to find something as simple as that.

I flew down to Cape Town to get the registration number. I managed to sneak into Parliament's parking bay with the help of a Member of Parliament, but it turned out Yengeni did not park his four-wheel drive in his designated parking spot that morning.

As I walked out of the Parliament buildings disappointed, and spoke to my colleagues back in Johannesburg over the phone about the bad news, I spotted the car at a traffic light from the corner of my eye. The conversation shifted: I was now, instead, reading out the registration number. We were back in business.

It was the start of a long journey: slowly the unit pieced together the history of the car, which raised questions that remain unanswered to this day.

After we had gathered enough information, I phoned Yengeni on 22 February 2001 and asked for an interview to discuss "rumours" about his vehicle. Yengeni invited me to come to his office in Cape Town so we could have a one-on-one "discussion".

As I walked into Yengeni's office in Parliament, we shook hands, but the politician stubbornly refused to explain how he had come to acquire the car. Instead, with all the grandiose arrogance of a politician, he challenged the *Sunday Times* to go out and seek the "truth".

South Africans woke up to a Yengeni exposé on 25 March 2001, with a story that took four months to investigate, after a mountain of evidence and thousands of documents that were perused.

The story was headlined on the front page, with full reports on page eight and nine: "Tony Yengeni, the 4x4 and the R43 billion arms probe".

Today we reveal how Tony Yengeni, the ANC's chief whip in Parliament, ended up with a luxury Mercedes-Benz 4x4 which manufacturer DaimlerChrysler says it never sold him. We also reveal:

- How the car was ordered as a "staff car" by DaimlerChrysler Aerospace South Africa (DASA), a company linked to the R43 billion arms deal; and

- How Stannic denies financing the car, although this is stated on Yengeni's registration records.

When the *Sunday Times* walked into Tony Yengeni's office in Parliament at noon 30 days ago, there were beads of sweat on his brow. Shaking reporter Mzilikazi wa Afrika's hand, the well-built MP said, "Why is your hand sweating like that?"

"No," said Wa Afrika, holding up his, "it's not my hand that is sweating, but yours, Mr Yengeni."

The award-winning investigative reporter was there to find out how a vehicle ordered by a company involved in the R43 billion arms deal had come to be in the possession of Yengeni, who, as chief whip of the ANC, is one of the most powerful men in Parliament. He was also head of the Joint Standing Committee for Defence, which had played a key role in the decision to buy the arms in the first place.

The vehicle in question is a state-of-the-art Mercedes-Benz ML320

4x4. The price tag when it was delivered nearly three years ago was R359 000 – without any fancy extras. Buyers were offered the choice of extras like an electric glass sunroof, tinted windows and a fabulous Bose sound system.

Yengeni's 4x4 had plush body-hugging beige leather seats, tinted windows and metallic green paintwork.

The first official records on the vehicle show that it was dispatched from DaimlerChrysler's East London plant on 15 September 1998. It arrived at the company's Johannesburg stockyard on 19 October.

Computer printouts from DaimlerChrysler which came into the possession of the *Sunday Times* show the 4x4 was ordered as a "private staff vehicle" by DaimlerChrysler Aerospace (DASA), which, through a joint venture, secured a contract to supply tracking radars for the corvettes bought in the arms deal package.

But on 22 October, three days after it was delivered to Johannesburg, the vehicle was registered in the name of Tony Yengeni in Pretoria. A few days later it was licensed in Cape Town – in Yengeni's name.

Traffic department records give the vehicle's details: registration number (CA 80233), chassis number (WDC 1631542A048577) and engine number (112942302 03839).

The same records list the titleholder – the banking institution, which owns a car until it is fully paid up – as being Stannic.

But bank sources deny this.

Stannic says it can find no record of any agreement on this vehicle and that the last motor vehicle financing agreement between Stannic and Yengeni was for a different car in 1993.

And then there is the puzzling matter of the insurance.

Banks which finance vehicle purchases are reluctant to hand the money over to motor dealers (who hold the car keys) until the buyer can produce proof of comprehensive insurance cover.

Elmarie Barac, customer liaison officer at Stannic, said the Credit Agreement Act made it the duty of a person getting credit to ensure that a car was comprehensively insured.

But this Mercedes-Benz, ostensibly financed by Stannic, appeared to remain uninsured for five months.

On 12 March 1999 – 14 days after the 4x4 was first registered in his name – Yengeni signed an insurance agreement with Millionsure.

But the records of traffic fines show he had been driving the car before it was insured.

His first brush with Cape Town's traffic officials was on 2 March 1999, when the driver of the 4x4 disobeyed a traffic directional arrow while cruising along the city's busy Klipfontein Road. The driver, who received a R150 ticket, was listed as the MP at his current home address.

Exactly a fortnight later, on 16 March, the dark green vehicle with tinted windows collected a second traffic violation for exactly the same offence along the same road. A second R150 ticket was made out to Yengeni.

Both remain unpaid – a matter traffic officers were unable to explain this week.

Nevertheless, the car then headed off for its first inspection service on 23 April.

Records show the inspection, which did not reveal any major mechanical problems, was done on behalf of Yengeni, named as the "customer".

A month later, rumours began circulating in the corridors of Parliament that Yengeni had received the car as a "gift".

This is where the whole saga took a puzzling turn that has left a trail of unanswered questions.

Documents in the possession of the *Sunday Times* show that it was only at this point that Yengeni started paying monthly instalments for the 4x4.

Seven months after the vehicle was registered in his name, Yengeni entered into a finance agreement with DaimlerChrysler Financial Services (Debis) on 28 May 1999.

The question, investigators probing the arms deals are asking themselves, is why? If, as Stannic states, it played no role in financing the deal, then Yengeni's registration forms contained incorrect, possibly fraudulent information. On the other hand, if Yengeni had entered into a finance agreement with Stannic, why did he need to enter into another one with Debis eight months later?

Had he been loaned the vehicle for seven months, he would have been obliged to record this fact in terms of Parliament's Code of Members' Interests.

Yengeni's signed list of declared items for 1998 makes no mention of a Mercedes-Benz.

What is known is that a Cape Town newspaper published a letter in

July 1999 suggesting that Yengeni should explain how he came to own the vehicle. Two months later, on 11 September, Yengeni summoned a group of journalists to his office where, waving a sheaf of papers in the air, he protested his innocence.

Yengeni told the journalists that the papers in his hands were bank statements and said they were proof that he was paying for his car. Three of the journalists present say he did not allow them to read the documents. Yengeni says he did.

Four days later, on 15 September, Cabinet announced it had concluded the controversial arms deal. PAC MP Patricia de Lille then made startling allegations of corruption relating to the arms deal, naming several prominent politicians, including Yengeni.

In the months that followed more allegations about bribery and corruption playing a role in the arms deal surfaced, but matters came to a head in September 2000 when Auditor-General Shauket Fakie submitted a report to Parliament's Standing Committee on Public Accounts suggesting that a forensic audit be carried out into aspects of the arms deal.

The committee was flooded with more allegations of corruption and shortly thereafter it was suggested that a whole team of investigators, including the auditor-general, the public protector and the Directorate of Public Prosecutions, be appointed to undertake a full-scale investigation.

Yengeni moved into the spotlight in January this year when Andrew Feinstein, ANC leader on the Standing Committee on Public Accounts, was removed from his post. Feinstein had been vocal in his support for a thorough investigation of the arms deal.

Yengeni, in his capacity as ANC chief whip, replaced him with Geoff Doidge. The move was seen by political observers as an attempt by the ANC to bolster the committee with party loyalists.

At the same time, President Thabo Mbeki announced that Judge Willem Heath would not take part in the investigation.

While these political developments were being played out, the *Sunday Times* started gathering documents on the arms deal and identified several issues which needed to be investigated. One of them was how Yengeni got his 4x4.

The newspaper telephoned Yengeni on 22 February requesting a meeting to discuss the allegations around the car.

Yengeni agreed to a meeting and asked reporter Wa Afrika to fly to

Cape Town the following day. Yengeni agreed to bring all the necessary vehicle documents to the meeting.

The sweaty handshake kicked off an hour-long meeting in which Yengeni described the allegations against him as "hogwash". Wa Afrika switched on his tape recorder, telling Yengeni he wanted an accurate record of their discussion.

Well-known as the nattiest dresser in Parliament, Yengeni was not wearing the R1 000 suit given to him by Fabiani, one of Cape Town's most expensive designer boutiques on the V&A Waterfront. He was casually dressed in a simple short-sleeved shirt and a pair of jeans.

Yengeni refused to produce any of the documents that could have, within minutes, proved his innocence once and for all.

"I am saying to you I am not going to answer your questions now or ever and if you still want to continue, you can go to the other guys, the journalists [summoned to his September press conference] who were here," said Yengeni.

He said he was aware that investigators had trawled through his personal and financial details. If they had questions, he would gladly answer them, but he would not respond to the *Sunday Times*.

"There is a due process under way in the so-called arms deal. I respect this process. I will submit myself to it, as well as fully co-operate with the investigation. I will not submit myself to a witch-hunt by the *Sunday Times*," Yengeni insisted.

He said three legal bodies were conducting the arms investigation: "Now we can't have an investigation by the police and the *Sunday Times* running its own parallel investigation."

He then challenged the *Sunday Times*, "Go to the traffic department to find the information about the car."

A number of traffic department records with details of Yengeni's car had already arrived anonymously at the *Sunday Times* office. As suggested, the *Sunday Times* approached the traffic department to seek the truth.

It was during this search that the *Sunday Times* traced the two unpaid fines.

Yengeni also said, "Everything is registered and it is legal. The information is with the banks."

We approached Stannic where sources said there was no record of the bank financing the vehicle.

Taking note of Yengeni's protest that allegations about him were "hogwash", the *Sunday Times* then ran a check through a company called Hire Purchase Information (HPI). Every hire purchase deal anywhere in the country is stored in a central database in Pretoria by HPI. But HPI's only record relating to the 4X4 was Yengeni's deal with DaimlerChrysler Financial Services on 28 May 1999.

Still searching for answers, the *Sunday Times* headed for Daimler-Chrysler whose representatives at first seemed to know less about the vehicle than us, and became increasingly nervous as we asked more questions.

In the meantime, our team succeeded in obtaining a full history of the vehicle from DaimlerChrysler's own computer system which showed clearly that DASA had ordered it as a "staff" car. The documents were delivered anonymously to the *Sunday Times*.

DaimlerChrysler spokesman Annelise van der Laan said: "Daimler-Chrysler South Africa has no record of selling an ML320 to Mr Yengeni."

Her statement did not, however, explain whether DASA had sold him the vehicle.

"As we have now been made aware of various allegations, we have launched our own internal investigation into the matter in order to establish the full facts," she said.

The *Sunday Times* waited for news of the DaimlerChrysler investigation. Two weeks later, we faxed DaimlerChrysler a complete list of questions.

These included whether DASA had ordered the vehicle as a staff car; whether there was any record at all of DaimlerChrysler ever having sold the vehicle to Yengeni or having any record of a finance agreement with him.

We asked if any deposit had been paid and whether the motor group had sponsored overseas trips by Yengeni.

The last question was asked because Yengeni, in a public disclosure to Parliament, acknowledged that DaimlerChrysler had sponsored his trip to an air show in Chile and the Daimler-Benz plant in Brazil in 1998.

Media relations manager Lulama Chakela responded: "It has come to our attention that the issues you are investigating are contained in a judicial inquiry which, as you are aware, the South African government has instituted on the much-publicised arms deal.

"The matter is therefore sub judice and any information Daimler-Chrysler may have at its disposal which may have material bearing on the case cannot be discussed with the *Sunday Times* or any other interested party outside the judicial process."

We then turned to DASA, hoping it could explain how its car had landed up in Yengeni's hands.

DASA was incorporated two years ago into the European Aeronautic Defence and Space Company (EADS). The company issued a brief statement signed by Melanie Grobbelaar, personal assistant to managing director Michael Woerfel. It said government had "instituted a judicial inquiry" and EADS was "obliged to respect this process". They declined to reveal any further information.

Yengeni told Wa Afrika, "I am very, very clear about this matter. Those that have information must take it to the police. I am a law-abiding citizen.

"I have got nothing to hide. The investigators must investigate this," he said.

An official investigation into how Yengeni obtained the car is under way by the Directorate of Public Prosecutions, the public protector and auditor-general. Yengeni's entire file at DaimlerChrysler has been attached and several staff members subpoenaed by the investigation team.

The story would make international headlines, quickly becoming a topic of discussion on different radio talk shows around the country and sparking heated debates in Parliament.

This would be followed by a series of other exposés about two more luxury cars in Yengeni's possession: a silver C180 Mercedes-Benz saloon for his wife, Lumka, and a sporty red SLK 320 for his Congolese girlfriend, Wivine Ndlandu Kavidi. The cars were ordered as staff cars and sold to Yengeni at a massive discount.

Yengeni refused to answer any further questions.

He would take out full-page advertisements, costing R283 000, in four different leading Sunday newspapers, except the *Sunday Times*, on 15 July 2001, protesting his innocence and claiming that the allegations against him "elevated my car issue to a major scandal of national and international proportion without any shred of evidence of wrongdoing on the part of anyone".

He added, "The manner in which this whole issue was handled at public level was characterised by an unprecedented concoction of distortion, rumour and gossip mongering; outright lies and half-truths.

"All this was deliberately intended to conceal the truth, and create an atmosphere of doubt and suspicion and thereby find those who are accused guilty without bothering with the tested principles like fairness and accuracy in dealing with issues of this nature."

The above notwithstanding, Yengeni would be arrested in Cape Town by the former elite crime busting unit, the Scorpions, on charges of corruption, fraud, forgery and statutory perjury on 3 October 2001.

Wearing a light brown suit, Yengeni sat in the dock, chewing gum, while Magistrate Petro de Villiers read him his charges. He was released on R10 000 bail.

The case was transferred to the Pretoria Commercial Crimes Court.

Yengeni told a press conference the following day that he was resigning as ANC chief whip in Parliament because he could not continue with "those kinds of charges hanging over my head".

He stressed, "I also reiterate my view that I'm innocent of all charges laid against me and I will prove that in court."

The *Sunday Times* investigations unit won the Nat Nakasa Award for Media Integrity two weeks after Yengeni was arrested, and he sold his fancy ill-gotten car for R220 000 in November of the same year.

Yengeni appeared in the Pretoria Commercial Crimes Court alongside his co-accused, Michael Woerfel, former managing director of the European Aeronautic Defence and Space Company (EADS), on 25 January 2002.

Woerfel was the man who organised the luxury cars and discounts for Yengeni. The perjury charge against the flamboyant gum-chewing politician was dropped.

The *Sunday Times* also reported in May 2002 that Ayanda Mbanga, a Johannesburg-based communications and advertising agency, was suing Yengeni for R200 000 after he failed to pay for the full-page advertisements that they had placed on his behalf. The court papers stated that Yengeni and his sponsors paid Ayanda Mbanga Communications only R70 000.

When Yengeni finally received his indictment in July 2002, the charge sheet read exactly like our first story.

Pretoria Specialised Commercial Crimes Court magistrate Bill Moyses later found Yengeni guilty of defrauding Parliament and sentenced him to four years imprisonment on 19 March 2003.

The magistrate said Yengeni showed no remorse.

Magistrate Moyses said, "What makes the crime even more serious is the planning and ongoing deceit after the benefit became public knowledge. Not only did you not disclose the benefit, but thereafter covered your tracks."

He ruled that Yengeni abused his position of trust as a Member of Parliament.

"Parliament is chosen by the citizens of this country, and they were all misled. I regret to say the example you set as the chief whip of the ANC is shocking."

All charges against German businessman Michael Woerfel were withdrawn.

Yengeni faced a fresh probe by the ethics committee in Parliament for his failure to disclose a substantial discount in the register of member's interests. He decided to jump the ship and resigned as a Member of Parliament on 5 March 2003 and the inquiry against him was stopped as he was no longer a member.

Yengeni appealed against his sentence and lost the appeal.

Scores of ANC supporters, including senior member Ebrahim Rasool, who was the premier of the Western Cape, provincial chairperson James Ngculu and the party's chief whip in Parliament at the time, Mbulelo Goniwe, gave Yengeni a "hero's parade" as he was driven to Pollsmoor Prison in Cape Town in a top-of-the-range Range Rover on 24 August 2006, where he began his sentence.

He would be immediately transferred to a modern correctional facility, Malmesbury Prison, where he was controversially released on parole after completing a mere four months of the four-year sentence, on 15 January 2007.

As for Yengeni's comrades, Mbulelo Goniwe made headlines about a month after the "hero's parade" for allegedly making sexual advances towards a 21-year-old administrative assistant, Nomawele Njongo, in the ANC's parliamentary office. He was suspended as the ANC chief whip in Parliament on 14 December 2006.

After Njongo officially complained, the ANC's National Disciplinary Committee (NDC) brought three charges against Goniwe: abusing his office to obtain sexual favours, bringing the ANC into disrepute and provoking divisions in the unity of the party.

He was found guilty on the first two charges in May 2007 and lost his parliamentary seat. The ANC suspended his membership for three years.

He later took the ANC to court for loss of income and the South Gauteng High Court ordered that the ANC must pay him R1.2 million plus interest of some R800 000 for loss of income.

Goniwe claimed the sexual harassment charge was a smear campaign against him because he was seen as a supporter of former president Thabo Mbeki.

He managed to get the ANC's National Executive Committee (NEC) to reverse his sentence and reinstate his membership.

The ANC fired Ebrahim Rasool as Western Cape premier in 2008 after it emerged that he had two senior political reporters, Ashley Smith and Joseph Aranes, from the independent newspaper, *Cape Argus*, on his payroll.

Whoever said birds of a feather flock together did not lie.

There is no doubt in my mind that Professor Jonathan Moyo, Zimbabwe's controversial minister of information, media and broadcasting, is the most colourful political chameleon on this continent.

Moyo began his illustrious career, politically and otherwise, as President Robert Mugabe's fervent critic, writing a column lambasting the Zimbabwean leader and his government and then morphed into becoming the greatest defender of Uncle Bob.

Not only did the charismatic and former political science lecturer from the University of Zimbabwe become Mugabe's hatchet man, he is also the self-appointed axe-man for the president for life: hackling and orchestrating the arrest of journalists and closing down independent Zimbabwean newspapers that were critical of Mugabe's regime and shenanigans.

Years before the PhD graduate (in public policy) from the University of Southern California in America became Mugabe's mouth and ears, he worked in Kenya for a Nairobi-based non-government organisation, the Series on Alternative Research in East Africa Trust (Sareat), which he had left. A US$6 million dollar corruption scandal was exposed at the company for the alleged siphoning from the Ford Foundation.

The millions squandered, according to independent auditors, PriceWaterhouseCoopers (PWC), were meant for Sareat, but instead the money allegedly found its way into another bank account.

The PWC report, dated 20 March 2000, hinted about "questionable expenditures of US$61 644 out of a grant of US$127 000".

Moyo was a programme officer at the Ford Foundation in Nairobi from 15 September 1993 to 31 December 1997, before he moved to the University of Witwatersrand, South Africa in 1998.

The report also states, "Expenditure on unapproved projects includes US$40 858 relating to scholarship costs to Milka Okidy [a former employee of the Foundation] and US$5 073 given as an advance to support *Generations* activities under Professor Jonathan Moyo."

The audit report also shows that the man from Tsholotsho North and Zimbabwe African National Union – Patriotic Front (ZANU-PF)'s propaganda machine – was a programme officer with the Ford Foundation in Nairobi, when he received US$6 215 000 from the foundation and spent it without properly accounting for it.

The report states that US$5 073 was removed from the first grant and another US$287 000 meant for Sareat. US$108 000 was transferred into the bank account of Moyo's lawyers, Edward Nathan Friedlands Inc.

The Talunoza Trust, named after Moyo's children, was used as a conduit to transfer the money that was later used to buy a R1 million house in the affluent suburb of Saxonwold in Johannesburg, South Africa.

Moyo and his former colleagues at the Ford Foundation in Nairobi became subjects of the US Federal Bureau of Investigation (FBI) probe, and were investigated for impersonation and money laundering.

The Ford Foundation sued Moyo and Sareat directors Mutahi Ngunyi, Joshua Nyunya, Milka Wanjiru Njuguna-Okidi, Monicah Wanjiru as well as the Talunoza Trust in January 2001.

Moyo's corruption woes continued in 2002 when Wits University together with Moeletsi Mbeki, the younger brother of former South African president Thabo Mbeki, and his company, Endemol, sued Moyo.

Mbeki, who is one of the directors of Endemol, a television production company, claimed Moyo was given the money to produce a Pan-Africanism documentary called *Generations: The Making of a New Africa* that was going to be called *Generations* and failed to deliver.

Mbeki told *Sunday Times* at the time: "Our company [Endemol] paid for the production costs of the documentary. We paid for the workshops, airfares and so forth. We paid the money on the undertaking that we would be the production company of the documentary. According to the agreement, if Moyo did not produce the documentary or chose another company, he would pay us the costs we would have incurred." Moyo denied the claim, saying, "I never got a cent from Endemol. I don't owe anybody documentary."

Wits University also sued Moyo for R100-million for allegedly absconding with part of a research grant.

Moyo allegedly received the money for a research project, *The Future of the African Elite*. He was a visiting lecturer with Wits University at the time and the university claims the project was never completed as Moyo resigned from Wits to take up his ministerial position in Zimbabwe.

Wits University registrar at the time, Derek Swenner, told *Sunday Times* that Moyo "told the university that he was conducting research, but instead, we found out that he was in Zimbabwe running Robert Mugabe's election campaign. When we asked Moyo to explain how the money was spent, he chose to resign."

Moyo claimed, "There was never a R100-million research grant. That claim is shamelessly fictitious."

As soon as Mugabe appointed Moyo as minister of information in Zimbabwe in July 2000, the man, who is sometimes described as the "Nutty Professor", started his onslaught on the independent newspapers and critical journalists in his country. He became the architect of the country's draconian media laws that were condemned around the world.

He ordered new changes at Zimbabwean Broadcasting Corporation (ZBC) and fired about 400 journalists, and replaced long-serving journalists on the state newspapers with his loyalists.

Moyo also introduced the Access to Information and Protection of Privacy Act, which banned foreign journalists and correspondents from working in Zimbabwe.

He forced local journalists to register for licences to work with the government-controlled Media Commission. Moyo had the powers to shut down any newspaper and also discouraged government departments and state-owned enterprises from advertising with independent newspapers.

One of Moyo's casualties was the critical *Daily News*. The newspaper was closed down after Moyo refused to renew its licence. Before its closure, the newspaper's printing press was bombed just a day after the minister threatened to ban it for "peddling British propaganda". Another newspaper that was compelled to shut down was *The Tribune*. More journalists found themselves on the streets looking for jobs other than in the newsroom.

Moyo became like a robot in the Zimbabwean political arena: changing from red, green and yellow from time to time and, depending which direction one is coming from, one would know which way to turn.

The maverick politician started flooding Zimbabweans with his opinions – others believed they were Mugabe's – writing different columns in state newspapers and using several pseudonyms. He was a real propaganda machine at work.

The New Zimbabwe, a London-based website reported, "Moyo is known to craft stories and send them to editors to publish, complete with quotations. When his editors publish stories which he considers not in line with government policy, he is known to have awoken them at 3:00 a.m. and forced them to hold the paper from print."

When there were reports of food shortages in Zimbabwe, Moyo sprang like a bulldog to defend his master's government calling the reports "weapons of mass deception".

Moyo proudly claimed, "What we are seeing here is the use of weapons of mass deception through the press. There is no food crisis in Zimbabwe."

He added, "It's a case of not having a balanced diet. Malnutrition is there, even in Britain and the US. People in the US are fat because they eat too many burgers. That's malnutrition."

He also claimed that Zimbabweans were living better than South Africans. "It is you people who have Mandela [squatter] camps all over the place, not us. In fact, the average black person in Zimbabwe is better off than the average black person in South Africa."

I received a tip-off in December 2002 that Moyo was in Johannesburg stocking groceries and other luxuries for his family while he publicly denounced media reports that millions of Zimbabweans were starving, some even dying of starvation, and I decided to put the hypocrite to the test – he failed the test dismally.

Award-winning *Sunday Times* photographer Sydney Seshibedi and I booked into a hotel in Bedfordview, east of Johannesburg, where Moyo, his family and bodyguards were enjoying their luxurious meals including takeaways. I chose a strategic room, the one directly opposite Moyo's.

Sydney and I spent days sitting by the hotel window, behind the curtains and watching Moyo, his family and bodyguards loading an assortment of groceries into their three vehicles. Sydney was taking photos while I was taking notes.

On New Year's Eve, while sitting by the window, I witnessed what looked like a physical fight between Moyo and his wife. A few minutes later, police officers arrived after one of their children called the reception to report that their parents were fighting.

Just after dawn on 8 January 2003, I noticed that Moyo and his entourage were leaving the hotel. I notified Sydney, who was staying at a different room, and we followed them to Pretoria. Sydney was taking photos while I was driving.

The *Sunday Times* published our exposé on the hypocrite Moyo on the front page on 12 January 2003 under the headline: "Hey, Big Spender". The story had a series of photos showing how Moyo was shopping up a storm in South Africa. Included was a piece about the fight between Moyo and his wife.

HEY, BIG SPENDEER
Mugabe's spin doctor stocks up on food in
SA as millions starve at home

Zimbabwe's propaganda chief, Jonathan Moyo, spent nearly two weeks in South Africa on a holiday shopping spree while millions of his countrymen face starvation.

The controversial minister of information, who wants to be the next president of Zimbabwe, booked into the Mercure Hotel in Bedfordview from 27 December to 8 January with four children and his wife, Betty.

While there, he went on a shopping spree – surrounded by his bodyguards – and bought thousands of rands worth of food to take home to Zimbabwe, where more than two-thirds of the population of 11.6 million are desperate for something to eat.

It was just one year ago that Moyo, referring to South Africa, said, "It is you people who have Mandela squatter camps all over the place, not us. In fact, the average black person in Zimbabwe is better off than the average black person in South Africa."

He bought a big-screen TV and a home-theatre sound system. When he ran out of packing space in his luxury vehicles – a 4x4 Pajero, a Mercedes-Benz car and a bakkie – Moyo filled a trailer with more than a dozen bottles of cooking oil, tins of canned food, packets of rice, sugar and mealie meal, polony, macaroni and bread.

On Thursday the *Sunday Times* called an OK Bazaars store in Harare and was told, "We have no stocks of cooking oil".

Just days before Moyo's shopping jaunt, Zimbabweans were bracing themselves for a miserable Christmas without basic goods like fuel, milk and fruit. They are forced to queue for hours just to buy a loaf of bread.

The *Sunday Times* booked into a room directly opposite rooms 804 and 806, where Moyo's family were staying. His bodyguards and children were seen packing groceries into the vehicles on Tuesday afternoon and again at 4.20 a.m. on Wednesday before leaving at dawn to go home.

After Moyo's departure, escorted by bodyguards, the *Sunday Times* went inside room 806 and found five staff members cleaning up the mess left behind.

It was clear the family had been enjoying sumptuous holiday take-away meals, including hamburgers and chicken. Bits of uneaten food were lying on the floor. Pots containing porridge and meat had been left, half eaten, on the stove.

Empty bottles of beer were scattered about. At least four unopened dumpies of Moyo's favourite beer had been left behind.

Staff had to move furniture out of the rooms so they could be cleaned properly. Two trollies were needed to remove the garbage.

The *Sunday Times* watched as the cleaning staff feasted on Moyo's leftovers before cleaning the room.

The leader of the opposition Movement for Democratic Change, Morgan Tsvangirai, said he was horrified by Moyo's behaviour.

"This man has no shame at all. He goes to South Africa to buy his food while Zimbabweans are struggling to buy salt and bread.

"Where did he get the foreign currency when we do not have any in Zimbabwe? [President] Robert Mugabe is ordering food from London and Moyo is shopping in South Africa. These people are hypocrites."

Attempts to get comment from Moyo were unsuccessful.

Also on the front page was the story about how Moyo assaulted his wife, under the headline:

MOYO'S WIFE FLEES FIGHT IN HOTEL ROOM AND CALLS POLICE

Zimbabwe's Information Minister Jonathan Moyo's wife, Betty, called police to intervene in a row in his Johannesburg hotel room on New Year's Eve.

The drama started when one of Moyo's children phoned a receptionist to report a fight in the room. The *Sunday Times* has established that a security guard was sent to the room to check if the hotel's property was being damaged during the row and to calm those who were fighting.

But the guard was stopped as he made his way to the suite by Moyo's wife, who ran out of the room. She warned him not to go into the room because her husband "was a senior politician and a government minister" who would never listen to a security guard.

"I want to see the police – please phone the police to come here," she was heard shouting.

Moyo's wife was taken to the reception area where she pleaded with the night staff to call the police or give her directions to the nearest police station.

Two police officers responded to the call but gave Moyo's party only a verbal warning. No assault case was opened.

"The receptionist said police must rush to room 806 because of the fighting, which might damage the hotel property," said Sam Baloyi, an official at Bedfordview police station. "I don't know what was discussed. I have never seen any report but I can confirm that no case was opened."

The hotel confirmed that the incident took place but refused to comment further.

Moyo went berserk that Sunday morning, claiming that our photos were taken by British intelligence operatives with expensive cameras and long lenses.

Realising that he had been caught with his pants down and exposed as a hypocrite of the highest order, Moyo later caused a diplomatic row by launching a scathing attack on South Africa, saying South Africans "are filthy and recklessly uncouth". He said our report showed South Africa should not be a preferred holiday destination where one could come with one's "family and enjoy the kind of privacy that anybody else could expect in a civilised country".

In a statement released in the state-owned newspaper, the *Herald*, Moyo said, "I have always had a nagging feeling that for all their propensity for liberal values and civilised norms, these people [South Africans] are dirty. In fact they are filthy and recklessly uncouth. Now the evidence is there for any decent person to see. If these people, in the name of South Africa, believe they can lead an African renaissance, then God help them because they are joking. Their barbarism will never take root or find expression in Africa."

He also added that the South African press, just like its British counterpart, was undemocratic, uncivilised and unfair.

"Can you imagine people ransacking your baggage as you prepare it, taking pictures without your knowledge and lying through their teeth about its contents, claiming you are carrying food and no clothes and that you have been there for two weeks?"

Sydney's photos proved Moyo wrong beyond any reasonable doubt. If he were an honest man with any integrity, he would have been ashamed of his conduct. If at all there was someone who is barbaric and uncivilised, it is Moyo.

Days later, the Zimbabwean government issued an apology of behalf of Moyo saying, "His criticism and anger was not directed at the people of South Africa nor indeed for that matter at President Mbeki. It was directed only at the *Sunday Times* journalists concerned."

Moyo slapped me with a banning order: I am *persona non grata* in Zimbabwe. He later told a friend of mine, who I asked to negotiate the lifting of my order, that I will remain banned in Zimbabwe as long as he is still alive.

I have never been to Zimbabwe since. I have no wish to end up in the notorious and filthy Chikurubi Maximum Prison, an overcrowded facility, where blankets are reported to be lice-infected.

Half of the prisoners at Chikurubi are reportedly dying of hunger. Some observers believe that Chikurubi is similar or even worse than Adolf Hitler's concentration camps in Germany where "ordinary people were enslaved, starved to death, tortured and killed".

Moyo had a fall-out with Mugabe and the ZANU-PF top brass after he was accused of instigating the so-called "Tsholotsho Declaration", which decided to block the rise of Joice Mujuru as the deputy president in favour of Defence minister Emmerson Mnanganwa. Mugabe had named Mujuru as his favourite for the post.

Mugabe fired Moyo in February 2005.

The same year Moyo stood as an independent candidate for Tsholotsho, in defiance of his party's resolution that the constituency was reserved for a woman candidate. He won and returned to Parliament as an independent MP in 2008. He soon began to work closely with ZANU-PF towards the 2008 presidential run-off and in 2009 he was re-admitted into ZANU-PF and moved into the party's politburo, ZANU-PF's highest decision-making body.

Moyo lost his parliamentary seat in Tsholotsho to MDC member Roselene Sipepa-Nkomo in the 2013 election.

Mugabe again came to Moyo's rescue and recycled him as the new minister of information, media and broadcasting when he announced his new cabinet in September 2013.

In his first interview, Moyo claimed he wanted to heal the media rift he had created during his previous term as information minister because it was a "war period". Speaking to reporters after he was sworn in, Moyo said, "I would like to use a word that was so common during the era of the inclusive government, which is, 'if we can find each other, let us look for one another'. If it means having an indaba with [media] stakeholders to find each other, we will do so."

Days later, addressing journalists, Moyo said, "I am promising that we [as a ministry] will ensure that all your grievances are addressed and will work for the betterment of the country."

For now it is too early to tell whether the leopard will change its spots. I for one do not believe anything that comes out of his mouth.

Even if he can do the charm offensive, I will not set my foot in Zimbabwe as long as he is still alive.

Chapter 15

MBABVA: A lion in a sheep's skin

"Do not get so comfortable in someone else's house that you forget to build your own." – African Proverb

The cabinet announced the appointment of Jacob "Jackie" Selebi as the new police commissioner on 20 October 1999. He became the first black police boss, taking over from John George Fivaz, who had joined the South African police in 1964.

When the former ANC Youth League leader took up his position in January 2000, President Thabo Mbeki gave him a list of 24 people he should investigate and possibly arrest during his term of office. At the top of the list was soccer boss and businessman Irvin Khoza.

Khoza is the chairperson of Orlando Pirates Football club, one of the most colourful and fervently supported soccer teams in South Africa. He later became the chairman of South Africa's 2010 FIFA World Cup bid, leading the team that successfully secured the hosting of the global joust in South Africa in 2010, making history as the first African country to host the FIFA World Cup.

President Jacob Zuma bestowed Khoza with the Order of Ikhamanga in Gold in April 2011 for "his hard work and dedication in helping South Africa win the right to host the 2010 FIFA World Cup, and for ensuring that the tournament becomes a success in the eyes of the football fraternity. He is also honoured for his contribution towards the development and transformation of the game of soccer in South Africa".

After the *Sunday Times* investigations unit heard and confirmed the existence of Selebi's list, I started investigating Khoza, trying to understand what drove the powers-that-be to place him high up on that list.

I established that the self-made millionaire did not make it to the top of Police Commissioner Jackie Selebi's list for nothing: he had managed to dribble past the prosecuting authorities for years.

At the time, there was little information available about his past except from the days after taking over at Orlando Pirates. After speaking to a number of people – from soccer bosses to soccer players and sports journalists – I established that Khoza's first brush with the law came in 1972 when he was expelled from Fort Hare University for being a "political activist". It is not known what it is exactly that Khoza did or which liberation movement he belonged to at the time, but it is strongly believed that he was a member of the Azanian People's Organisation (AZAPO).

Khoza was born in Alexandra, north of Johannesburg, on 27 January 1948. He is affectionately known as the "Iron Duke" and though he never played professional football he was appointed secretary of Alexandra Football Association at the tender age of 14.

He joined Orlando Pirates as its general secretary in 1976, but was forced to leave the club six years later when he was convicted of fraud. Khoza became embroiled in criminal activities when a case of fraud was opened against him at Johannesburg Central Police Station in September 1978 (case number 88/8/1978). In February 1979 he was later sentenced to 12 months in jail or a R3 000 fine after being found guilty of a fraudulent life insurance claim amounting to R50 000.

A year later, another fraud case was opened against Khoza at Johannesburg Central Police Station in June 1980 (case number 100/6/1980). He was, once again, caught in another insurance scandal when he tried to claim R42 918 from a fictitious insurance policy. He was sentenced to nine months imprisonment or a fine of R2 000 in September 1981.

After paying the fine, Khoza decided to start a legitimate business career: exporting wines from South Africa to Zambia. It was during one of those trips to Zambia that Khoza was introduced to "Vicky" Goswami and Milanos Constantino.

In 1983 Khoza was arrested at Lusaka International Airport after he was caught with a box of mandrax tablets while boarding a flight to South Africa. The ANC placed Khoza on its list of "most wanted" after the soccer boss told the Zambian court that he had been given the mandrax by the party's representative in Kenya. Khoza did not name the ANC representative. Little did the court know, at the time, that the ANC did not have a representative in Kenya.

ANC members in Zambia were given instructions to arrest Khoza on sight for scandalising the name of the organisation. Khoza paid a fine of K95 (kwacha – Zambian currency) after he was found guilty of possession of narcotics, but managed to sneak out the country, avoiding the airport and major border gates where "ANC police" were waiting to arrest him. He returned to South Africa.

Constantino, a Greek national, fled Zambia for Europe after Khoza's arrest. There was also a warrant out for his arrest in the country for drug dealing, but was never sentenced for such a crime. It is believed that Khoza was placed on top of the list given to Selebi because the ANC at the time (before its president Zuma had a baby with the soccer boss's daughter, Sonono Khoza, out of wedlock) had a score to settle with him for the Zambian incident.

Meanwhile Goswami remained in Zambia and continued dealing in drugs and greasing the palms of some of the country's top politicians including then home affairs minister Newstead Zimba, wining and dining former Zambian and Football Association chairperson Winson Gumboth and other influential personalities.

Goswami became comfortable. He thought he had everyone eating from the palm of his hand – but he was wrong. The Anti-Corruption Commission (ACC) started investigating him after it was suspected that he was amassing his wealth from drug trafficking.

The investigation recommended that Goswami be deported to India, his home country, and declared a "prohibited immigrant" in a Government Gazette released on 28 January 1994. However, before Goswami was served with deportation papers in November 1993, Zimba, who was also in charge of police and immigration, gave the drug baron a tip-off and the Indian national fled to South Africa, where he had some friends, among them Irvin Khoza.

Goswami bought a house in Bryanston and had another property in Sandown as well as offices in Sandton. He was back in business – trading in drugs, flying his consignments from Lanseria Airport on his private jet.

Goswami operated his mandrax-manufacturing factory in Johannesburg and had some of the South African Narcotic Bureau (SANAB) officials on his payroll.

Goswami's friendship with Khoza took a new twist when a Soweto businessman and a self-confessed drug dealer, Robert "Rocks" Dlamini, disappeared while he was on his way to meet the Orlando Pirates boss on 6 April 1995.

He was reportedly picked up by two men in a car who were to take him to the meeting.

Dlamini, according to his family, was supposed to collect R1.5 million owed to him by Goswami. The money was from a drug deal that went sour and Khoza was supposed to be Goswami's messenger.

Neither Dlamini nor his remains have been found to date despite the fact that there has been a R250 000 reward offered for any information about his whereabouts since 1996.

Meanwhile, *The Star* newspaper's investigation unit, headed by Chris Steyn (before she became known as Chris Steyn-Barlow), had started probing Goswami's activities in South Africa. Their exposé under the headline: "Biggest drug lord in SA builds huge empire", hit the streets on 28 March 1996 and Goswami went underground before skipping the country for Mumbai, India. He left behind luxury cars, a Learjet and properties worth millions of rands.

After a short spell in Mumbai, Goswami moved to Dubai where he tried to rebuild his troubled empire. He bribed senior government officials before setting up two mandrax-manufacturing plants.

But his tail was cut short after a joint sting operation in Mozambique and South Africa exposed his drug manufacturing factories in Dubai. Goswami was arrested after he was found with mandrax worth US$6 million in 1997 and he was given life imprisonment. But for reasons, still unexplained, Goswami's arrest and conviction was kept secret.

A source – a police officer who was part of the joint operation – tipped me off me in June 2000 that Goswami was in a prison in Dubai.

"Try your luck, Vicky might talk about what happened to 'Rocks' as he is so frustrated there in prison," the source said.

A few days later I landed at Dubai International Airport, in scorching 30 ^{0}C weather at 5:00 a.m.

I arrived on Thursday and by Friday I was harassing the authorities in my attempt to speak to Goswami. I was told to fill forms explaining my status and the reasons I wanted to speak to a convicted drug dealer. I was told to return on Monday to check whether my request to see him had been approved.

Saturday, in the hot Dubai weather, I left my hotel, heading to the nearest bank to do my forex. Across the bank was a McDonald's where I decided to have my meal.

I was halfway through my meal when three young men (two local lads and a third who was clearly African) walked in and cheerfully greeted me, acknowledging the FUBU cap I was wearing.

I was glad to see another African brother after two days in Dubai. After ordering their meals, my three new friends came to share a table with me.

We talked about everything and they promised to take me to a "tourist beach" after the meal. I happily agreed.

One of the men could not speak English at all and the other one could speak "small English". My fellow African brother and I were doing most of the talking.

After the meal, we jumped into their car, a black Nissan Maxima parked outside. I was sitting in the back seat next to one of the guys who could not speak English, behind the passenger seat. The "small English"-speaking guy was the driver.

"We must fetch our swimming gear and towels first," said my African brother.

After driving for about five minutes we took a dirt road. I do not know what Mr Small English said to his friend – they were speaking Arabic. The guy just suddenly jumped on me and pressed me harder on the seat while trying to strangle me.

I was kicking and screaming, fighting for my life. My African brother also joined in the skirmish.

"If you don't shut up, we will kill you!" he screamed.

I used all the energy I had, any chance that came my way to kick any-one within my reach, bite whatever hand or finger came close to my mouth while trying to raise my head pressed down on the seat.

This fight for my life lasted a few minutes before the door was opened and I was thrown out of the moving vehicle, but my wallet, with all my cash, and my camera were gone. All but my passport – still in my back pocket – was stolen.

I managed to dust myself off and tried to find my way to the hotel, where I phoned the office and explained what had just happened.

"Unfortunately, you can't open a case because it means we have to spend money flying you there every time there is a court appearance should these men be arrested," responded Jocelyn. "Just thank God you are safe and alive. We will send you money as soon as we can."

I spent that weekend living on hotel food until the money arrived on

Monday. When I went back to the police offices that same day, I was told that my request to see Goswami had been turned down. I was informed that they could only let him speak with a South African government official. Not a journalist.

On my way back home, as I was walking towards the departure gate at Dubai International Airport, I heard someone calling my name from the business section. I looked around and I saw a familiar face with a gloating smile, beckoning me to come closer to him. He whispered, "It was just a warning."

Former *City Press* investigative journalist Phalane Motale, who was also investigating Khoza, phoned me one night to say he had scooped me. Motale had met a source who had given him information about Khoza. He decided to visit his mother in Soshanguve, north of Pretoria, the Saturday after his "exclusive" interview. He was shocked the following morning to find that his car, which had been safely parked inside the yard with high walls, had been broken into. The only thing stolen was his notebook. His leather jacket, camera and other valuable items, resting on the seat of the car, were not taken. On his way back to Soweto where he was renting a house, he was followed by two unknown men.

Days after my return from Dubai, I received a phone call from Khoza, who invited me to a face-to-face meeting, "if there is anything you want to know about me". He added politely, "You have been going around asking people a lot of questions about me."

We debated Khoza's invitation at the office. Some of my colleagues suggested that it was a trap and that I would be walking into the lion's den.

I asked my colleague Jessica Bezuidenhout to accompany me and told everyone that I "will cross the bridge when I get there".

I told my worried and concerned colleagues that Julius Caesar once said, "Cowards die many times before their deaths, the valiant never taste of death but once."

On that Saturday morning Jessica and I walked into the Orlando Pirates offices on the second floor of the Oakhurst Building, situated at St Andrews Road, Parktown, Johannesburg, and Khoza welcomed us with a radiant smile and a warm handshake.

Wearing a striped shirt, Khoza ushered us into a neatly furnished boardroom with leather seats and offered us mineral water.

"No, we are fine," we responded politely, declining his offer of refreshments.

Getting down to business, Khoza fired the first salvo, accusing me of harassing his friends and acquaintances by asking questions about him.

"You think you are smart and we don't know anything about you," said Khoza.

"Whatever you know, or you have been told, won't make me a suspect to any crime or criminal activities. All my life I have obeyed the rule of law and I am not ashamed of my past because there is nothing that I did then that I would try to hide today," I explained to Khoza.

Khoza was silent for a moment – either thinking about what I had just said or his next move.

"So what have you found out about me?" he asked.

Without fear, I told Khoza everything I had found out about him during the course of my investigation: from his first criminal record to his arrest in Zambia. I mentioned his thorny relationship with Goswami – I gave it to his face, not behind his back. When the allegations of his business with Goswami were put to him, Khoza neither confirmed nor denied them.

After I finished with my story, Khoza broke down and cried. With his arms folded on the table and his head down, trying to hide his tears, he was quiet for more than 20 minutes.

Jessica began to panic and gave a hand sign that we should run. Khoza had his head buried in his arms. I indicated to her we could not run.

After Khoza regained his composure, he asked, "What are you going to do with this information?"

"I hope to write a story one day," I said.

"Can you write my biography?" he offered.

"I don't think it's a good idea," I said.

Khoza thanked me for honouring his invitation. We shook hands and left his office in one piece.

On our way back to the office, I decided to pull over at Nando's in Rosebank for some lunch. Soon after I placed my order, Khoza phoned me and read me back my order.

"I am watching your every move," he said laughing.

My investigation into Khoza was disrupted when I was offered a Harry Brittain Fellowship (a training programme for Commonwealth journalists started in 1960 that was discontinued in 2003). I left for England in April 2001 and I spent three months there. Shortly after my return, I was offered another scholarship to the United States of America – a foreign exchange programme sponsored by the State Department.

I had just arrived in my room at the Henley Park Hotel in Washington DC on 17 August 2001 when I made the call to the office back in South Africa, only to be told that Khoza had been arrested and that police and South African Revenue Service (SARS) had raided his house.

"I want you to be part of this story. You know Irvin like the palm of your hand," said Jocelyn.

The next call I made was to Selebi. "You guys wait for me to come to America then you arrest Irvin?" I asked, fuming.

"It's not me but Pravin [Gordhan, who was SARS commissioner at the time]," Selebi protested.

It was during this interview with Selebi that he confirmed that a document allegedly detailing the smuggling of gold and diamonds from 1991 to 1996 was found at Khoza's house during the raid.

"The document has names of several prominent people who are suspected to be involved," the police commissioner said, refusing to divulge any names.

I did most of my interviews – I already knew the majority of the officials linked to the Khoza investigation – before filing my part of the story.

The story about Khoza's arrest was on the front page of the *Sunday Times* on 19 August 2001 with the headline, "Why the taxman bust Khoza", with my byline along with my three colleagues, Celean Jacobson, Ranjeni Munusamy and Jeremy Lawrence.

The first paragraphs of the story read: "Tax authorities raided soccer boss Irvin Khoza after subjecting him to a new 'lifestyle' analysis of how he built his business empire. Khoza, chairman of the leading soccer club Orlando Pirates, was granted bail of R3 000 on Friday night after being arrested on charges of illegal possession of a rifle. The gun was discovered during a raid on his double-storey home in Diepkloof, Soweto, by about 20 SA Revenue Service officials. Yesterday National Police Commissioner Jackie Selebi confirmed that two further charges had been brought against Khoza under the Income Tax Act. The two charges were contravening the Income Tax Act by failing to declare income, and giving false information to the Revenue Service, Selebi said."

Khoza was accused of owing SARS about R66 million after he failed to declare his income and gave false information. It was also alleged that he failed to submit tax returns between 1996 and 1998.

He was also charged for possessing an unlicensed firearm after a .303 rifle was found in his house during the raid, but the charge was later withdrawn after it was established that the rifle was "decorative" and could not be fired.

Khoza managed to settle his tax matters with SARS almost a year later. A joint press statement released by SARS and Khoza on 2 August 2002 stated, "Mr Khoza has accepted personal tax liability for an income tax assessment for the periods 1984 to 2000 in the amount of R10 342 631. An amount of R3 126 475 has already been recovered leaving an outstanding balance of R7 216 156 which amount includes capital, interest and penalties."

My longer investigation about Khoza was published a week later on 11 August 2002 under the headline, "Murky past of soccer's Iron Duke: Irvin Khoza has a history of trouble with the law dating back to 1979 and the origin of his fortune remains a mystery":

The man who will head South Africa's bid for the 2010 World Cup has dribbled past authorities for over two decades, but will now face a new investigation.

Affectionately known as the Iron Duke, Irvin Khoza is a self-made millionaire whose road to riches is tainted with allegations of drug dealing, fraud and tax evasion running into millions – none of which has been proven to date.

The police's elite Scorpions Unit is now probing where he got his money from.

Khoza is also the focus of an ongoing probe by the South African Revenue Services which claims he owes R66 million.

As boss of one of the top soccer clubs in South Africa, Orlando Pirates, and vice-president of the South African Football Association, Khoza mingles in the top social circles. But he has also been a close associate of some shady operators.

Yesterday Khoza said, "In discouraging people from praising themselves, my mother always said 'let one's deeds speak for themselves'. Please understand when I now choose to heed my mother's advice.

"Concerning the ongoing probe by the state, I would like the record to show that I respect the rule of law and the spirit of its practice."

Khoza's home is a plush mansion in Diepkloof, Soweto. Outside is likely to be parked a Mercedes-Benz, but police say no car is registered in his name and he doesn't have a driver's licence. He is driven around by chauffeurs in one of two luxury vehicles.

He flies first class on his many international trips, but he never carries more than one small piece of hand luggage. He says he "does not want drugs to be planted in his bags".

In Lipton he owns Freedom Square, a shopping centre that he bought for R42 million.

For a public figure, his private life is very secret.

His wife of many years, Elsie Matina Khoza, is rarely seen in public with him.

And how he made his fortune is shrouded in secrecy.

Khoza was born on 27 January 1948 in Alexandra township, north of Johannesburg. He grew up at house 58 on 10th Avenue. His mother was a cleaner at the local clinic, but little is known about his father.

He went to the Roma Mission School in Alexandra before he went to Orlando High School in Soweto. He was expelled from Fort Hare University in 1972, reportedly for his opposition to apartheid.

As a teenager he developed his great love for soccer and at the age of 14 became secretary of the Alexandra Football Association. But he has never played professional football which is now the centre of his life.

In 1976 Khoza joined Orlando Pirates as general secretary, but six years later left the team after he was found guilty on two fraud charges.

On 5 February 1979 he was sentenced in Johannesburg to a R3 000 fine or 12 months in jail for a fraudulent life insurance claim amounting to R50 000.

On 18 September 1981 he was again sentenced in Johannesburg to a R2 000 fine or nine months in jail for fraud after trying to claim R42 918 from a fictitious insurance policy.

But the woes of the Iron Duke were not over. In 1995 he again became embroiled with the law when a prominent Soweto businessman and socialite, Robert "Rocks" Dlamini, mysteriously disappeared.

Khoza was questioned by police as it had been established that Dlamini, a self-confessed drug dealer, went missing while on his way to collect money from Khoza.

Police said the money was a payment from a R1.5 million drug deal which turned sour.

Dlamini is now presumed dead although the 55-year-old's body was never found.

Khoza's business career began in Zambia in the early 1980s when he imported wine from South Africa.

It was in Zambia where Khoza was introduced to Vijay "Vicky" Goswami and Milanos Constantino.

In 1983, shortly after he befriended Constantino, Khoza was arrested at Lusaka International Airport for possession of mandrax. Constantino's arrest for operating a mandrax factory in Zambia followed.

Constantino soon fled the country and a warrant of arrest is still outstanding for him in Zambia. Police believe he is now living somewhere in Europe.

The Zambian Drug Enforcement Commission confirmed this week that "Irvin Khoza was fined K95 [kwacha] or three months in jail".

Goswami also fled Zambia for South Africa in 1994 after a senior government official warned him about an order for his arrest in connection with drug dealing and money laundering.

Once in South Africa, Goswami revived his friendship with Khoza. Goswami is now in jail in Dubai, United Arab Emirates, on charges of drug dealing.

Goswami was also linked to Dlamini's disappearance and fled South Africa for Dubai in April 1996, after he was exposed as a major drug lord.

Within a few months of being in Dubai, Goswami was arrested when local police raided two of his mandrax factories and confiscated tablets worth millions of rands.

He was initially given the death sentence but it was later changed to life imprisonment.

After Khoza paid the admission of guilt fine, he returned to South Africa where he started a company building houses in Diepkloof. Today he is a director of more than 20 companies.

Khoza made a dramatic comeback at Orlando Pirates as a general manager in 1992.

Pirates was going through a financial crisis and Khoza was their saviour.

Khoza again hit headlines in 1999 when he and Sizwe Mthembu, a senior official from the National Intelligence Agency, spent R3 million in state funds to buy 30 luxury vehicles for the agency.

They registered the cars in the name of SAFA.

The agency gagged Khoza from speaking about the deal and Mthembu was suspended.

Goswami, who was sentenced to life imprisonment, was released after 16 years for "good conduct" on 15 November 2012.

The *Mail & Guardian* newspaper reported that "a life sentence in Dubai is in effect 25 years, but prisoners can apply for early release on various grounds. Apart from good conduct, these include learning to recite passages from the Qur'an or converting to Islam."

Goswami, who wanted to boost his clemency appeal, converted to Islam and now calls himself Yusuf Ahmed. He even learnt how to recite some of the passages from the Qur'an.

He moved to Kenya after spending a few weeks in India after his release.

He secretly married a former Bollywood actress Mamta Kulkarni on 10 May 2013. The couple live in Nairobi where she started an events management company. Goswami is believed to be its funder, although they are keeping a very low profile. Kulkarni also converted to Islam and she is now known as Ayesha Begum.

Kulkarni is no stranger to controversy. Famous for posing topless on the cover of *Stardust*, a popular Indian film magazine in September 1993, she came under attack from conservative religious and women's groups in her homeland. She was charged with obscenity and convicted in July 2000. During one of her court appearances, she was plunged into another scandal when she appeared in court in a burqa "to evade photographers". She received severe condemnation and even death threats from the Islamic community.

Whether or not Goswami is on his way back to South Africa to reclaim his long-deserted assets remains to be seen.

My investigation is still pending. As they say, it's not over until the fat lady sings.

When I interviewed Selebi for this book, the former police commissioner said, "I have done my best to solve Rocks Dlamini's murder and bring those behind it to book. I even went to visit Vicky in jail in Dubai. We had a 40-minute session and he told me that he doesn't want to betray his friend.

"I did everything I could to locate Rocks' remains," Selebi continued. "We searched the Vaal Dam for a week after we were told that his body was thrown there. The source claimed Rocks' body was put in a drum, which was loaded with concrete before it was thrown in the dam – we came back empty handed. We also dug behind Orlando Stadium, the home ground of Orlando Pirates after another source claimed that Rocks was buried there but all in vain."

Ironically it took another convicted drug smuggler, Glenn Agliotti, to bring Selebi down.

Selebi's friendship with Agliotti became the subject of an investigation by the former criminal investigative elite unit, the Scorpions.

Selebi's world came crumbling down when the NPA issued a warrant of his arrest for corruption, fraud, racketeering and defeating the ends of justice on 10 September 2007.

Former president Thabo Mbeki was forced to put Selebi on an extended leave in January 2008 after the chief admitted that Agliotti was his friend "finish and klaar". Selebi was the president of Interpol at the time.

Agliotti, who turned state witness, told the court during Selebi's trial that he had paid the police boss R1.2 million in bribes since 2000.

The court found Selebi guilty of corruption in July 2010 and he was sentenced to 15 years imprisonment. Selebi, who is suffering from diabetes and kidney disease, was released from prison on medical parole on 20 July 2012.

Chapter 16

RS452: Sorry, wrong number

"Make the lie big, make it simple, keep saying it, and eventually they will be-lieve it." – Adolf Hitler

Sometime in January 2003 a source working for the South African Reve-nue Service (SARS) whispered in my ear that Durban businessman Schabir Shaik was facing a tax-related probe.

Shaik was at the time the "self-appointed" financial adviser to Jacob Zuma, who was then the deputy president of South Africa.

My source said SARS's investigators had stumbled across interesting documents, namely proof of payments that the charismatic businessman al-legedly made to a number of politicians including Zuma and former trans-port minister Mac Maharaj.

The documents, the source said, had been forwarded to the Scorpions for further investigation.

For weeks my source refused to tell me more about the matter and ig-nored my pestering, sometimes annoying messages, until one day he agreed to meet for coffee. He then proceeded to give me and my colleague Jessi-ca Bezuidenhout a blow-by-blow account of the investigation including a number of the documents.

We went through the documents for two weeks, corroborating some of the financial transactions, and trying to make sense of them.

When Jessica phoned Maharaj for comment, the veteran politician refused to confirm or deny whether or not he had received any payment from Shaik.

The story was on the front page of the *Sunday Times* on 16 February 2003 with the headline "Shaik paid money to Maharaj":

Former transport minister Mac Maharaj and his wife received payments and gifts worth more than R500 000 from Durban-based businessman Schabir Shaik, who is under investigation by the Scorpions for his role in the arms deal.

Most of the payments and gifts were given before Maharaj left the Cabinet in 1999.

Shaik, who is the personal financial adviser of Deputy President Jacob Zuma, is also the chief executive of Nkobi Holdings and a director of Nkobi Investments.

Nkobi Investments is part of the N3 Toll Road Consortium, which was awarded a R2.5 billion tender to upgrade the road from Johannesburg to Durban by the department of transport while Maharaj was the minister.

An Nkobi Holdings subsidiary, Kobitech, is part of the consortium Prodiba, which won a R265 million contract to produce new credit-card driver's licences.

Maharaj yesterday declined to comment on the payments or on his relationship with Shaik.

He said: "All contracts awarded by the department of transport during my term of office are a matter of public record."

Documents scrutinised by the *Sunday Times* suggest that six payments totalling R260 000 were made to Maharaj and his wife in the four months after he announced the N3 Toll Road Consortium as the preferred bidder.

It is believed that the Scorpions' investigation of Shaik has been extended to include Maharaj and a number of other government officials.

Maharaj said he was unaware of a government investigation, but would co-operate if asked to do so.

Sipho Ngwema, spokesman for the National Directorate of Public Prosecutions, said: "Our policy is not to comment on an ongoing investigation. There is an ongoing probe against Schabir Shaik and we cannot comment on the status of the probe or any of those involved."

Documents, including bank statements, invoices, financial records and faxes show that Shaik or his companies paid a total of R525 352 to Maharaj, his wife, Zarina, or her company, Flisan Investments.

The *Sunday Times* has established that:

- R50 000 was deposited into Maharaj's Absa cheque account on 15 December 1997 by Kobifin, the finance division of Nkobi Holdings; and

- R25 000 was deposited into Maharaj's Absa cheque account by S Shaik on 25 May 1998.

Notes on Shaik's financial records refer to payments made to Maharaj, his wife and her company. Maharaj declined to say if he received the money from Shaik or his companies.

Among the payments recorded in the notes were:

- R25 000 on 10 May 1998;
- R25 000 on 30 May 1998;
- R50 000 on 17 August 1998;
- R55 000 on 19 August 1998;
- R75 000 on 4 September 1998;
- R10 000 on 9 October 1998;
- R25 000 on 20 November 1998 as a "social facilitation cost";
- R20 000 on 24 November 1998;
- R25 000 on 18 December 1998; and
- R13 157 on 28 February 1999.

The notes also detail payments of R60 000 to Maharaj or his wife after he stepped down from the Cabinet in June 1999. They were made between 15 October 1999 and 1 March 2000.

Two payments, of R50 000 and R55 000, were made within a week of the N3 announcement.

In addition to the payments, an invoice shows that Shaik, through Nkobi Holdings, paid R49 857 for computers installed at Maharaj's home in Hyde Park, Johannesburg, in 1997.

An Nkobi Holdings official facilitated payment of import duties totalling R18 338 for a marble-top table imported from India by Maharaj's wife.

Shaik also arranged a trip to Disneyland for Maharaj and his family in July 1996.

Asked to comment, Shaik said: "I don't want to answer any of your questions. Tell the Scorpions to ask me those questions in court or ask Mac Maharaj to answer for himself."

Under the parliamentary code of conduct, gifts and benefits worth more than R350 received by members, their spouses, companions or dependent children must be declared.

But not a single one of the gifts or payments is logged in Maharaj's parliamentary register of members' interests.

After this story was published, Maharaj accused the former Scorpions boss and National Prosecution Authority director Bulelani Ngcuka of being the source of the story.

Maharaj subsequently joined FirstRand Bank after he resigned as a government minister and became one of the bank's highest paid non-executive directors at the time.

Paradoxically, FirstRand Bank was one of the beneficiaries of the R2.6 billion toll-road contract awarded by Maharaj's former department of transport.

FirstRand Bank launched an internal investigation after our story was published. Maharaj was forced to take three months paid leave while he was being investigated.

Sunday Times came with another front-page story; a sequel to the above story on the 3 August 2003 with the headline:

SHAIK PAID MAHARAJ DISNEYLAND BILL

By Jessica Bezuidenhout, Andre Jurgens and Mzilikazi wa Afrika

Former transport minister Mac Maharaj's future at FirstRand hinges partly on a family holiday to Disneyland that was paid for by Durban businessman Schabir Shaik.

Maharaj is expected to respond by Wednesday to the findings of an audit by Deloitte & Touché of payments and gifts, including the trip that he and his wife got from Shaik and his company, Nkobi Holdings.

The audit report was submitted this week to the board of FirstRand, of which Maharaj is a director. A decision on Maharaj's future at First-Rand will be made only once he has responded to the findings.

He is on leave pending the outcome of the inquiry.

But today the *Sunday Times* can reveal that the Scorpions Investigating Unit issued a subpoena compelling a major international company to explain why it was billed for the Maharaj's holiday to Orlando, Florida, in the US.

Halliburton, a company with controversial ties to US Vice-President Dick Cheney, was subpoenaed by the Scorpions after it emerged that its construction and oil subsidiary, Brown & Root, had arranged the Disneyland trip.

The *Sunday Times* this week tracked down a former Brown & Root employee who was responsible for arranging the trip.

Mike Elsip, who was managing director of Brown & Root at the time, said although the company had been billed for the trip, it had recovered the money from Nkobi Holdings or Shaik himself.

Elsip said his company was at the time engaged in "exploratory talks" with Nkobi Holdings, which was keen to establish a joint venture with Brown & Root.

Yesterday Shaik, speaking from Mauritius, confirmed that he had asked Brown & Root to handle the arrangements for the Maharaj family's stay, including hotel accommodation and a limousine, for the duration of their trip to Orlando in July 1996.

Shaik said he had been forced to foot the bill after receiving an invoice from Brown & Root months later.

"Mac (Maharaj) told me he had settled the bill directly at the hotel, so it was not clear why the hotel still invoiced Brown & Root. It was awkward.

"What was I supposed to do? I had a potential business partner on one side and a minister on the other so, yes, I just paid it," Shaik said.

As he did not wish to spoil his relationship with Maharaj or with Brown & Root, he settled the full amount by electronic transfer and a subsequent cheque.

On Friday, Halliburton's former financial director, Dave Gerrard, confirmed that the company had submitted an affidavit to the Scorpions, but said he was not in a position to divulge details of the 11-page document.

Gerrard said the company was aware that its name had been linked to the investigation, and wished to state categorically that it had at all times conducted its affairs in South Africa in full compliance with the law.

The *Sunday Times* has established that Shaik described the Disneyland trip for Maharaj, then minister of transport, as "strategically important" to Brown & Root and Nkobi Holdings.

He said one of Nkobi's subsidiaries, Procon Africa, had at the time been in talks with Brown & Root about projects in various parts of Africa, including South African airport developments.

Maharaj yesterday refused to comment on the matter, saying he was co-operating with investigators and did not intend to comment until the case against him was concluded.

Elsip said he had met Maharaj "once", at a lunch arranged by Shaik, and that the nature of his engagement with Shaik or Nkobi Holdings centred on a proposed airport development at La Mercy in KwaZulu-Natal and development of a new terminal building at Johannesburg International Airport.

Elsip said his company was not interested in the venture proposed by Shaik and never pursued it.

Shaik, who had to submit to questioning this week, is also at the centre of the Scorpions' investigation of Deputy President Jacob Zuma.

He is personal financial adviser to Zuma, who is alleged to have tried to solicit R500 000 from Thomson-CSF/Thales, a company that benefited from South Africa's multi-billion-rand arms deal.

Maharaj resigned from FirstRand Bank after the institution released the outcome of its investigation against Zuma's spokesperson. In the meantime, the Scorpions' probe against Shaik and Zuma continued. Commentators and various newspapers had a field day.

Around the third week of July 2003, I received a tip-off that the Scorpions had sent Zuma a list of questions. We tried every source and every trick in the book to gain access to those questions, but to no avail.

The unit approached Ranjeni Munusamy, who was a senior political reporter with the *Sunday Times*, to see what she could do through her political contacts.

A breakthrough came days later when Munusamy told us on 25 July 2003 that Zuma had agreed to leak the questions to the *Sunday Times* and that she must fly down to Durban to collect them.

Munusamy flew to Durban on the morning of 26 July 2003 and later that morning phoned to say "the chief could only give us those questions on condition that we agree to publish a story next week that Bulelani was a spy".

Although I suspected there was somehow a motive behind Zuma volunteering to leak us those questions, this came as a shocker.

"I have all the documents," Munusamy told us.

After a lot of discussions with my colleagues and our editor at the time, Mathatha Tsedu, it was agreed that if it were true that Bulelani was a spy as Munusamy claimed the documents could prove, then the *Sunday Times* would definitely publish such a story.

A few minutes after I called Munusamy to explain our position, the fax was rolling out the questions, which were being sent from the offices of one of Zuma's lawyers. I personally stood by the fax machine and collected them. The following day – 27 July 2003 – the *Sunday Times* had a front-page story with the headline "Scorpions to grill deputy president":

ZUMA TO ANSWER 35 QUESTIONS ABOUT
HIS FINANCES AND THE ARMS DEAL
By Ranjeni Munusamy, Jessica Bezuidenhout,
Mzilikazi wa Afrika and André Jurgens

Deputy President Jacob Zuma has been sent a list of questions by the Scorpions investigation unit about his financial interests since 1994 as part of a probe into the multi-billion-rand arms deal.

The list of 35 questions, sent to Zuma's Durban attorneys on 9 July, relate to the deputy president's relationship with his financial adviser, Durban businessman Schabir Shaik, and Shaik's company Nkobi Holdings. Questions are also asked about financial benefits from various sources, including former president Nelson Mandela, and Zuma's debts.

The Scorpions have asked Zuma to provide details of all expenses he paid on behalf of the ANC since 1994 as well as his personal income since then, suggesting that the investigation has expanded beyond the arms deal.

All diaries, official and private, travel plans and itineraries kept since 1995 have been requested.

The delivery of questions to Zuma comes after months of speculation that the deputy president was under investigation by the National Prosecuting Authority. He is alleged to have tried to solicit R500 000 from a company that benefited from the arms deal to protect it during a subsequent investigation.

The Scorpions have, among other things, asked Zuma to explain:

- His knowledge of or involvement in a business relationship between Shaik and the Nkobi Group, on one hand, and Jean-Paul

Perrier, Alain Thétard and Pierre Moynot of Thomson-CSF France, the company that allegedly paid the bribe;

- His knowledge of the R265 million contract to supply credit card driver's licences, a contract to build a new international airport in Durban and a contract to supply new national identity cards; and

- His knowledge of or involvement in the acquisition of armaments by the department of defence, and specifically the role of Parliament in the acquisition process and the involvement of the Nkobi Group in the corvette programme.

The *Sunday Times* can also reveal today that former transport minister Mac Maharaj and his wife Zarina have been subpoenaed and subjected to questioning by the Scorpions.

The Maharajs are being investigated in connection with their relationship with Shaik and Nkobi, payments and gifts worth more than R500 000, and the credit-card driver's licence contract. One of Shaik's companies, Kobitech, is part of the consortium, Prodiba that won the contract.

In addition, Shaik – also slapped with a subpoena – is to report to the Scorpions' Pretoria office on Tuesday to answer questions about his relationship with the Maharajs. He lost a court bid challenging an earlier subpoena to answer questions about Zuma.

The developments coincide with claims by National Director of Public Prosecutions Bulelani Ngcuka that he is a target of a smear campaign by members of the ANC under investigation by the Scorpions, who fall under his authority.

Scorpions' spokesman Sipho Ngwema confirmed yesterday that Zuma had been sent the questions but said he could not comment on them.

He would not say why investigators were examining Zuma's personal and ANC financial activities since 1994 except that they were "looking for certain preliminary information". Zuma has been given until Thursday to respond to the questions, but his lawyers are likely to request more time.

In a letter to Zuma's attorney Russel MacDonald, Deputy National Director of Public Prosecutions Leonard McCarthy said Zuma was "invited to respond in writing" to the questions.

"He is, however, not compelled to submit an affidavit or to offer any incriminating evidence since his evidence is not obtained in terms of Section 28 of the National Prosecuting Authority Act," McCarthy said.

Zuma's spokesman, Lakela Kaunda, said: "If there are any allegations against the deputy president they should be investigated properly and professionally through the correct legal structures and concluded.

"The investigation and quasi-prosecution must not be conducted through the media. We therefore question the motives of people who keep leaking information to the media and believe the public should do the same."

Furthermore on page six of the same newspaper, we had the questions in details under the headline "The questions Zuma is being asked":

The Scorpions yesterday confirmed that a ten-page letter containing a list of questions was sent to Zuma's attorneys on 9 July 2003.

The *Sunday Times* has obtained a copy of the document. Among the questions is a request for Zuma to supply:

- Particulars of your relationship with Schabir Shaik, with specific reference to the circumstances surrounding your introduction, the nature of your acquaintance and details of any business relationship that exists or existed;

- Particulars of your relationship with any of the entities within or related to the Nkobi group of companies, with specific reference to the commencement and nature of such relationship, any shares directly or indirectly held in any of the entities and any financial interest in the business of any of the companies in question;

- Your knowledge of and/or involvement in the business of any of the shareholders of Nkobi Holdings, to or with Star Corp, Clanwest Investments, Floryn Investments and Workers College;

- Particulars of your relationship with any of the entities within or related to the Thomson/Thales group of companies, with specifically the commencement and nature of such relationship, any shares directly or indirectly held in any of the entities, any financial interest in the business of any of the companies in question;

- Particulars of your relationship with Jean-Paul Perrier, Alain Thétard, Pierre Moynot and/or any of the directors and/or office bearers of any of the entities within the Thomson/Thales group of companies, specifically the circumstances surrounding your introduction, the nature of your acquaintance and details of any business relationship that exists or existed;

- Particulars of your relationship with African Defence Systems, any shares directly or indirectly held in the company, and any financial interest in the business of the company;

- Your knowledge of or involvement in the establishment of a business relationship between Schabir Shaik, Nkobi Holdings, Nkobi Investments and/or any company with the Nkobi Group and Jean-Paul Perrier, Alain Thétard, Pierre Moynot, Thomson-CSF-France, Thomson-CSF Holding or any other entity within the Thomson group;

- Your knowledge of the business relationships and detail of joint ventures, with specific reference to the national contract for the driver's licences, the contract in respect of the Durban airport and the national ID card contract;

- Particulars of the following meetings between Jean-Paul Perrier, Alain Thétard and/or any other representative of the Thomson/Thales group, Schabir Shaik and with, specifically, the reason for the meetings, the identities of the parties present and the nature of the discussions that took place at:

  a) London on 2 July 1998,
  b) Paris during the period 1997 to date,
  c) Durban on 11 March 2000,
  d) All other meetings in South Africa during the period 1997 to date.

- Particulars of any involvement on your part ensuring Nkobi's participation in the corvette bid through its effective shareholding in African Defence Systems, with specific reference to the meeting on 18 November 1998 attended by Schabir Shaik and representatives of Thomson CSF/Thales;

- Details of any undertaking on your part to protect Thomson-CSF in respect of the investigations regarding the award of the contract for the supply of the corvette, and particulars of any actions taken in this regard.

The Arms Deal

- Your knowledge of and/or involvement in the acquisition of armaments by the department of defence, with specific reference to the role of Parliament in the acquisition process and the business interest and involvement of the Nkobi Group in the corvette programme;

- The office of the Presidency issued a statement on 9 September 1999 in which allegations of your involvement in the arms deal were denied. Details of your knowledge relating to the initial allegations and the content of the presidential statement are requested.

Financial Benefits

- Financial benefits received directly or indirectly from 1995 to date from:

   a) Schabir Shaik,
   b) Nkobi Holdings,
   c) Thomson CSF/Thales entities,
   d) Jurgen Kögl and/or Cay nominees,
   e) Former president Nelson Mandela,
   f) Bohlabela Wheels,
   g) Durban businessman Vivian Reddy,
   h) The amount of money received, any repayment agreements, if these were loans and an explanation of how the money was used is requested in all of the above.

Nkandla Development

- Particulars of the development of a traditional village and Nkandla in northern Kwazulu-Natal with reference to:

   a) All dealings with and agreements reached with Tusker & Schumann in respect of the drafting of sketch plans and construction drawings for the development, whether the interaction was in person or with the assistance of an agent, representative and/or a friend or relative;

b) Details of the financing of and all payments made for the plans drafted in respect of the development;

c) Details of all dealings with and agreements reached with Eric Malengret and/or Eric's Industrial Plumbing and Building cc;

d) Particulars of the financing of all payments made in respect of the development in question.

Financial Position

- Particulars of your debts in respect of AQ Holdings and Development Africa, with specific reference to the incurrence thereof, the amount involved and the settlement thereof;

- Particulars of your debt in respect of Michigan Investment cc for the period 1994 to date, with specific reference to the incurrence thereof, the amount involved, action taken by Standard Bank and settlement thereof;

- Particulars of the overdraft facilities and status of your Nedbank, Standard Bank, WesBank and SA Permanent Bank accounts during the period 1994 to date;

- Particulars of all expenses paid on behalf of the ANC during the period 1994 to date;

- Particulars of your income during the period 1994 to date;

- Code of Conduct and disclosures to Parliament;

- Particulars of your disclosures during the period 1999 to date in the Register of Members' Interest.

Documents Requested

- All diaries (official, as well as private), travel plans and itinerary kept during the period 1995 to date;

- All documents in your possession or under your control relevant to any of the transactions referred to in this document, including correspondence, contracts, agreements including loan agreements, documentary proof of financial benefits received, acknowledgements of debt and share agreements.

Just hours after the *Sunday Times* hit the streets, Zuma gave different radio stations interviews where, without any shame, he publicly accused Bulelani Ngcuka of leaking those questions to our newspaper.

Zuma made me angry. I was mad. I felt that he used me and my colleagues to fuel his political agenda and conspiracy. It made me sick to my stomach. But there was nothing I could do about it. That day I lost complete respect for the man.

For the purpose of this book I interviewed my former boss, Mathatha Tsedu, who said, "Ranjeni got the questions on the basis that the source is not going to be identified and I committed myself not to say who the source is."

I told Mathatha that I would like to identify the source in my book and how it all happened.

Without naming anybody, Mathatha added, "We all know that they woke up with a prepared press statement to accuse Bulelani for something they know he didn't do."

On Tuesday, as part of the commitment we had made to Zuma, Munusamy brought the documents to the investigations unit, which she claimed were from ANC intelligence structures. Zuma had been the overall commander of Umkhonto we Sizwe intelligence from mid-1980s to 1994. The documents suggested that Ngcuka was an apartheid spy whose agent code was RS452.

She also refused to explain Zuma's outburst that Ngcuka leaked the questions to the *Sunday Times*.

Since Zuma's interviews on Sunday my colleagues and I were aware that we were bystanders caught in the crossfire. We had to treat this information with caution and great care.

I immediately phoned a friend of mine, a former Umkhonto we Sizwe operative who was working for the NIA. I asked him if he could verify for me who agent RS452 was without giving him too much information on why I required it. He promised to come back to me in a day or two.

Two days later, my friend called to say agent RS452 was a white woman and a former Port Elizabeth-based lawyer. It was believed that she was living somewhere overseas.

Towards the end of that week, I informed Munusamy that the story was not ready to be published as it had too many holes, but that it would be published once we were ready. I must be honest, I didn't tell her what I knew already about RS452 – something in my guts told me to withhold the information.

For the following three weeks, with the help of my friend from NIA, I tried to trace agent RS452 until one day, he called to say he had her full name and a contact number for me. Agent RS452's real name was Vanessa Jacinta Brereton and her home phone number was somewhere in England.

Without any hesitation I called the number and a man answered the phone. I explained that I was a journalist and asked to speak to Vanessa Brereton.

"What do you want from my wife?" the man asked me aggressively.

"It's personal, sir," I said.

"You can tell me, I am her husband," the man insisted.

I explained to the man that I was doing a story about a former apartheid agent RS452 and that it was believed to be his wife. I explained I just wanted confirmation from her.

After a long silence – I guess the man was thinking long and hard about it – he said, "Just hold on, I will ask my wife to talk to you about it."

After about five minutes or so, a woman was on the phone sobbing. She asked, "What do you want from me?"

I asked her a number of questions and waited for her response.

She said, "Can I speak to you completely off the record?"

"Yes," I said.

Vanessa Brereton confirmed that she was agent RS452. Her handler had been Karl Edwards, a security branch captain at the time. She was recruited as an informer sometime in 1985 and had resigned from it in April 1991.

"I am so ashamed of what I did, that's one of the reasons I relocated to London. I thought my past was dead and buried but it looks as if it has come back to haunt me," she said sobbing bitterly over the phone.

Brereton said she was a human rights lawyer and a political activist, trusted within the political circles and even elected treasurer of the Walmer branch of the ANC in the Eastern Cape.

"I turned my back on my people at the time they needed me the most. I am ashamed of myself," she said.

After a lengthy discussion, I thanked her. She asked me not to publish her story – there was no good reason to do so at the time.

171

"Please don't give anybody my contact numbers or maybe I should change this number," she said before hanging up.

We had a discussion as a unit and it was agreed that Munusamy should be told that we were not going to do the story because the information given to her was false.

The following day, I informed her that the unit was not going to do the story because we were 100 per cent sure that Ngcuka was not a spy. I did not give her all the details about Brereton, as I did not want her to be traced and victimised.

What happened next, only Ranjeni Munusamy can explain.

Soon thereafter we started hearing rumours that Ranjeni was trying to leak the story to other newspapers. Honestly, I thought it was just hogwash as I trusted her integrity. She was still a *Sunday Times* employee above all else.

On Sunday, 6 September 2003, we woke up with a screaming *City Press* headline: "Was Ngcuka a spy?"

The story stated, "Documents leaked to *City Press* this week by a senior investigative journalist, which are said to have been sourced from the NIA database, identify the head of the DPP as possibly, but not conclusively, an apartheid police spy nicknamed Agent RS452".

Munusamy's judgement as well as that of *City Press* editor at the time, Vusi Mona, was disappointing. The story was written by Elias Maluleke, a former *Sunday Times* reporter who had left the company.

Munusamy had good reasons to choose Vusi Mona as her blunt instrument. I had told her around July in the presence of our former editor Matha-tha Tsedu and investigations unit colleagues that the disgraced former *City Press* editor might face an investigation by the Scorpions after his public re-lations company, Rainbow Kwanda Communications, co-owned with Moss Mashamaite, was awarded a dodgy multi-million-rand tender in Mpuma-langa.

One of the losing bidders had phoned me to say he had reported the matter to Ngcuka. I drove to Nelspruit, met with one of the losing bidders, received some documents, as well as a lowdown of how Mona's company – which he had not declared to his employers – was given the deal on a platter.

There were allegations that bribes were paid to some of the government officials to win the deal. So Mona had every motive to deal with Ngcuka before the Scorpions boss and his team could investigate or arrest him.

After the *City Press* story ran, Thabo Mbeki, who was the country's president at the time, appointed a commission of inquiry headed by former judge Joos Hefer. The Hefer Commission, as it was known, was to look into the allegations made against Ngcuka. During the Hefer Commission Mona admitted to not declaring his company and he was officially investigated for allegedly receiving bribes.

Mathatha had to write a column explaining to readers the reasons we did not publish the story:

The *Sunday Times* answers to no one but you, our readers. Stories that we print have to pass a test to ensure that the information they contain are as accurate as possible. Any story, no matter how important it might be, will not go into the paper until and unless the editorial executive team and I are satisfied that it passes a number of tests.

These include accuracy, public interest, balance and fairness. They must be legally defensible and, importantly, well written, easily digestible and not shot through with jargon.

Since July, a member of our staff, Ranjeni Munusamy, had worked on a story based on allegations that the National Director of Public Prosecutions Bulelani Ngcuka had been investigated by an ANC intelligence unit for spying for the apartheid government.

The investigation, which involved Moe Shaik, Mac Maharaj and Jacob Zuma, had found that agent RS452 "could be BN" – Ngcuka's initials. The documents at hand did not contain the information used to arrive at that ambiguous conclusion.

It emerged in the course of discussions that the investigation file had been given to Zuma more than ten years ago, and the question had to be asked: why was this information only being revealed now that Zuma, Maharaj and Shaik's brother Schabir were being investigated by Ngcuka?

We also had to ask ourselves: was the report we had in our hands a true version and not a latter-day fabrication to achieve other ends? In an attempt to answer these questions, Munusamy travelled to Port Elizabeth where she met one of the security policemen who was alleged to have been RS452's handler.

The ex-policeman is said to have confirmed that Ngcuka had been a spy, and identified a Karl Edwards as Ngcuka's direct handler. The ex-policeman did not want to be quoted in the story. Munusamy could not find Edwards, who has since publicly denied having anything to do with Ngcuka. The story was tabled at one of *Sunday Times'* editorial executive meetings where it was turned down for having too many holes.

Munusamy later brought in a copy of a telex which appeared to be a report by agent RS452. That still did not prove that Ngcuka was in fact RS452; it merely showed that agent RS452 existed and had reported on meetings of a lawyers' organisation. Munusamy told me she had been shown a database compiled by ANC intelligence operatives which contained more than 200 names of people investigated by the ANC unit and found to be spies. These names included those of Cabinet ministers, journalists and Ngcuka, she said.

Munusamy said the telex copy would have to be returned to the people who gave it to her once we had finished with it.

I directed her to confront Ngcuka and see what his response would be. Ngcuka would not return calls and later said through his spokesman that he would not comment. Munusamy was adamant that we should run the story to the effect that Ngcuka had been investigated, but I told her we could not do that unless:

- The initial ANC investigators gave us all the information that was at their disposal at the time so that we could see what made them reach their conclusion;

- Having looked at the information, we were satisfied that we would come to the same conclusion; and

- The intelligence unit that had shown her the database gave us the list of over 200 names so that we could subject all of them, or as many of them as we needed, to an investigation.

Munusamy said she would not be able to meet these conditions and that the people who gave her the telex copy wanted it back. I told her that if the owners of the copy wanted it to be returned I could not stop her from obliging.

A few weeks later she gave her information to another paper, which ran the story. Subsequent investigations have suggested that RS452 was a white woman.

I am satisfied that our decision not to run the story with the information at hand was correct.

Journalists are by nature curious people and obtain information from many sources. In almost all instances, the giver has a cause to fight for. Sometimes the motivation is sincere public interest but sometimes there is a personal agenda.

Our role as a newspaper is not to refuse such information, but to subject it to rigorous tests for accuracy, and to ask ourselves whether publication is in the public interest. The latter is done by answering, as best one can, the question: what purpose or interests are we serving by publishing this?

I remain convinced that publication of the story with the information we had at the time would have served interests other than those of the public and exposed our newspaper to litigation.

The *Sunday Times* has not, and will not, take sides on this issue. We will continue to report fairly so that our readers are able to consider the matter with all the facts at hand. Where there is a need for the paper to take a stand on a point of principle, we will continue to do so without fear or favour on our editorial pages.

A lot has been made of the off-the-record briefing by Ngcuka to a select group of editors where I was also present. Journalists often attend such briefings to gain insight into an issue. But information gleaned at such briefings must be subjected to the same rigorous tests as that obtained from any other source prior to publishing, and this was the case in this instance.

We believe we have striven harder than many to give as unbiased a view of the Ngcuka/Zuma fiasco as possible. We respect our readers too much to give you information that we ourselves are not convinced is correct or which is patently designed to serve personal agendas.

Munusamy was suspended last Friday after admitting that she passed the story to *City Press*. She resigned this Friday.

Munusamy refused to testify to the Hefer Commission as she claimed it would go against her journalistic principles.

Zuma was also asked to testify but he turned down the offer claiming that, "When I was deployed by the ANC as Chief of Intelligence, I was tasked by my organisation, the ANC, to undertake this most sensitive duty. The information of various categories that I dealt with was the property of the ANC. I, as an individual, had no right or authority then, and still have no right, to discuss such matters outside the ANC. I therefore regret that I will not be of any assistance to the commission without the permission or instructions of my organisation."

The commission heard how Maharaj and Riaz Shaik, affectionately known as Moe, had made the allegations that Ngcuka was agent RS452 and had passed this over to Munusamy as part of a smear campaign against Ngcuka and the Scorpions.

Mona, who boldly accepted to testify before the commission, lied under oath and was slapped with a perjury charge. He admitted to the Hefer Commission that he lied, but the perjury charge was later withdrawn when he publicly apologised for this act. He was later fired from *City Press* and the newspaper issued a front-page apology, branding Mona as "reckless".

"We recognise that the dignity and reputation of Ngcuka and his office have been harmed by the inaccuracy and untruthfulness of the reports that he may have been a spy for the apartheid government." The apology was penned by then acting editor Wally Mbhele.

In the end Mona conceded defeat and testified that, "I want to apologise unreservedly to Ngcuka, his family and to the National Directorate of Public Prosecutions for the pain the story caused. I still regard him as a man who can do his work."

In his report, Judge Hefer said Mona "admitted that his evidence had been untruthful in certain respects. The result was that, when the cross-examination ended, his credibility had been reduced to nil."

The commission concluded that Ngcuka was not a spy. Vanessa Brereton submitted an affidavit confessing that she was agent RS452. Her affidavit was accepted without question.

Ngcuka decided not to sue anybody involved including *City Press*. During an interview for this book, Ngcuka said it would have been "a waste of time" to sue.

"We took a decision as a family not to sue. These were not just attempts to destroy me, but also to derail the NPA's progress in other investigations. I would have won the defamation case simple, but it was going to be an empty victory. I am still standing strong after all what they tried to do to me," he said.

Ngcuka also confirmed that Mo Shaik and later Mona came to him and apologised for their roles in the saga.

"In his apology, Vusi said he was sorry as there were superior forces at work and that he felt used," Ngcuka explained.

He said Munusamy and Maharaj decided not to apologise. He added that he did not expect Zuma to apologise, as the president believed his hands were clean.

Ngcuka explained, "You must also remember that Zuma never said publicly that I was a spy, but he got his people to say what he was afraid to say in public. We all know that Zuma was working with them from day one. Zuma and I speak about anything from time to time but the spy saga is one thing we don't discuss."

Ngcuka said he regrets making a decision not to charge Zuma along with Schabir Shaik.

"We had prima facie evidence against Zuma but I wasn't convinced to take it to court as I had no full backing of my team; they were divided on the matter. Once you put a deputy president on the dock, you must know you are putting the whole country on trial. And I couldn't go to war while some of my soldiers didn't believe in my course. But now with hindsight, with more evidence that later came out, I think it would have been better to charge Zuma along with Shaik."

Ngcuka said he did not try to convince his team to support the decision to prosecute Zuma. "I didn't want my personal views on the matter to cloud my professional judgement and at the end I decided not to prosecute. I thought long and hard before making such a decision and consulted extensively with our senior counsel," he said.

Ngcuka confirmed that he was made aware that there had been a plot to assassinate him after the attempts to discredit him as being a former spy failed.

"One of the people who warned me was Madiba [former president Nelson Mandela]. He said I must beef up my security and be very careful. I decided not to be paranoid but to be cautious and accept my fate. If there was a bullet out there with my name on it, I was ready for it."

He added that he received a lot of threats and warnings from a lot of people.

When asked if he was aware as to who was behind the plot to assassinate him, Ngcuka answered, "You leave those for people to read between the lines."

It was payback time when Zuma was elected as the president of the ANC on 18 December 2007 after defeating incumbent Thabo Mbeki at the ANC conference in Polokwane, Limpopo.

Zuma was appointed president of South Africa in May 2009. Vusi Mona would be appointed acting communications head in the presidency two months later. Ranjeni Munusamy would be part of communications in the department of higher education and training, whose minister, Blade Nzimande, is a close associate of the president.

Munusamy later resigned and started writing for the online publication *Daily Maverick*. Mona moved from the presidency to the Government Communication and Information System (GCIS). He has since moved to South African National Roads Agency as communications manager at the time of writing this book.

I have nothing against Ranjeni Munusamy. I speak to her from time to time. We all make our own mistakes and bad judgements in our lifetimes.

Schabir Shaik, who was serving a 15-year jail term for fraud and corruption, including that he, through one of his companies, paid Zuma R1 340 078 for his influence in his business dealings, was released on medical parole in March 2009 after serving two years and four months of his sentence.

Shaik had spent most of his prison sentence in the prison sanatorium or in a private ward in a private hospital. He eventually admitted he had bribed Zuma "with the intention to corrupt him".

His brother Moe Shaik was appointed head of the South African Secret Services in October 2009 and Maharaj became Zuma's spokesperson.

The *Sunday Times* once more found a paper trail proving how Shaik had paid Maharaj and his wife.

Another front-page story on 20 November 2011 ran with the story.

MAC'S DODGY MILLIONS
Paper trail leads from arms company Thales to Maharaj and his wife Zarina
By Rob Rose, Stephan Hofstatter and Mzilikazi wa Afrika

President Jacob Zuma's spokesman Mac Maharaj stands accused of receiving millions in bribes from French weapons maker Thales, the company that will be at the centre of the government's arms deal inquiry next year. A two-month *Sunday Times* investigation has uncovered a paper trail that leads from the arms company to Maharaj and his wife Zarina. Schabir Shaik, Zuma's former financial adviser who was convicted of corruption in the arms deal trial, was the conduit used by Thales to channel the money to Zarina Maharaj.

The "missing link" obtained by the *Sunday Times* is a consultancy agreement, never before disclosed, between Thales predecessor Thompson CSF and Shaik's company Minderley Investments, registered in the British Virgin Islands. The agreement shows that secret payments totalling 1.2 million French francs (R2.3 million) went from the arms dealer's French bank to offshore bank accounts belonging to Maharaj's wife Zarina just two months before her husband's department awarded the French company a controversial credit card licence tender worth R265 million.

Documents from the Swiss district attorney's office, which obtained court orders for statements of Zarina and Shaik's Swiss bank accounts show Shaik's company was used as a conduit to channel the Thales money to Zarina's accounts. It is believed the Scorpions were unable to obtain this agreement, and that this ultimately torpedoed their corruption investigation into Maharaj in 2007. Investigators believed at the time there was a "reasonable suspicion" the money was destined for Mac Maharaj, according to documents seen by the *Sunday Times*. This week Maharaj declined to respond to detailed questions on his wife's secret offshore payments from Thales via Shaik's Swiss bank accounts. "These issues" had been investigated by the Scorpions who "did not bring any charges against either of us", he said.

"Neither Mrs Zarina Maharaj nor I are prepared to subject ourselves to a separate and additional investigation by a member of the media."

On Thursday, Maharaj prevented the *Mail & Guardian* from publishing a separate story relating to his links with Thales. It involved evidence he gave to a confidential section 28 inquiry.

The *Sunday Times* first exposed payments from Shaik to Maharaj and his wife in February 2003, when it revealed they had received gifts and payments of more than R500 000 from the convicted businessman, including a trip to Disneyland.

The payments were made between 1997 and 1999, while Maharaj was minister of transport. During this time his department awarded a R2.5 billion tender for the N3 toll road between Johannesburg and Durban and a R265 million contract for credit-card driver's licences to consortiums in which Shaik's Nkobi Holdings held stakes.

At the time Shaik was also a director of Thales, which owned a 33.3 per cent stake in the Prodiba consortium that won the shady credit-card driver's licence deal. No one has been able to prove a direct link between gifts and payments received by the Maharajs and Thales – until now.

A secret "consultant" agreement obtained by the *Sunday Times* reveals that Shaik would be paid a fee of 1.2 million francs to negotiate the driver's licence contract with the Department of Transport. Half would be payable when the department signed a letter of intent and the rest "at the coming into force of the contract". The deal was dated 5 July 1996, just two months before Maharaj's department awarded the driver's licence tender.

The deal was signed by Alain Thétard – the Thales country manager who also sent a fax to Shaik confirming that his company would pay R500 000 a year to Zuma for "protection" during any arms deal probe.

The "consultancy" deal unearthed by the *Sunday Times* relates to the transport department tenders. It specifies that Thales' company IDMatics in France would pay Shaik's company Minderley Investments' account in Switzerland to "keep our company regularly informed of all operational, financial, technical and commercial matters pertaining to the above business", and to provide "assistance for any negotiation".

Documents from the Swiss district attorney's office, which in 2004 obtained the court order for statements of Shaik and Zarina's Swiss bank accounts, show that Shaik's company Minderley Investments was merely a conduit to channel the Thales money to Maharaj.

The statements show the money was paid from Thales's BNP Paribas account to Minderley Investment Inc.'s account 95436 at Banque Alliance SCS in Geneva on 11 October 1996 and 11 March 1997. Each time the transfers from Thales to Shaik's Minderley account are matched days later by Minderley's payments to Zarina's accounts.

On 11 October 1996 IDMatics paid Fr600 000 to Minderley. Five days later Minderley paid Zarina Fr579 999. Zarina then transferred the dollar equivalent – $96 000 – to her Isle of Man account number 11444107 at Allied Dunbar bank. Then, in 1997, there is a similar trail of money. IDMatics paid Fr600 000 to Minderley's account at Banque SCS on 11 March, and two days later, Minderley transferred the equivalent $100 000 to Zarina's Swiss account. Shortly thereafter, Zarina transferred $65 000 to her Isle of Man account.

Maharaj's defence that his wife was simply being paid for work she did for Shaik was rejected by prosecutor Gerrie Nel in 2007.

"Further investigation itself revealed a reasonable suspicion that other offences had been committed [by] 'Mac' Maharaj [and] Shaik," Nel said in a request for mutual legal assistance to the Swiss authorities in 2007. His letter, addressed to Fridolin Beglinger of the Federal Department of Justice and Police in Bern, concludes that "the defence of Mac Maharaj and Shaik that Zarina Maharaj received money from [Shaik's companies] cannot be true. Why were such huge amounts transferred from the account of Minderley Investments [to] Mrs Maharaj's overseas bank account?"

Contacted this week, Shaik confirmed a "long-standing relationship with the Maharaj family" but declined to discuss the secret deal that allowed Thales funds to be channelled to Maharaj through his Swiss bank account. "I have no comment on that matter," he said.

Pierre Moynot, who headed the South African arm of Thales at the time, refused to discuss the payments. "I am not aware of who paid this or that, so please leave me alone."

In a corruption case in Paris earlier this year, Thales and the French government were ordered to pay a record US$920 million fine to Taiwan for paying bribes to push through a deal in 1991 to supply the Taiwanese navy with six Lafayette frigates. As part of the notorious arms deal in South Africa, Thales' predecessor Thompson-CSF was part of the consortium that won the R6 billion bid to supply the navy with four corvettes in 1998.

Thales spokesman Carol Davies said the company would investigate the allegations.

Maharaj yesterday laid charges against the *Mail & Guardian* newspaper and two of its journalists.

In a statement, Maharaj said, "Attorneys acting on behalf of Mac Maharaj laid charges against [the newspaper and journalists] for contravening the provisions of section 41(6) of the National Prosecuting Act of 1998." Maharaj also requested police to investigate whether records of National Prosecuting Authority inquiries had been stolen.

The matter is still pending and has not yet been finalised. The story won our investigations unit the Taco Kuiper Award for Investigative Journalism in 2011. Maharaj is still at the helm as the president's spokesperson.

Chapter 17

TIMBILA: Music is the weapon of the future

"Treat a sick man with the medicine and a sad man with the music."
– Amit Kalantri

My love for music is innate, an inborn inclination. I confess I am addicted to it, but there is no need to drag me into rehabilitation at Music Anonymous. Music is in my blood: I breathe it, talk it and eat it – even dream about it.

Music has been my bosom friend, in good times and bad times.

My intrinsic love for music is invigorating, the fuel I need in my daily journey. From an early age the pen was my secret paramour: I managed to write what I like, the way I wanted. I had an obsession with words and a serious crush on poetry. Several times I had been tempted to elope with beautiful poetry until one day, music showed up at my door and stole my heart.

I come from the generation of disco and funk icons but I didn't bite their sound. I have always searched for that African sound, an authentic African melody that would take me to bed at night and wake me up with a smile in the morning. I am an African to the bone, even my dreams are Africanised. I have been a proponent of black consciousness from an early age.

I have been collecting music for years. I started with buying cassettes before graduating to CDs and DVDs. In fact, I had my first record, a 45 vinyl, when I was eight years old and wrote my first song when I was 11.

My mother was not a professional singer but boy, did she have an amazing voice. She loved music and cherished her collection of country music and some local acts. I grew up listening to the sounds of Dolly Parton, Don Williams, Kenny Rodgers and John Denver, to mention just a few. There was also the music of mbhaqanga icons, Soul Brothers and Steve Kekana as well as Babsy Mlangeni.

When I was 12 years old, living in Bushbuckridge, my best friend Robert Khosa and I started a no-name band: Robert was on vocals, Thomas Matlhabane was on bass, Johannes Shabangu was on guitar and I was on drums.

All the musical instruments belonged to Shabangu. We used to play for fun, doing cover versions, but as a band we had no sense of direction.

Before the politics, activism and books came along, music had been one of the strongest bonds between Robert and me. Long after the no-name band fizzled out, Robbie and I continued writing songs. We later recorded an album together as a duo in 1998 calling ourselves R5, like the semi-automatic assault rifle. Our single, "Muthavini", was on high rotation at Munghana Lonene FM and dominated the charts.

When I was working in Nelspruit for AENS, I befriended Joe Silinda who had a studio in Matsulu, a township near Malelane, along the Kruger National Park border. I began to spend most of my free time there learning the ropes.

I started studying African musicians, their way of writing songs and singing. I was hooked on Nigerian afro-beat legend Fela Anikulapo Kuti whose protest songs mesmerised me. I was also under the spell of Senegalese superstar Youssou N'Dour, Malian icon Salif Keita, and later Busi Mhlongo's debut album *Babhemu* got me on her groove.

African musicians might not be keeping the world on its dancing feet but those who care to listen to the beautiful music from our continent can sing with tears dancing down their faces, and at the end of the song, they would have been educated and entertained. There is more to Africa than a picture of poverty and half-naked, sometimes undernourished, children running down the dusty streets like hobos – we have a very rich history and culture. My ears were not saturated with the pop sound.

I had been listening to Miriam Makeba, Hugh Masekela, Caiphus Semenya, Jonas Gwangwa, Bayete, Sankomota, Mzwakhe Mbuli, Stimela, Mbongeni Ngema and Oliver Mtukudzi as well as the "Shangaan disco king" Paul Ndlovu for years.

On the international front, I was influenced by Curtis Mayfield, Tracy Chapman, Bob Marley and later Tupac Shakur.

When I joined *Sunday Times* in 1999, I asked former entertainment reporter Lesley Mofokeng to introduce me to the legendary Sello "Chicco" Twala, one of the best producers in the country, and sometimes described as the "Quincy Jones" of South Africa.

Chicco allowed me to come to his studio any time of the day. One of the musicians he was busy recording at the time was Brenda Fassie. I witnessed the recordings of Mabrr's album, *Amadlozi*, released in 2000. It was destined to become a multi-platinum album.

The South African Music Awards' (SAMA) organisers named Fassie's song, "Vulin'dlela", the Song of the Decade and her album, *Memeza*, as the Best-selling Release of the Decade in 2004. *Time* magazine later named Fassie as the "Madonna of the Townships".

During this time, before they became multi-platinum-selling musicians, I met and befriended the twins, Tshepiso George and Tshepo Joseph Mothiba, a house-music duo better known as Revolution. In 2002, Revolution released their debut album titled *The Journey* featuring a guitar wizard Phillip Tabane on a song simply titled "Vhavenda". The song became a club anthem across the country and neighbouring states.

It was the twin brothers from the dusty streets of Alexandra township who encouraged me to build my own home studio, which they helped me set up. I recorded a world music album deeply inspired by Africa's soul and sounds under my name Mzilikazi titled *Afrika*. In 2004 I signed a deal with Gallo Records.

I wrote all the songs on the album and produced the album myself, assisted by former Harari 80s afro pop band front man Oom Alec Kgaodi. The title song "Afrika" had lyrics in Swahili, Zulu, English and Shona and was a collaboration between maskandi legend Phuzekhemisi (who honoured my invitation to join me in the studio), Tshepiso Mpotle, before he became a gospel megastar, Max Mhlanga from Zimbabwe and myself.

Below are the lyrics of the title track, "Afrika".

From Cape to Cairo
Children are armed and dangerous
They don't know how to read and write
They are taught how to shoot and kill
Someone must be blamed
Our children don't want tea any more
They want more alcohol and tequila
Our children don't want bread any more
They want more cocaine and mandrax
Someone must be blamed

The album was well received – it became an album of the week on various radio stations – but it was poorly marketed which compelled me to terminate my deal with Gallo Records. I headed back to the drawing board.

One song from the album titled *Ijazi* (Condom) was licensed for an international release by a London-based record company.

Revolution and another house legend, Oscar "Oskido" Mdlongwa, asked me to change my style of music to house. I chose to do deep tribal house music.

I started my own record label, Bomba Records, with Gallo Records doing the distribution. I released a house album called *Dance or Die* in July 2007 using my stage name Mzee (Swahili for "your highness").

The album featured the hit "Mahuwelele" with Candy "N'wa-Yingwane" Mokoena on vocals, a collaboration with the Kora award-winner Pop Mohamed, whom I call the minister of music. It also includes the vocals of Khoisan people recorded in the Kalahari Desert in Namibia, on a song titled "T txoroca" (pronounced Tiqorosa), which is a!Kwe language for "we can dance".

I also featured another Kora award-winner, the Nigerian-born guitarist now based in South Africa, Kunle Ayo, on a song simply titled "Fela: Afrika man original", a tribute to Fela Kuti.

I sampled the album among a number of DJs around the world and months later, in 2008, I was offered an international recording deal by Ocha Records, an American-based record company owned by house-music doyens, Osunlade and Carlos "Casamena" Mena. They heard my song "Mahuwelele" and were so impressed that they wanted to do an international release of it.

When Ocha Records released *Mahuwelele Remixes EP* in February 2009, the song became an international club anthem. The remixes were on the playlist of every house DJ across the globe, reaching number-one status as the best-selling album on Traxsource, a house music billboard.

The EP featured remixes from Manoo, who is based in Paris, Halo from City Deep Music, Tommy Bones and Steve Rigmaiden, based in the USA, and Boddhi Satva, born in Central African Republic (CAR) but based in Belgium. Another remix by our very own house maestro, Black Coffee, followed later.

The EP made me an internationally renowned house musician and put me on the global map.

The Ocha Records press statement stated, "Mzee might need an introduction in the international music arena but his single 'Mahuwelele' is about to take the world by storm and make a name for the little-known South African musician."

"Mahuwelele" was one of the songs that changed the way people around the world perceived South African music, paving the way for deep tribal house music around the globe. It made most producers change the way they were making their music: it was a simple global game-changer.

I became one of the most sought-after producers, producing songs for Caribbean-born American actor Antonio David Lyons (*American History X, Hotel Rwanda* and *False Prophets*), South African-based Senegalese hip-hop crew Nomadji, the award-winning Ethiopian reggae star Johnny Ragga, Israel-based diva Elisete as well as multi-award-winning Shangaan Disco queen Esta M, among others.

In 2009, there was another smash hit called "Diteki", which I did for DJ Lucky and Lacosta on their debut album, *Reloaded*. Though there were three songs produced by me for the album, "Diteki" became the crowd favourite.

I did a remix of Oliver Mtukudzi's classic "Neria" for DJ Sly in Botswana and the song became the number-one hit in that country.

When the legendary Louie Vega, American-based and Grammy-award-winning house icon, was asked during an interview with online magazine, *Soul Heaven*, in March 2010, what other producers out there were really pushing boundaries or making a big impact on the music scenes, he said, "Hot producers worldwide cooking up a storm are Black Coffee, Mzee, Culoe de song, Anane Vega and Antonello Coghe at Nulu music, Boddhi Satva, Fabio Genito, Duce Martinez, Louie Gorbea, Phil Asher, Atjazz, Ezel, Abicah soul, Radio slave, Luciano, there are quite a few."

Louie Vega also licensed one of my songs titled "Ancestral Calling", featuring the powerful voice of Prince Malatji, for his album *10 Years of Soul Heaven* released by Ministry of Sound in 2010.

It is an incredible feeling to have a Grammy-award winner and house master like Louie Vega feature one of your songs on his internationally released album.

I released three EPs with Ocha Records: *Mahuwelele, Umoja* and *Zvinosiririsa*. They all did well and reached the top five bestselling albums on Traxsource. I also released one EP, *Ancestral Calling*, with Nulu Records, another US-based record label owned by Louie Vega's wife, Anane, and Antonello Coghe.

In the summer of 2009 I released a double album with 31 songs titled *Tamanini*, featuring some of my best friends in the industry like Boddhi Satva, Black Coffee, Culoe de Song, Fabrizio Ortella, Halo and The A Team. The album was just what the doctor had ordered for the dance floor.

"This album is legendary," Black Coffee said to me after listening to it.

The album's first single "Zvinosiririsa", (Shona for "what a shame"), featuring Oluhle Ncube on vocals, was on high rotation on national radio station. Its video, shot with the help of a helicopter at the top of the Drakensberg Mountains in KwaZulu-Natal, became one of the most requested songs on different television channels and was also included on the *House Flavaz Fo Sho! 3* – a compilation of various music videos released on DVD by Soul Candi in conjunction with SABC 1.

The second single from the album, titled "Umoja" ("unity" in Lingala, a language from the Democratic Republic of Congo), featuring the late Congolese export Kampi Moto on vocals, was still receiving massive radio play years later.

There is no day that goes by without one of my friends sending me a tweet or Facebook message asking me when I am dropping my next album. And now finally, the questions have been answered: my new title *Timhamba*, Xitsonga for "ancestral rituals", is available at your nearest music store.

I made good friends in the industry: Revolution, Black Coffee, Oskido, Boddhi Satva, Max Pela, Culoe de Song, Pops Mohamed and Casamena are by far some of my closest friends. Boddhi Satva has been to South Africa at least three times (and counting) and he was one of the guests at my birthday party and album launch in 2009. Our friendship goes beyond music.

Commenting for the book, Sello "Chicco" Twala said, "I met Mzilikazi when he started visiting me in my studio in 1999. I didn't know at the time he was a musician or had interest in music. But when he started making positive inputs to the beats that I was working on, I told him that he should consider releasing a solo album or be a music producer. His African melodies are unique and very exciting to listen to. I think his busy schedule as a journalist is preventing him from being one of Africa's top musicians and arrangers."

Oskido said, "Mzee's music is touching the roots of the African culture that most of us are lacking. His unique way of fusion authentic African voices gives his music a better global appeal. Music legends like Louie Vega have made great comments about his music. Mzee became the king of Traxsource with the release of his classic EP, *Mahuwelele*; every house deejay in the world had that song on his set. It was a club banger and still is even today."

And about the new album, Oskido said, "This is a highly anticipated album; everyone wants to see which direction Mzee will take this time around. We are all eagerly waiting for it."

George Mothiba from Revolution said, "When we first met Mzee back in the days, we could see that he was different from others who wanted to be in the music industry. Mzee is a scholar of music, he knew some songs we didn't even know about and his interest to learn was encouraging and most of all he is a quick learner.

"From the beginning, we could see that he was not coming to the industry to play or for fame. Mzee is unique, even though we spend more of the time together, he didn't try to copy us or anybody in the industry but he came with his own style and made a name for himself."

About my new album, George said, "Obviously I am expecting to be blown away; we are looking forward to hearing something we haven't heard in a long time. We are looking forward to the next level of Mzee's music."

The legendary Pops Mohamed said, "Mzee is one of the most fantastic human beings I have ever come across; he is a brother, a friend and a very creative musician. Apart from that, he is kind and understands people. I could call Mzee any time of the day or night when I am in desperate need of a friend and he will always be there for me or anyone else for that matter.

"I have worked with Mzee on many projects over the years. As a producer, he knows what he wants and always makes sure that artists feel comfortable and not intimidated when in his studio.

"I love working with him because he knows exactly what he wants. I am comfortable in allowing him to explore my music to the fullest, because he knows where I'm coming from and I feel I have known him all my life. We have a mutual understanding when it comes to working with hard-core traditional music and the use of ancient African musical instruments.

"He is a true pro in every sense of the word and I am therefore very grateful to know someone like him because he is a true friend. I think he is one of the future producers of true African music in a modern context, and I am looking forward to collaborating on many of his future productions."

My friend, Robert Khoza, said, "During our younger days you had always put together politics, music, reading and football as a combo. Initially it was music that brought us together but politics cemented our bond.

"We made music against all odds, learnt whatever we wanted to learn about music regardless of the fact that Bushbuckridge had nothing to offer at the time."

Robert said he was surprised that I became a journalist. "I thought you were going to be either a musician or a politician," he told me.

I have also discovered some amazing and talented musicians like Jason "Jaso Moke" Beukes, who was just 15 years old when I met him, and my Congolese brother from another mother, Guaylord "G'Sparks" Mbolela, to mention but a few.

This is what Jason had to say: "There are many things that I've come to appreciate from knowing Mzee. He's shown me that there are no limitations to what you can do, and achieve. He would always have an open mind about music, which I hold dearly.

"Mzee taught me how to look beyond the superficial exterior of humanity and find truth through music and literature. I would never have been the musician that I am if I never met Mzee."

Meanwhile G'Sparks said, "For me Mzee is a brother, mentor and a friend. He believed in my talent and gave sense to my music production. He helped me to understand and be proud of what I am able to produce. Mzee, who is a perfectionist of note, does whatever it takes to get what is important to be accomplished."

Music knows no boundaries and it is a universal language. Sometimes it talks to your heart; sometimes it becomes fuel for your feet. From time to time, it comforts you more than any pastor can, heals you more than any doctor can and mesmerises you more than any person can. It can take you far and beyond, more than any car can take you. Music is not just great melodies and beautiful sounds, but it is food for your soul, if you listen without prejudice.

Until then, let the music play. Let music steal your heart, feed your soul and ease your pain. Music won't leave you with a broken heart, but a good vibe and great memories. After all, music is food for the soul, when cooked well without dissonance; it is rich with nutritious melodies and sounds that speak directly to your heart and command respect from your feet.

This memoir is a soundtrack of memory lane; after all, a long and lonely journey becomes shorter when one is accompanied by good music.

Chapter 18

MAMPARALANGA: There is a bullet for everyone

"It is better to die for an idea that will live, than to live for an idea that will die." – Steve Biko

Sometimes as a journalist you do not have to go out looking for news: it comes looking for you.

An integral part of this is intuition and faith. Some people will have faith in you and trust you with their lives, sharing with you the deepest of their secrets, or give you some of the most explosive documents. They see you as someone who might bring closure to a certain matter or give exposure to a hidden reality that is in the public interest.

So it was not a surprise when I received a frantic phone call from Jimmy Mohlala, speaker of Mbombela municipality in Mpumalanga at the time, requesting an urgent meeting with me on 24 December 2008.

Jimmy said he was in Johannesburg and that the issue at hand could not wait. "Sorry, I didn't want to make an appointment because I don't trust my phone. I didn't want to be followed," he explained.

I told Jimmy that I was away but we could make arrangements to meet in the first week of January.

"If I am still alive by then, we will," he replied.

"Are you planning to commit suicide?" I asked, as I was puzzled by his answer.

"No, they want me dead," he responded.

At the time, I had never met Jimmy Mohlala face-to-face, but I had spoken to him several times over the phone. The last time I had spoken to him was around October that year, when I asked him for a certain document I had been told was in his possession.

"I will give it to you at the right time," he had said.

Jimmy was a whistle-blower of the tender fraud and corruption related to the building of the R1.2 billion Mbombela Stadium that was constructed as part of the FIFA World Cup 2010 in South Africa. Mbombela municipal manager Jacob Dladla was initially dismissed after Jimmy exposed his role in the corrupt tender process.

During that brief phone call in December, Jimmy and I agreed to meet early in January 2009 as soon as I was back at work. At the time I was the investigations editor at *Sunday World* newspaper, a sister publication to the *Sunday Times*.

It still came as a shock to me when I received the news that Jimmy was gunned down outside his house in KaNyamazane, outside Nelspruit in Mpumalanga, on 4 January 2009.

I attended Jimmy's memorial service in Nelspruit on 8 January 2009. Soon thereafter, while I was having lunch at News Café with my cousin, Simon, SABC current affairs producer and former AENS colleague Landiwe Dlamini, a man I did not know came over to our table to chat with Simon.

It was only when Landiwe introduced me to the man that he froze for a second, before he said, "Are you Mzilikazi wa Afrika, the journalist?"

"Yes, I am," I responded.

"I am Fazaki Gama. I was with Jimmy, in Joburg, the day he phoned you," the man said.

"What did he want to tell me?" I asked.

"I was just a driver but his best friend, who was with us, can tell you more."

Fazaki made a phone call. "Where are you? Hurry up, I am with Mzilikazi wa Afrika at News Café."

About 20 minutes later a trendily dressed man in a suit arrived and introduced himself as Themba Mbokani, a local businessman.

"Jimmy wanted to speak to you before he was killed," he said after we exchanged greetings.

Themba said Jimmy had documents that could expose serious corruption involving Lefika Emerging Equity, a company that was awarded the tender to build the stadium. Lefika is owned by Kaizer Chiefs' manager Bobby Motaung and businessmen Herbert Theledi and Chris Grip.

Themba phoned someone and asked where they were, requesting an urgent meeting. He took me to a local hotel where I met someone whose identity I cannot divulge, and pleaded with the person to give copies of the documents that Jimmy had handed over before he was killed.

This person made another phone call. I was then sent to meet another someone, whose identity also cannot be divulged, at the Mbombela Legislature. This person told me that there was a hit list of councillors who must be killed and Jimmy Mohlala was number one on that list. He was scared to share with me the documents that Jimmy gave him for safe keeping because he was also on the list.

He gave me the name of the councillors on the hit list and said that Jimmy had the list given to him by one of the hitmen, who had been turned and had blown the whistle on the murder plot.

After a lot of persuasion and begging, the man agreed to give me one of the documents. This was an official document Lefika allegedly sent to First National Bank, when asking for an overdraft on 22 December 2008. The document was on the official municipality letterhead with the signature of the acting municipal manager Sigananda Siboza, who later confirmed that he was not the author of the letter and that his signature had been forged.

The municipality was also concerned about how Lefika had access to their letterhead.

"Jimmy was killed just a day before he was going to open a fraud case against Lefika. There are a number of other supporting documents but unfortunately, I can't give them to you. I don't want to be killed," said the man, visibly shaking and sweating.

When I phoned Bobby Motaung on Saturday morning, 10 January 2009 for comment, the soccer boss refused to comment and literally told me to go to hell. But on the same afternoon, just before our deadline, *Sunday World* sports editor Louis Mazibuko handed me his phone, saying Motaung was on the line and wanted to talk to me.

When I answered, Motaung said, "My brother, drop the story and name your price."

I told him that I was not for sale.

"Everybody has a price, what is yours? I have R1 million here for you, if you agree to drop it," Motaung insisted.

"My price is to see you rotting in jail," I said to him before I switched off the phone.

The story appeared on page five of the *Sunday World* the following day:

MOHLALA 'SILENCED'
Speaker was to blow whistle
By Mzilikazi wa Afrika

Mbombela municipal speaker Jimmy Mohlala, who was "assassinated" last week, was about to open a fraud case against Lefika Emerging Equity, a company co-owned by Kaizer Chiefs manager Bobby Motaung.

Mohlala was shot dead in his house in Kanyamazane, outside Nelspruit, last Sunday. His son Tshepiso (19) was shot in the leg.

Mohlala is the man who blew the whistle on Lefika, the project manager for the R1-billion World Cup 2010 Mbombela Stadium, three years ago.

A forensic investigation later established that Lefika was paid R43-million in an irregular transaction.

Sunday World can exclusively reveal that Mohlala was to open a case of fraud against Lefika on Monday, alleging that they submitted a letter to their bank using a fraudulent letter from Mbombela municipality to motivate a request for an overdraft.

He was also going to lobby the municipality to fire Lefika as the Mbombela Stadium project managers when the council re-opened tomorrow.

Sunday World is in possession of the letter Lefika allegedly submitted to First National Bank (FNB). We couldn't get comment from FNB yesterday.

The letter was "signed" on behalf of the acting municipal manager, Sgananda Siboza, who confirms that he knew nothing about it or its content.

Siboza says he started getting death threats after he told the bank official the letter was fraudulent.

He is also reported to be next on the hit list of eight officials to be assassinated – along with everyone in possession of the letter, including Mbombela executive mayor, Lassy Chiwayo.

Chiwayo says: "I have been getting death threats, as well as the acting municipal manager."

Mohlala's ordeal started the day the bank faxed him the letter.

That night he was attacked in the street. A source close to the police investigations says the men who attacked Mohlala wanted to use his own gun to shoot him, but he was not carrying it.

Police are looking for Vincent Nkosi, who might help them with their investigations.

Yesterday Motaung distanced himself and his company from the letter: "I don't want to get involved in the matters involving Jimmy Mohlala and I don't know anything about this letter.

"As far as I know, we have never requested an overdraft."

Mohlala will be buried today in Kanyamazane, Nelspruit.

The police were on the lookout for Vincent Nkosi, who they wanted to question about Jimmy Mohlala's murder. Police later issued a statement that "Nkosi was detained, questioned and then released because police found that he was not linked to the crime". The morning after the article was published, Motaung went to the Pretoria High Court to try to gag me from publishing further "defamatory" stories about him and his company. In my responding affidavit I explained how he had tried to bribe me to drop the story.

The court noted that although initially I had no intention to write a follow-up story on the matter, "Motaung's efforts to silence him [me] have prompted him [me] to research the matter further".

Motaung lost the case with costs after findings were in my favour.

Judge Cynthia Pretorius added that no reasonable reader, when reading the article published, would make the deduction that Motaung and Lefika were responsible for Mohlala's death.

"The sting the applicants want to read in the article does not exist as far as I am concerned. The only mention made of the applicants relates to the allegation of fraud by the deceased in connection with the Mbombela Stadium," Judge Pretorius said.

Judge Pretorius stressed that when I approached Motaung for comment, it was only in connection with the fraudulent letter and not the assassination of Mohlala.

She concluded that it was important not to deprive the media and the public of relevant information.

Media law expert Dario Milo, who represented me and the *Sunday World*, said the judgement was a victory for freedom of the media.

"Lefika and Motaung dragged the *Sunday World* to court, attempting to get an interdict on the basis that they would suffer some hypothetical and speculative harm based on the article that had already been published. If they were aggrieved by the article, their remedy is to issue a summons for defamation – not to rush off to court seeking to gag the media," Milo said.

A week later, *Sunday World* published an article that the municipality was about to cancel Lefika's multi-million-rand contract.

MUNICIPALITY RED CARDS MOTAUNG
and SARS Plans to Arrest Lefika MD
By Mzilikazi wa Afrika

The Mbombela municipality will this week launch its bid to terminate its contract with Lefika Emerging Equity, a company co-owned by Kaizer Chiefs manager Bobby Motaung.

This after the South African Revenue Services (SARS) informed the municipality that Lefika used a fraudulently obtained tax clearance certificate to win the tender to build the R1-billion 2010 World Cup Stadium, Mbombela Stadium.

The municipality will also try to recoup the R40-million it has already paid Lefika, as well as an additional R3-million that was allegedly irregularly paid to Lefika for a job that was worth only R200 000.

Sunday World can also reveal that SARS has obtained a warrant of arrest for Lefika MD Chris Grib after their investigation established that the company used a fraudulent tax clearance certificate.

Grib skipped the country immediately after the warrant was issued.

He went to Dubai, where he is CEO of global property developer, Jafkamber.

The other Lefika directors are Motaung and businessman Herbert Theledi.

If SARS decides to charge Motaung as Lefika's director, it won't be the first time the soccer boss faces the taxman.

Motaung and seven others were arrested in connection with a syndicate scam that allegedly defrauded SARS of more than R100-million in 2000.

One of the suspects, Robert Mokhonki, was a senior SARS employee and one of Motaung's friends.

Now another SARS employee, whose name cannot be divulged for security reasons, is in trouble after it was established that she helped Lefika obtain the fraudulent tax clearance certificate.

The employee has been suspended pending the investigation.

SARS spokeswoman Karen Nelmapius yesterday said, "I can confirm that the investigation into the fraudulent issuing of Lefika's tax clearance certificate is continuing.

"In the case of Grib, even if the person skips the country their tax matters remain as a matter between SARS and the company – not the individual."

Three weeks ago *Sunday World* reported that Mbombela municipality speaker Jimmy Mohlala was assassinated a day before he was to open a fraud case against Lefika.

This after they allegedly submitted a fraudulent letter deemed to be from Mbombela to motivate their application for an overdraft with their bank.

We also established this week that Mohlala was also going to open a criminal case against a senior municipal official who allegedly received a R375 000 bribe from Lefika. The official allegedly used the money to buy a luxury vehicle.

The municipality will also force Lefika to pay back R16-million it short-changed consultants working at the stadium.

A source says: "Lefika also short-paid some of the consultants by R16-million after we paid them the full amount. The municipality had to open a new bank account, into which all the money for the consultants will be paid."

On 16 August 2012 Bobby and his two business partners, Herbert Theledi and Chris Grip, were finally arrested and charged with fraud relating to Mbombela Stadium tender.

Motaung and Theledi were released on R50 000 bail each, Grip was released on R10 000 bail.

The case had not gone to trial at the time of writing this book, but Motaung, Theledi and Grip have pleaded not guilty in court.

Fast forward to 2010, few days after Mpumalanga's arts, culture and sport communications director Sammy Mpatlanyane was shot dead in his bed. He was killed on 5 January 2010, just a year after Jimmy Mohlala was assassinated. My former colleague Charles Molele and I were assigned to probe the hit-list saga in the province. The investigation was a joint venture between *Sunday World* and *Sunday Times*.

When Charles and I arrived in Mpumalanga in January 2010, little did we know that we would spend the next six months in that province, moving between Mozambique and Swaziland, and that we would also become potential victims.

What we discovered in Mpumalanga was shocking: a cover-up by police, bungling of the investigation and intimidation of witnesses. It was clear that the police were not there to investigate these murders, but instead to contaminate the scenes and conceal evidence.

To start with, the last man to see Jimmy Mohlala alive was only interviewed more than a year after the former speaker was killed. When we interviewed him, he alleged that he had a video footage of Mohlala's killers as the hitmen also came for him. Little did they know he had CCV cameras on his premises.

The last man to see Sammy Mpatlanyane alive was also not interviewed. The man told us how the former government spokesperson borrowed his car, disappeared to meet someone, and was killed shortly after he had returned the vehicle.

Within a short space of time, Charles and I had become unpopular with the local police and politicians. We were hated for asking the right questions of the right people and turning the heat on the potential culprits – the brains behind these murders.

We published the first series of our investigations in the *Sunday Times* on 7 February 2010.

INSIDE MPUMALANGA HIT SQUADS
Murder Inc. in Mbombela
Special report by Charles Molele and Mzilikazi wa Afrika

An ANC boss used to have opponents shot, but switched to poison last year.

A 25-year-old contract killer has accused an influential ANC leader in Mpumalanga of offering him R100 000 and a cushy government job if he poisoned government officials who were blocking access to tenders linked to the 2010 Soccer World Cup.

The ANC boss, whose name is known to the *Sunday Times*, was fingered by more than a dozen other sources interviewed during a three-week investigation into the killings of at least a dozen senior politicians in Mpumalanga starting in 1998.

The would-be assassin said he had been given the poison and had been ready to do the job, but had pulled out after a disagreement with his "client" over an advance fee.

Though his three intended victims are still alive, six officials were murdered or died in suspicious circumstances in Mpumalanga last year alone and another has been killed this year. Local party leaders and officials who spoke to the *Sunday Times* mentioned a "hit list" of other proposed victims and said they were living in fear.

The *Sunday Times* has been given the full name of a Mozambican gangster known as "Josh" and told that he was responsible for the murder of Mbombela (Nelspruit) council speaker Jimmy Mohlala in January 2009.

"Josh" agreed to speak to our reporters in Mozambique, but then changed his mind.

ANC national spokesman Jackson Mthembu – the former speaker of the Mpumalanga legislature – said the ruling party was aware of the alleged hit list and had sent a task team to investigate those responsible for the killings of its members in the province.

The *Sunday Times* investigation took reporters to sources in Gauteng, Mpumalanga and Mozambique. Those interviewed included senior ANC members, municipal officials and NIA sources, as well as the province's former ANC Youth League leader, James Nkambule, and Mpumalanga Democratic Alliance leader Anthony Benadie.

The *Sunday Times* has given details of the plot to police Superintendent Sibongile Nkosi and Mpumalanga's deputy provincial commissioner, Rex Machabi. They said the would-be killer would be interviewed soon.

The assassin said many people lived in fear of the ANC leader he had named. "This politician must be exposed and expelled from the ANC in order to stop his reign of terror in Mpumalanga. I am scared of him. Even those in the higher echelons are scared of him because he is too dangerous. I don't want to go on killing innocent people," he said. However, he did not admit to any killings.

A former ANC regional leader Alfred Monareng said the ANC boss and his cabal used to have their opponents shot, but had switched to poison last year.

He said the assassin interviewed by the *Sunday Times* had confessed to him that he had planned to spike a bottle of Johnnie Walker whisky on Christmas Eve while drinking with him at his home in White River, where he works as a senior waste manager in the Mbombela municipality.

"He told me he was about to poison me, but decided not to," said

Monareng. "The motive behind the plot to kill me is apparently to force me to vacate my post in order to make way for a preferred Samwu [municipal workers' union] candidate who is known to me. They cannot find any case of misconduct, irregularities or corrupt activity, so they have resorted to poisoning me," he said.

Monareng said he had not believed the confession, but then discovered that other suspicious deaths, including that of his brother, could have been as a result of poison.

"We now suspect that my brother, Themba [regional secretary], Mthandazo Ngobeni [chairman of the ANC Youth League], Vusi Sibiya [regional secretary], Lucas Shongwe [regional secretary] and the fiery ANC member Michael Sifunda were allegedly poisoned, as they've all shown similar symptoms before they died."

They all vomited white foam before dying.

Nelspruit mayor, Lassy Chiwayo, whose name is on the hit list, said he was living in fear after receiving death threats on his cellphone. He has sent a report to ANC headquarters at Luthuli House about his victimisation.

"I have been warned that I will go back home in a coffin," said Chiwayo.

Deputy Mayor Nackie Ndlovu said she had been told of plans to poison her. "I fear for my life and cannot trust anyone. There have been so many killings in Mpumalanga. We are pleading with the ANC to do something because we are really not safe anymore," she said.

At least 12 local leaders have been murdered or have died in suspicious circumstances in Mpumalanga since 1998. Police say they are investigating, but no one has been arrested.

People who spoke to the *Sunday Times* said they were afraid to give information to police because they did not know which faction of the party the law enforcement agents supported.

DA provincial leader Benadie slammed Mpumalanga premier David Mabuza for his silence on the deaths of three senior officials who had been on the alleged hit list.

"Why have we not heard [from] the premier on these murders, the hit list and poisoning claims? The premier is a feared man. Our constitutional democracy is at stake if people won't talk because they are afraid of being taken out," said Benadie.

Former Youth League leader Nkambule said he knew who was behind at least one of the killings of senior officials in government and had given the information to crime intelligence officials. He said some of the murders were planned at a farm outside Nelspruit owned by another ANC politician.

Nkambule made headlines when he alleged that premier Mabuza had contributed R400 000 to sponsor President Jacob Zuma's wedding to his second wife, Nompumelelo Ntuli.

Mohlala was shot dead at his house in Kanyamazane, outside Nelspruit, after he allegedly blew the whistle on the abuse of power and corruption relating to the construction of the province's R1 billion Mbombela Stadium intended for use during the 2010 World Cup.

Four weeks ago, Sammy Mpatlanyane, communications director in the provincial department of arts, culture and sport, was also gunned down at his home in Nelspruit.

Mpatlanyane allegedly was regarded as an obstacle by the ANC boss and his powerful allies to winning irregular tenders involving the World Cup.

ANC national spokesman Mthembu said: "We are aware of the hit list and allegations against the politicians allegedly involved in these killings, but we cannot do anything until the police crack these cases.

"We are particularly incensed that nobody has been brought to book since the murder of Mohlala. His murder happened so many months ago, but until now we still have not received any information that makes us confident that the matter is being dealt with properly."

On the same day, there was also a story on how Mpumalanga Premier David Mabuza had remained mum on these killings.

PREMIER 'TURNING MPUMALANGA INTO A BANANA PROVINCE'

The ANC is under mounting pressure to recall Mpumalanga Premier David Mabuza.

Critics within the ruling party blame Mabuza for deepening factionalism and accuse him of nepotism and patronage, but few are willing to confront him in public.

Mabuza, known locally as "The Hurricane", is also under fire for his silence on the killings of senior politicians in the province, where spending on preparations for the 2010 Soccer World Cup has fuelled political rivalry.

In September last year, a group of ANC members organised a press conference to discuss Mabuza's removal as party chairman. But it was called off after they received threats.

They then wrote an anonymous letter to President Jacob Zuma, asking him to "help before we become a banana province".

"Mr President Sir, may you please relieve our premier of his duties if you want to see progress in the province," the letter reads.

"He is busy destroying the legacy left by former Premier [Thabang] Makwetla. He does not have management skills to run the province. We are asking ourselves that with the irregularities that he has committed while MEC for Roads and Transport how he was chosen [as] premier of the province."

Besides roads and transport, the letter also accuses Mabuza of a litany of irregularities while he was MEC for education and agriculture. He is further accused of buying cars for journalists employed by the *Sowetan*, *City Press* and a local news agency to write positive stories about him.

ANC spokesman Jackson Mthembu confirmed that the letter and additional reports and documents had been received at Luthuli House.

"We are investigating all these reports and documents and we are currently verifying their authenticity before acting on the matters raised," said Mthembu.

Mabuza's spokesman, Mabutho Sithole, said it was unfair to criticise Mabuza's silence on the killings. "Our position is that any killing of an individual is wrong and very painful to the families of the deceased.

"However, we believe the law enforcement agencies must take the lead in the matter, investigate and apprehend the people behind these senseless killings," he said.

A source close to Mabuza accused those opposed to Mabuza of funding service delivery protests. "We will defend him from people like [Mbombela Municipality Mayor Lassy] Chiwayo and former premier Matthews Phosa, who are behind the plot to oust him," he said.

A source told the *Sunday Times* that the ANC NEC wants the provincial executive of the party disbanded immediately.

A source close to Mabuza said the premier was aware of a plot to oust him including those behind it and named Chiwayo as being involved.

Mabuza beat Chiwayo to the post of ANC chairman of Mpumalanga with 388 votes to 305 votes in 2008.

At the centre of the problems in Mpumalanga is a fierce fight for multi-billion-rand contracts and tenders related to the FIFA World Cup, and other projects such as roads and construction contracts circulating among a few individuals.

Mthembu said the ruling party in the province was in "a state of paralysis".

"There are serious difficulties in ANC structures such as factionalism, but we have appointed a task team to investigate all the problems affecting service delivery in Mpumalanga."

The ruling party has deployed NEC members to deal with the problems in the province in the next few weeks. They will report back before the end of March.

The task team's convener is Deputy Home Affairs Minister Malusi Gigaba, ANC Deputy Secretary-General Thandi Modise, Justice Minister Jeff Radebe, Deputy Minister of Police Fikile Mbalula and ANC Women's League President Angie Motshekga.

We also carried a list of some of the victims of the Mpumalanga killings.

SURGE IN MPUMALANGA KILLINGS

Chasing the FIFA millions and other lucrative deals has been fatal for many in Mpumalanga.

The following people have either been killed, received death threats, disappeared or survived assassination attempts on their lives. The hitmen – most of them alleged to be Zimbabwean and Mozambican nationals – are still at large.

Saul Shabangu, (killed in 1998);
Hebron Maisela (killed in 1998);
Sydney de Lange (killed in 1998);
Rose Aletta Mnisi (killed in 1999);
Caswell Maluleke, (survived assassination in 2000);
Joshua Ntshuhle (disappeared in 2005);
Sizile Ndlovu, (survived assassination in 2006);
Thandi Mtsweni (killed in 2008);
Jimmy Mohlala (killed in 2009);

Isaac Mohale Matsoabane (killed in 2009);

Samuel Mpatlanyane (killed in 2010);

Themba Monareng (died 2009);

Mike Sifunda (died 2009);

Simon Lubisi (died 2009);

Lucas Shongwe (died 2009).

Shortly after the newspaper hit the streets, the propaganda machines were hard at work. That same Sunday afternoon, Colonel Rudolph Gerald Adolph from the Crime Intelligence office in Nelspruit called *Mpumalanga News* journalist Lungile Dube on the pretext that he had a story for her. When she arrived at his office, Adolph asked her to sign a prepared affidavit that alleged Lungile had witnessed Mathews Phosa paying me a lot of money to tarnish Premier Mabuza's image.

"If you sign this affidavit, the premier will take good care of you," he told Lungile.

Lungile refused to sign the affidavit and stormed out of the office. Lungile made me aware of what happened and said she was willing to file an affidavit to that effect.

Charles and I lodged an official complaint about Adolph with his boss Brigadier Dan Maropeng. Months later Maropeng was arrested for drinking and driving and suspended before he could conclude his investigation into Adolph's conduct. Colonel Christopher Mabasa, the same police officer who arrested me later, arrested Maropeng, who had been travelling with his family at the time. Maropeng was forced to take an early retirement and his position was given to Adolph.

After refusing to sign the affidavit, Lungile was summoned to a secret meeting by the premier where Mabuza told her he was disappointed that she had refused to sign. At the same meeting Mabuza asked Lungile to spy on me, even giving her a small digital recorder to record my every move, if possible, including everyone I spoke too.

After Lungile failed to deliver me on a platter, windows of a house she was renting were broken and she started getting death threats.

Her boss at the time, Irma Green, who is the group managing editor for *Lowvelder*, took Lungile to the ANC head office and provided party Secretary-General Gwede Mantashe a blow-by-blow account of Premier Mabuza's conduct and how he had been trying to intimidate me.

To this day, I do not know what Mantashe did with the information, but all I know is that Lungile was forced to relocate from Mpumalanga to Johannesburg and forced out of journalism.

Molele and I came out with a sequel to our Mpumalanga investigation, on 28 February 2010.

I KILLED MOHLALA
Hired hitman fingers top politician and soccer boss
By Mzilikazi wa Afrika and Charles Molele

The Mozambican gangster who claims to have been hired by top Mpumalanga government officials to eliminate opponents has now been linked to the death of former SA National Defence Force secretary January "Che" Masilela.

The police believe the thug, known in the criminal underworld as Josh, is also responsible for the unsolved murder of Morris Mothibi, a well-known Joburg drug lord, in 2006.

Masilela, a high-flying ANC cadre from Mpumalanga, died on the N4 highway near Bronkhorstspruit at about 5.20 a.m. on 25 August 2008 after his BMW X5 overturned and burst into flames.

Police sources told *Sunday World* this week that Josh seems to have been hired to kill Masilela and that his murder was made to look like a car accident.

"The information in our possession is that Masilela's accident was a hit," says a police source. "Our investigation has fingered Josh, also known as Joseph Khoza and Orlando Maziya, as responsible for his death." Both are Mozambican nationals who have returned home and were never arrested. The Masilela case is still pending and no one has been arrested for his murder.

At the time of his death senior ANC members in Mpumalanga were lobbying with the party's deployment committee at Luthuli House for Masilela to replace Thabang Makwetla as premier when his term ended in May 2009.

The current Mpumalanga premier is David Mabuza, who was elected provincial chairman at the party's provincial conference in August 2008.

Sunday Times can today reveal that Josh has also made sensational claims in an affidavit against at least one senior ANC politician and a top soccer boss regarding the death of former Mbombela speaker Jimmy

Mohlala, who blew the whistle on irregularities in the tenders to build the R2-billion FIFA 2010 World Cup stadium in Nelspruit.

The police want him to make a confession before a magistrate.

Arrangements are being made for his safety when he makes the confession and for his placement in the witness protection programme.

He will then testify against the senior ANC politician, two Mpumalanga businessmen and a prominent soccer boss.

The Mozambican claims he was hired by the Mpumalanga government officials and the soccer boss as a "cleaner" from 2000 until 2009 to eliminate the four men's political and business opponents.

His work included smuggling drugs, moving cash, burying dead people and murdering opponents, some by poisoning.

He alleges that he planted drugs in councillor Isiah Khoza's house, poisoned ANC Youth League provincial leader James Nkambule, tried to kill former mayor of the Gert Sibande District Council Andries Gamede and Standing Committee on Public Accounts chairman Fish Mahlalela and Mbombela Mayor Lassy Chiwayo.

He further alleges that Govan Mbeki's chief financial officer Joshua Ntshuhle's car was driven to Malawi to make it look like he vanished while driving to Malawi.

Ntshuhle vanished in December 2005, days before he was scheduled to testify in the fraud and corruption trial of the municipality's marketing manager Sibusiso Sigudla, who was acquitted after the State star witness disappeared and his car found burnt in Malawi.

His body is believed to be buried on a farm outside Nelspruit, along with two others.

"I buried these bodies at the farm," claims Josh.

The Mozambican gangster also claims he and three Zimbabwean nationals and a fellow Mozambican were hired to assassinate Mohlala.

They were offered R40 000 each for the hit, which they dubbed "Mbombela Clean-up Operation".

"After following Mr Mohlala's movements, we split [sic] into two groups," claims Josh in the affidavit.

"One group of three was stationed at one of his two houses and the other group, myself and [name withheld] was stationed at the other house.

"We followed Mr Mohlala into the house and I shot him twice or thrice. He was with a child who was shot by [name withheld] while I had to make sure that Mr Mohlala was dead. This was January 2009.

"I called [name withheld] and told him the job was done. [Name withheld] sounded very happy on hearing this news."

"He told me the rest of our money will be paid sooner [sic]. He also told me to 'shake' Mr Chiwayo with threats on his phone. I threatened Mr Chiwayo on his phone at least five times."

Chiwayo confirms he got threatening phone calls shortly after Mohlala was killed from "a very aggressive person".

He says: "I was told that I will go back home to Witbank in a coffin."

Nkambule made a statement to Barberton police's Senior Superintendent Harry Shabangu about his alleged poisoning.

"Josh confirmed to have poisoned me with a substance that activated an otherwise benign cancer in me which is now killing me softly," he says in his statement.

Four of the hitmen who carried out the hit on Mohlala have since been killed to destroy evidence.

The Mozambican national claims he fears for his life but is willing to co-operate with the South African police if placed in a witness protection programme in order to testify against the Mpumalanga government officials and the soccer boss.

On Friday Mpumalanga police spokesman Superintendent Sibongile Nkosi confirmed that they had received the affidavit from Josh.

"We can confirm that the police have obtained an affidavit and that our members are still investigating allegations made in it," he said.

Shortly after this story was published, police arrested James Nkambule, who they considered as one of our sources.

There was also a rumour doing the rounds that there was a reward of R1 million for anybody who would kill me. Three different people confirmed the rumour, claiming they were at the same meeting when a senior politician made the offer. These three sources said they had reported the matter to Luthuli House, the ANC head office, and had allegedly submitted the recording from the same meeting, during which the R1 million reward was offered.

I was never given the recording.

One night on 12 April 2010 as I was parking my car at the hotel in Nelspruit, three men came from nowhere and tried to force me into the boot of a BMW parked nearby. What went down was the fight of my life. I managed to fight them off but a verbal war ensued and they told me they were going to get me sooner or later.

My colleague, Charles Molele, who was lodging at the same hotel, is one of many witnesses to this incident, which was also captured on camera by the hotel CCV cameras. The hotel security guard, the two receptionists who were working that evening, as well as the hotel manager who was phoned later that night, are also witnesses. The hotel also provided us with the CCV footage of the incident.

Within ten minutes of the incident at the parking lot, a convoy of about 15 cars arrived at the hotel, led by Welcome Nkuna, who was then head of security in the premier's office, and his lieutenant, Thomas Bongo, who was a senior official in the department of human settlements in the province.

Bongo, who was more vocal than the rest of his crew, threatened to shoot the hotel receptionist unless he gave him my room number or booked him in a room next to mine. The hotel manager was called and Nkuna and his people were asked to leave or the police would be called. Bongo, who lives about two kilometres from the hotel, booked himself into the hotel but not into the room next to mine.

The following day I confronted one of the three men who had cornered me in the parking lot, businessman Walter Sithole of Sithole Computers, a company supplying most provincial departments with computers. Sithole denied that he was part of the cabal.

"I saw everything that happened to you, as I was in that parking lot too, but I swear to God, I am not part of these guys. It just happened that I was at the right place at the wrong time. I don't even know those guys," Sithole said.

After the incident, we took a break from the Mpumalanga investigation and went back to Johannesburg where I was asked to re-join the *Sunday Times*.

In Johannesburg, a friend whom I have known for many years invited me to his office in Sandton and gave me the documents which suggested that the national police commissioner at the time, Bheki Cele, was planning to move the police head offices in Pretoria to a building owned by businessman Roux Shabangu without putting it out to tender.

I had to put Cele's lease investigation on hold, however, as Charles and I were heading back to Mpumalanga to continue with our murder probe.

During the FIFA World Cup, Charles and I were based in Mpumalanga.

One night, while having dinner at one of the local restaurants, Welcome Nkuna arrived with a different crew.

Five of the men took a table by the door, while Nkuna and two others sat near my table. The communication between the groups was via text messages. I could see messages going to and fro, fast and furious, and decided to pay our bill and leave.

The following day I received a phone call from Riot Hlatshwayo, who was the Mpumalanga bureau chief for the *Sowetan*, one of our sister publications, asking to meet me urgently.

I have known Hlatshwayo for years as my homeboy from Bushbuckridge. I had been a friend of his brother, Ephraim, for ages.

In fact, I was the one who paved the way for Hlatshwayo to be a journalist, when I took him to AENS editor Justin Arenstein and begged Arenstein to give him a chance.

Hlatshwayo is a small-town criminal. His rise to fame came when the well-known musician Peta Teanet was gunned down when he was with Riot at a pub near Acornhoek in Bushbuckridge. Riot phoned Munghana Lonene FM to report the incident. Each day, Hlatshwayo continued to give the radio station updates. In the end, he was hired as a newsreader for the station.

Not long after he joined the station, Hlatshwayo was arrested and sent to jail for attempting to steal one of the station's cars. He claimed he took the car without permission but he did not intend to steal it. He phoned me while he was in jail in Polokwane. During my visit to him, he told me he had changed and needed a chance. When Hlatshwayo was released from jail, he asked me to help him find a job. I turned to Arenstein, cautioning the AENS editor with the man's criminal history and background. But Arenstein took him in and promised to keep a close eye on him.

Later, when *Sowetan* was looking for a bureau chief in Mpumalanga, I recommended Hlatshwayo to Thabo Leshilo, who was the chief editor and had initially offered me the job.

When I arrived at Hlatshwayo's office that afternoon, he told me that I was lucky to be alive as the men who came to the restaurant the previous night were sent there to kill me. He described the situation in detail, what I was wearing and eating when the men arrived. I asked him how he knew of all this.

"You know there is a R1 million reward for anybody who can kill you?" he asked.

"Of course I do," I said.

"Those five men you saw were fetched from KwaZulu-Natal to come and do the job. They arrived yesterday," he said.

"How do you know all this?" I asked again.

"I have sources in high places, my friend," he said while making a phone call on his cellphone and putting it on the speakerphone.

"Yes, my chief," the other person on the line said.

"Tell me what happened last night?" Hlatshwayo asked.

"That dog Mzilikazi managed to escape again. This boy must be paying his sangoma too well. Yesterday we thought we got him. We would be rich today – we would be sharing the R1 million. This dog is beginning to piss me off now. He doesn't need a gun, just a knife; stab him straight in the heart and finish with this bastard," the man explained.

Hlatshwayo promised to phone the man later as someone had just walked into his office. He refused to divulge the identity of the man he was on the phone with or how the information came to him.

"Don't say I didn't warn you, when you get harmed or killed," said Hlatshwayo. I thanked him and left. I have a witness to this incident.

Before the end of the FIFA World Cup, Hlatshwayo told Charles and me that there was a rumour that the premier had written a letter to President Zuma tendering his resignation. We checked our sources, but nobody else had heard the rumour. After the World Cup, Charles and I returned to Johannesburg.

I then received a call from an unknown person on the morning of 21 July 2010. The caller asked if I was aware that Premier Mabuza had resigned and had written a letter to Zuma. I told the person that I had heard that rumour but nobody could confirm it.

"I have the letter," said the caller.

The caller said he was in White River. I told him that I was in Johannesburg but I knew a friend who resided in White River.

I asked the man to call me after five minutes as he refused to give me his number. I then called my friend Victor Mlimi who, fortunately, was at home in White River and asked him to be on standby. When the man called back, he told me he was at a KFC restaurant and that Victor would find him there.

Minutes later, Victor called to say he had the letter. I asked him to fax it to me as soon as possible. The faxed letter arrived at 10:57 a.m. on 21 July 2010. I scanned it and emailed it to my former political editor Wally Mbhele and colleague Charles with the message: "Now that we have the letter, let's verify the signature as I have never seen Mabuza' signature before."

The three of us discussed the letter and it was agreed that we should verify the signature. I phoned Hlatshwayo to ask if he had any document with the premier's signature, but he said he did not. I phoned Tom Nkosi, the publisher of *Ziwaphi*, a weekly newspaper based in Nelspruit, and asked him the same question. He too did not have the premier's signature. I phoned a couple of people I knew in Nelspruit but none of them had seen Mabuza's signature.

Without the premier's signature, there was nothing we could do. I left everything like that and kept it on hold but continued with my police lease investigation, working with my other colleague Stephan Hofstatter.

The *Sunday Times* broke the police lease story on 1 August 2010.

BHEKI CELE'S R500M POLICE RENTAL DEAL
Brass baffled as top cop suddenly signs lease
for new HQ – without tendering
By Mzilikazi wa Afrika and Stephan Hofstatter

A billionaire businessman has clinched a dodgy R500 million property deal with police chief General Bheki Cele that will result in the police moving their headquarters to a building he bought this week.

The *Sunday Times* can reveal that Cele signed the deal to move SA Police Service top brass – including Minister of Police Nathi Mthethwa, his deputy, Fikile Mbalula, and administrative staff – to Roux Shabangu's building almost two months before he bought it.

The deal never went out to tender, violating Treasury regulations that all contracts over R500 000 must go through a competitive bid process. After three days of queries from the *Sunday Times*, the department of public works could not explain why it had flouted Treasury rules.

"We will give you a written response by Monday or Tuesday," said spokesman Lucky Mochalibane.

Shabangu confirmed he bought the 18-storey Middestad Sanlam Centre in Pretoria on Wednesday for R220 million and claimed he was still "negotiating" with the police to move in.

But the *Sunday Times* is in possession of a lease agreement for Middestad between Shabangu's company, Roux Property Fund, and the SAPS, signed by Cele and public works official MB Tlolane on 1 June.

The lease will run for ten years from today and specifies that cheques should be made out to Shabangu's company. Projected expenditure under "actual cost calculations" totals R520 947 435. The police will occupy 21 747m² of office space. The remaining 16 000m² is mostly made up of shops on the ground floor.

SAPS headquarters is housed in the Wachthuis building just around the corner.

It is owned by Encha Properties, which declined to disclose the rental it charged. However, a police insider said the Wachthuis lease was also worth about R500 million, and was set to run for another ten years.

This is supported by the fact that Encha registered two bonds with Investec over the property for a total of R415 million.

Unless the Wachthuis lease is cancelled, taxpayers could be forking out almost R1 billion in the next decade to house SAPS headquarters.

Several senior officials apparently have serious reservations about the move. "They don't understand why you should rent a new building when there is enough space [at Wachthuis]," said one official close to police management.

For R500 million, at least 10 000 new constables could be patrolling South Africa's streets.

Cele said the new space was needed to house the top brass and between four and six specialised units. He could not specify how many police officials would move.

"There are so many units that come under my direct command and they have to be where I am. The minister, the deputy minister and some of the commissioners are moving into the new building with me."

Cele could not explain why he signed the lease in June for a building that was bought this week. "Every day I sign piles and piles of documents and the lease is one of them. If there were any irregularities maybe supply chain management can answer that."

Cele's choice of landlord suggests political considerations trumped efficient use of taxpayers' money at a time when the government claims it can't afford pay hikes for striking public servants.

Wachthuis owners Encha Properties belongs to the Moseneke family, who are close allies of former president Thabo Mbeki.

Shabangu, on the other hand, appears to be well connected to President Jacob Zuma's government, having attended Zuma's inauguration as a VIP guest. He denies using his political clout to close deals.

"I am a businessman and not a politician," he said. "Not everyone who attended that function was there because of political connections."

The billionaire whose family hails from Swaziland started as a humble maize distributor in Mpumalanga.

Today his R1.4 billion property empire includes Protea and Jabulani Malls in Soweto and Alex Plaza in Alexandra. He's also a partner in a massive R1.5 billion office and retail development in Mbabane, Swaziland, and a R1.2 billion mall in Mogale City.

He was previously accused of colluding with bank officials to buy properties on auction and sell them back to the government at a handsome profit, but denied this emphatically. "Ag no – that is not correct. We negotiated [farm sales] on behalf of the government and were paid a fee – that is all," he said this week.

Meanwhile, SAPS officials told the *Sunday Times* that Cele has also signed a deal to move police in Durban to another building Shabangu is negotiating to buy.

Shabangu was in Durban on Friday trying to clinch the deal, which he refused to elaborate on, saying negotiations were "at a sensitive stage".

He would only confirm that police would be moving into his Pretoria building. "I [have] just bought [the] building and police want to move in as Wachthuis is apparently flooding and horrible."

He also claimed the validity of Encha's Wachthuis lease was questionable. "There is a big controversy over the validity of [that] lease."

But Encha Properties CEO Dr Sedise Moseneke told the *Sunday Times* that his company had a "lawful lease" to accommodate police headquarters at Wachthuis.

He denied there was anything wrong with the building, "The property is maintained to the highest standards and to date we have not received any complaint whatsoever from our tenant."

I was arrested three days after this story was published and one of the police officers admitted that my arrest was for political and not criminal reasons. That admission was on the *Sunday Times* front page the following day:

"ARREST WAS POLITICAL" SENIOR POLICEMAN'S
STARTLING ADMISSION
By Stephan Hofstatter and Charles Molele

There is mounting evidence that political pressure lay behind the arrest this week of *Sunday Times* journalist Mzilikazi wa Afrika despite furious denials from police top brass.

A senior police official close to the case admitted yesterday that police were feeling the heat from ANC politicians to crack down on Wa Afrika, because of his reporting.

"Ja – it's political pressure," he told the *Sunday Times*.

Yesterday, Mabutho Sithole, a spokesman for Mpumalanga premier, David Mabuza, confirmed the premier had laid the initial complaint, at the Kabokweni police station in Nelspruit, which culminated in Wa Afrika's arrest.

Mabuza, a controversial figure in Mpumalanga, has been the subject of various articles in the *Sunday Times* and other publications.

The complaint was sparked by a letter faxed to the *Sunday Times*, in which Mabuza supposedly states his intention to resign as premier. Mabuza insisted the letter was a forgery and that he had no intention of resigning.

No article relating to the letter was published.

"He [Mabuza] complained to the police here at Kabokweni after we got a copy of the letter and received information that there were people in possession of a letter bearing his name and signature," said Sithole.

Wa Afrika was arrested at 11:15 a.m. on Wednesday outside the *Sunday Times* building in Rosebank, Johannesburg.

Minutes earlier *Sunday Times* lawyer Renier Spies had been negotiating with Kabokweni station commander, Lieutenant-Colonel Chris Mabasa, at Rosebank police station not to arrest Wa Afrika at his office, but rather to allow the journalist to hand himself over at the station.

"In the meantime [Mabasa] contacted a 'general' whose further particulars are unknown to me, via his cellphone," said Spies. "According to [Mabasa], the general he spoke to was on his way to the station and wanted to join us."

Minutes later, several police vehicles with sirens blaring pulled up alongside Wa Afrika outside the *Sunday Times* building while he was walking to the police station. Police bundled him into an unmarked vehicle and drove off at high speed.

At 7:00 p.m. on Thursday night, the *Sunday Times* went to the High

Court in Pretoria to bring an urgent application for Wa Afrika's release. Just before 10:00 p.m., acting Judge Johan Kruger ordered his immediate release following an agreement with the state. Wa Afrika was released at 10:30 p.m. on Thursday night.

He appeared in Nelspruit Regional Court on Friday on charges of fraud, forgery and uttering. He was released on bail of R5 000 and is scheduled to appear again on 8 November.

Spies said he was convinced there was "political pressure on [Mabasa] to effect an arrest".

This is borne out by the line of questioning police adopted when interrogating Wa Afrika and fellow suspect Victor Mlimi, a senior provincial government official, at the Nelspruit office of the police's provincial Organised Crime Unit on Thursday.

"I was asked whether I was directly or indirectly involved in discrediting senior ANC office bearers in Mpumalanga," said Wa Afrika. "That made me wonder whether the police were investigating a criminal or a political case.

"They also wanted to know who the big politicians I'm working with behind the scenes are. This made me conclude the police were sent by politicians to harass and intimidate me."

Mlimi's lawyer, Daniel Mabunda, said his client was questioned for two hours about the ANC's provincial leadership succession battles, and which political camp he supported.

"I was present when my client was asked, 'Are you destroying the image and integrity of the ANC in Mpumalanga?' I advised my client not to answer that question. It struck me that this has more to do with politics than a criminal case."

The day before the arrest, police chief General Bheki Cele had referred to Wa Afrika as a "shady journalist", in response to an article he co-authored about the police chief's involvement in clinching a R500 million lease agreement, without going to tender, with billionaire businessman Roux Shabangu.

The vigour police used to pursue Wa Afrika also raised eyebrows. The case was opened at Kabokweni police station on Monday and Wa Afrika was arrested two days later.

Police have yet to arrest anyone connected to the deaths of Mbombela speaker Jimmy Mohlala and provincial arts and culture spokesman Sammy Mpatlanyane – both of whom appeared on an alleged hit list that emerged last year.

Mohlala was gunned down outside his house by three masked men in January 2009 in Kanyamazane township outside Nelspruit. Mpatlanyane was shot in his Nelspruit home in January 2010.

"Those murders are still under investigation," Hawks spokesman Musa Zondi told the *Sunday Times* yesterday.

The visible lack of progress in these cases contrasts with the swift action taken against Wa Afrika, one of the journalists who exposed the alleged hit list.

Cele's spokesman Nonkululeko Mbatha told the *Sunday Times* yesterday "the semblance and impressions you have are not factual".

"Police have instituted a probe which is ongoing and appealed to members of the public who might have information to come to the fore," said Mbatha.

Asked about the negative impression created by the police's heavy-handed action against Wa Afrika, she said: "I cannot undo that impression, but the fact of the matter is no one is immune from investigation of what is of a suspicious or of a criminal nature.

"Lastly, insinuations about a directive issued by the general [Cele] to apprehend or intimidate the journalist are incorrect and a figment of imagination."

Mabuza's spokesman also denied exerting any political pressure on police, or that the arrest was an attempt to intimidate Wa Afrika and derail his investigative reporting on the murders.

The matter was set to go to trial on 21 November 2012 but the state agreed to settle out of court.

Bheki Cele was fired as the national police commissioner in June 2012 when a board of inquiry headed by Judge Jake Moloi and appointed by Zuma found he was not fit to hold office. Cele bounced back when President Zuma announced him as the new deputy minister of agriculture, forestry and Fisheries on 25 May 2014.

Mabuza has not been arrested or charged for any crime or officially questioned by police.

Chapter 19

N'WA-TINTANGU: Circumcising a mosquito

"Don't blame the messenger because the message is unpleasant." – Kenneth Starr

When Stephan Hofstatter and I joined the *Sunday Times* in April 2010 I was coming "back home" from the *Sunday World* where I had served a stint as investigations editor. Rob Rose was on his way to Harvard University as a Nieman Fellow for a year.

Even though Stephan and I had not worked together before, we had written similar stories over the years and spoken to the same sources in most instances.

Against all odds we started plotting and planning how to revive the *Sunday Times* investigations unit.

While Charles Molele and I were busy with the Mpumalanga investigation, Stephan and Rob would share with us what they had (or had been told by their sources), supporting us all the way. From time to time, the four of us would meet, discuss stories and compare notes.

So when I received the five-page documents about the new police lease implicating the former national police commissioner Bheki Cele, Stephan was a perfect candidate to work with. He too had written stories about businessman Roux Shabangu during his investigation into the looting of funds at the Land Bank. In short, he was no stranger to more than a few of the players.

After the FIFA World Cup ended on 11 July 2010 and Charles and I had packed our bags and left Nelspruit for Johannesburg, Stephan and I started concentrating on the police lease investigation. Slowly but surely we were starting to rebuild the *Sunday Times* investigation unit.

When Rob, a multi-award-winning journalist, returned from Harvard

University after a year, the unit was already rebuilt from the ruins, like a phoenix rising from the ashes. He was the best choice to join us.

The unit started making waves. We won the Taco Kuiper Award for investigative journalism, the Mondi Shanduka Newspaper Awards for a hard news story, the Vodacom Award for the story of the year as well as the Vodacom Award for journalists of the year.

With Rob on board we became the infamous three musketeers. We worked on a number of investigative stories including ones on the former ANC Youth League president and now Economic Freedom Fighters (EFF) commander-in-chief, Julius Malema, his money trail, his farm and his joyride on businessman Mohamed Dada's private jet. Dada was getting tenders from the Limpopo government whose premier at the time was Cassel Mothale, a friend of Malema's.

As journalists the three of us thought we had done it all, seen the worst criminals, exposed atrocious corruption, unearthed unbelievable venality, untangled webs of lies and survived dirty tricks campaigns and malicious propaganda. That is until Dina Deliwe Pule, our former minister of communications, entered the fray and floored us with some jaw-dropping experiences.

Just a day after the inaugural ICT Indaba ended in Cape Town on 7 June 2012, an angry whistle-blower approached Rob alleging that Phosane Mngqibisa, who is romantically linked to Pule, had looted the sponsors' cash. The ICT Indaba was one of the projects under Pule's department.

Pule, the source said, had called up the telecom companies, who reported to her, and had "basically extorted" sponsorship cash of R25.7 million from Vodacom, MTN and Telkom. This was a serious conflict of interest for Pule: her own department chipped in an additional R10.5 million for the event.

When we confronted the conference organiser Carol Bouwer (of Carol Bouwer Productions) she confirmed that Mngqibisa had been subcontracted and that he was a "second signatory" to her company's bank account – where all the millions for the event were supposed to be deposited. The *Sunday Times* published a simple front-page story about Pule's shenanigans on 17 June 2012.

Minister's 'romantic link' to R25.7m telecoms conference row
By Mzilikazi wa Afrika, Rob Rose and Stephan Hofstatter

Telecoms companies lobbied by Communications Minister Dina Pule to pay R25.7 million towards this month's high-profile ICT Indaba are furious that millions in sponsorship fees were drawn from the account of the event organiser by a man alleged to be romantically linked to her.

The *Sunday Times* has established that millions paid in "sponsorships" by Telkom, MTN and Vodacom were withdrawn within days by Phosane Mngqibisa, who is said to be romantically linked to Pule. The minister personally lobbied Telkom, MTN and Vodacom to sponsor the event, held in Cape Town last week.

Vodacom, MTN and Telkom together forked out R25.7 million, with her department chipping in another R10.5 million.

Senior executives at the telecoms companies contacted by the *Sunday Times* were furious.

Insiders at MTN said this was "serious, as it might warrant an internal review of our processes over how we pay sponsors", saying the marketing department "facilitated these questionable payments to alternative accounts".

The money trail followed by the *Sunday Times* shows that Telkom paid R5.7 million and Vodacom R5 million into a First National Bank account in the name of Carol Bouwer Designs, while MTN paid R15 million into the bank account of a company called ABR Consulting. Pule's department appointed Carol Bouwer Designs, a company owned by former *Generations* star and businesswoman Carol Bouwer, who is close to President Jacob Zuma, to put the indaba together.

All three telecoms companies confirmed that they paid those amounts only after they were approached directly by Pule's ministry and asked to sponsor the event.

In February, Pule sent a letter to Bouwer, seen by the *Sunday Times*, in which the minister said her department "will make a financial contribution amounting to R10 million". She said she would "sign off a letter of endorsement, which Carol Bouwer Productions will use to approach other potential sponsors".

The event drew political heavyweights, including Zuma, his deputy, Kgalema Motlanthe, Pule, Trade and Industry Minister Rob Davies and foreign dignitaries.

Approached by the *Sunday Times*, Bouwer confirmed that Mngqibisa was a "second signatory" to her company bank account and that he had "access to the account until the conclusion of the [ICT Indaba]".

Bouwer admitted she hired Mngqibisa's company Khemano to handle the "event management" part of the indaba. "It was clear most of the payments would have to be effected by him, so I entrusted this responsibility to him to ensure suppliers can be paid timeously."

She would not reveal how much money Mngqibisa withdrew from her account or confirm whether he did pay the suppliers, saying only that "a full financial reconciliation is under way".

"Until I receive the audited statements from the project team, it would be premature of me to comment on payments being irregular or otherwise."

She said she had no idea of his relationship to the minister, but had she known, "such a relationship would simply disqualify him from working with me on this project".

Though Mngqibisa refused to reveal the exact nature of his relationship with the minister, a number of those close to the minister confirmed the link.

Though asked explicitly to clarify this "relationship", Mngqibisa sent a statement to the *Sunday Times* shortly before going to print, saying: "I prefer to keep my private personal life private, since I am not a public figure. I strongly deny all allegations of impropriety against me, and challenge anyone making such allegations to [provide] evidence."

He would not reveal whether the money he withdrew was spent appropriately to pay the suppliers, saying: "I have an obligation to maintain the privacy of my clients."

In a written reply, Pule's spokesman Siya Qoza did not address questions on the nature of her relationship with Mngqibisa. He said, "Questions regarding subcontractors and/or service providers engaged by [Bouwer] should be referred to the company."

He said an audit of the finances of the indaba "is expected in July".

He said the budget for the indaba was R102 million, which was largely raised "through sponsorships", and it was necessary for the department to partner with Bouwer "because the ICT Indaba is in the domain of the department".

He confirmed that the department paid R10.5 million for "securing the venue, conference speakers, the audio systems and interpreters".

MTN, Vodacom and Telkom confirmed that they were told by Pule's ministry to deal with Bouwer's company.

Pynee Chetty, a spokesman for Telkom, said, "[We] will engage with [Bouwer's company] to seek the necessary comfort on these matters to ensure that all promised rights were met, as well as proper governance followed."

MTN SA's chief human resources officer, Themba Nyathi, said his company put the money into the ABR Consulting account because the original account it was given, that of Carol Bouwer Designs, "did not comply with MTN's procurement requirements".

ABR Consulting president, Sheryl Manchisi said MTN's R15 million was used to pay suppliers. "Everything is accounted for and in black and white. We're being audited right now."

Vodacom spokesman Richard Boorman said his company had "performed a full due diligence on Carol Bouwer Productions, including an anti-corruption questionnaire".

Little did we know that we had touched a raw nerve. In the weeks and months to come we were subjected to all manner of dirty tricks and smear campaigns. Press conferences were organised to smear us, all at the expense of the taxpayer.

Several editors and some journalists were called to secret meetings where we were portrayed as corrupt journalists who had a vendetta against Pule. A six-page "intelligence report" was also produced and circulated to a number of newsrooms with allegations that a "rich Mpumalanga politician has paid R2 million in bribery cash for any work that they can do to defame Pule".

The report does not name the politician or the recipient(s) of the cash. The report added, "The amount was paid in cash on the 6 June 2012 in Cape Town."

It all started the day the first story was published. I received a phone call from soccer legend Ephraim Jomo Sono. He had been approached by Mngqibisa at a hotel in Sandton who had asked Sono, whom I have known for years – and this is public knowledge – if he could arrange a face-to-face meeting between Pule and myself.

"The minister wants to give you her side of the story," said Sono.

After a brief discussion with my colleagues it was agreed that I should go ahead and meet with Pule.

I met her at the Southern Sun Hotel in Sandton on 19 June 2012 and she asked that our meeting be off the record. I agreed. This is a common journalistic practice when exploring stories. But Pule broke the off-record agreement when she spoke about the meeting during a press conference months later.

Present at the meeting was Themba Phiri, Pule's deputy director-general at the time, and a former government official, Robert Nkuna. Nkuna is the former adviser to Pule's predecessor, Roy Padayachee.

During the meeting she accused President Jacob Zuma and fellow cabinet ministers of different misdemeanours and protested that she was a victim of an orchestrated smear campaign.

"Imagine," she said, "just three days after he [Zuma] appointed me as the minister of communications, his son Duduzani and the two Gupta brothers showed up at my house and demanded that I must give them a 24-hour news channel. They said Zuma sent them to me. When I phoned Zuma, out of anger, he denied that he said I must give them the news channel but claims that he asked them to talk to me about it."

Pule then turned her attention to deputy minister of public service and administration Ayanda Dlodlo.

"Ayanda knew about this story, she even asked someone to talk to me about it. I know she is one of your sources, because she is angry with me for refusing to facilitate a business deal between her business partners and Telkom," Pule explained.

She also accused former deputy minister of communications, Obed Bapela, of sour grapes and being a bad loser after she was appointed as minister instead of him.

"Obed had a party celebrating that he was going to be appointed as minister. He even bought a couple of brand-new suits and he was very disappointed when I was appointed. Obed is the man who wanted to loot the sponsorship funds for the ICT Indaba. He tried to interfere when I took over and I told him to go to hell." Obed was given the opportunity to respond to these allegations and stated that he could not give them any merit.

Pule promised that Phiri would deliver some explosive documents to support her allegations about the Guptas and their 24-hour news channel as well as how Bapela allegedly gave tenders to his cronies while he was deputy minister.

Yet when Phiri called for a meeting at another hotel in Midrand two weeks later, he did not bring any documents with him. But he did bring a bag full of money as my "present from the Minister".

I told Phiri that my salary comes from the *Sunday Times* and that I do not accept presents from politicians. "I would rather remain poor than accept bribes," I told him.

That same evening, Phiri deleted me from his BlackBerry contacts – I did not give a damn anyway but I told my colleagues about the attempted bribe.

In the meantime we had received confirmation from the three telecom companies that had sponsored the ICT Indaba that they wanted a forensic investigation to verify how their money was spent.

We sent Pule and Phosane a list of questions.

On Saturday night, a day before our story was to come out, I received a phone call from an unknown man who asked for an urgent meeting with me. He claimed Pule had sent him.

After another brief discussion with my colleagues, it was agreed that I would meet this man and hear what he had to say. We met at a parking lot of a restaurant in Woodmead with a friend of mine watching and observing everything from another car.

The man claimed he was an intelligence operative who had been seconded to help Pule. He explained that Pule was a victim of business people and politicians who had interests in the Telkom and Korean deal. A Korean company KT Corp had made an offer to buy 20 per cent of Telkom's equity as part of a deal to come in as a strategic equity partner and to provide management services.

Former communications minister Roy Padayachie and Telkom CEO Nombulelo "Pinky" Moholi, as well as the board, had supported the deal. However, the transaction was blocked at Cabinet level on Pule's recommendation when she took over as the new minister. Nobody knows the reason for her decision.

The man said Pule was willing to give us all the relevant documents implicating all the players who were involved in that deal if we promised to protect her as our source. I told the man that we always protect our sources and he promised to deliver the documents early in the week. The following day, on 8 July 2012, *Sunday Times* published a follow-up story:

Minister, "boyfriend" and actress face forensic
probe over "missing" ICT millions

By Rob Rose, Stephan Hofstatter and Mzilikazi wa Afrika

Communications Minister Dina Pule, a man said to be her boyfriend, and former *Generations* actress Carol Bouwer face a forensic probe into how R36 million in "sponsorship fees" for last month's ICT Indaba was spent.

This follows an exposé in the *Sunday Times* three weeks ago detailing how businessman Phosane Mngqibisa, who is said to be Pule's romantic partner, withdrew large sums of money soon after it was deposited into Bouwer's FNB bank account.

New details emerged this week of how Pule lobbied three companies regulated by her department – Vodacom, MTN and Telkom – to provide R25.7 million in "sponsorships" for the indaba organised by Carol Bouwer Productions. Pule's own department paid R10.5 million in sponsorship fees. In total, R36.2 million was raised.

Unbeknown to the telecoms companies, Mngqibisa was a second signatory to Bouwer's account – a potential conflict of interest, given his relationship to Pule. Now Telkom is considering launching its own forensic investigation into how its donation of R5.7 million was spent, and Vodacom is demanding answers from Bouwer.

Mngqibisa is close to a number of politicians, including Free State Premier Ace Magashule. He repeatedly refused to answer questions from the *Sunday Times*.

This week, he cited two deaths in his family for declining to respond.

Vodacom and Telkom confirmed this week they had demanded answers from Bouwer about what happened to the money for the event, which was attended by, among others, President Jacob Zuma and Deputy President Kgalema Mothlanthe.

Telkom spokesman Pynee Chetty said the company had "not received a satisfactory response as yet" from Bouwer.

"Carol Bouwer should deal with the inquiries regarding this matter transparently and expeditiously, failing which Telkom will have no choice but to appoint its own auditors," he said.

Vodacom corporate affairs chief Maya Makanjee said his company had also demanded "further information" from Bouwer "relating to the use of the sponsored amount", which was R5 million. Although MTN provided the largest amount, R15 million, it is taking no action.

MTN, which was accused this year of bribing politicians to get a cellular licence in Iran in 2005, said it was taking no action because it says it has no "competence" to trace the R15 million it gave.

Themba Nyathi, MTN SA human resources executive, said: "The allegations that came up [about] what transpired outside of MTN, is something beyond MTN's competence.

"That is something that the Department of Communications will investigate through the Auditor-General. We will wait for the outcome of the Auditor-General's report."

The companies provided the sponsorship money after Pule sent letters to them "inviting" them to "cooperate with the Department of Communications and Carol Bouwer Productions" to ensure the indaba was a success.

Though the ICT Indaba, which was held in Cape Town, is believed to have raised more than R50 million in sponsorships and delegates' fees, experts say the cost of hosting the event was likely to be less than half that.

Fears that the scandal would be covered up escalated this week.

Cosatu general secretary, Zwelinzima Vavi, raised the issue of Mngqibisa's withdrawals at the Union Federation's eleventh KwaZulu-Natal Conference this week. Vavi reportedly said it was "disappointing" that ANC and government leaders ducked the issue, hoping "our people forget about [allegations] in no time".

Cosatu has already called for a "thorough, independent investigation into the allegations", which it says highlights the danger of a government official having an arrangement with a private company run by a close friend or family member.

Although the matter is being probed by Auditor-General Terence Nombembe, his office has no authority to delve into private-sector bank accounts such as that of Carol Bouwer Designs cc – the account into which most of the money was paid.

It has emerged that Public protector Thuli Madonsela has turned down a request by the DA to probe the scandal because of "resource constraints" in her office.

"I have decided to suspend proceedings and allow the Auditor-General's process to run its course," Madonsela said in a letter to DA MP Marian Shinn.

Pule refused to answer nine detailed questions from the *Sunday Times*, including what her relationship was with Mngqibisa, saying only that "the Auditor-General is looking into the matter [and] the department is awaiting a report in this regard".

Pule's spokesman, Siya Qoza, said the auditor-general's investigation would be finalised in about two weeks. "At this point, all we can say is we have not received any feedback from the Auditor-General or Carol Bouwer [sic]."

Mngqibisa refused to clarify his relationship with Pule, reiterating his statement that "I prefer to keep my private personal life private".

Shinn said, "It is telling that Dina Pule has chosen not to clarify the nature of her relationship with [Mngqibisa]. The public deserves to know whether there was a conflict of interest in him having rights to the sponsorship money."

Shinn said the worry is that the auditor-general probe could be a smoke screen, as Nombembe "can't follow the money in private entities' accounts. He can just check whether the proper processes were followed with the department's R10 million, but not what happened to the cellphone companies' money," she said.

After the *Sunday Times* exposed how Mngqibisa withdrew cash from that account, Bouwer wrote a letter to all three companies and Pule's department, claiming she had no idea about Pule's relationship to Mngqibisa.

Bouwer's letter confirms that she gave Mngqibisa "the responsibility to be the secondary user on the ICT Indaba account due to our shared responsibility on the project". She added, "I certainly did not have any knowledge and in fact, still do not have knowledge of wrongdoing or misappropriation of funds on the part of Mngqibisa."

When asked again how much money he withdrew and why, Mngqibisa refused to answer questions, saying, "Please seek information about the accounts of Carol Bouwer Productions from [her]".

Bouwer told the *Sunday Times* that she had nothing more to say on the subject.

A number of questions remain unanswered, including why MTN paid its R15 million sponsorship fee into the account of a company called

ABR Consulting – a Woodmead-based company with virtually no track record – rather than that of Bouwer's.

MTN's Nyathi said this was because the Bouwer account "did not have a tax clearance certificate", so they paid this money into an "alternative account".

MTN's explanation is contradicted by Vodacom. Maya Makanjee, Vodacom corporate affairs chief, said, "A full due diligence was performed. We also obtained a tax clearance certificate in relation to the entity, being Carol Bouwer Designs cc."

The "intelligence operative" that promised to deliver the documents exposing people involved in the Telkom and Korean deal never called for months. But he had made one mistake: he had called me from his personal number and we used it to find his real identity.

His name is Hlukanisa Richard Zitha, and he was not employed by the NIA. In fact Zitha, one of Pule's confidants, used to own an Internet café in Hazyview. Zitha and Pule come from the same village in Mpumalanga and they are very close.

Pule was the chairperson of the committee and the selection panel that appointed Zitha as one of the 15 members of the Digital Dzonga Advisory Council back when she was deputy minister of communications in 2010. Another member of this advisory council, also nominated as the deputy chairperson, was none other than Ruddy Rashama, Mngqibisa's business partner.

The Digital Dzonga Advisory Council's job was to "advise the minister and oversee the complex process of migrating South Africa's analogue broadcasting services to a new digital technology known as digital terrestrial television".

As we continued with our investigation into the Pule affair it emerged that Mngqibisa had used money from ICT Indaba sponsors to buy Pule luxury designer shoes. I phoned the shop in question several times. They confirmed the purchase, but refused to give me the copy of the invoice because I was not the buyer. The story made another front page on 2 September 2012.

DINA'S RED-SHOE BLUES

By Mzilikazi wa Afrika, Rob Rose and Stephan Hofstatter

Minister Dina Pule's eagerness to show off a pair of expensive Christian Louboutin shoes, with their distinctive red soles, has confirmed her link to the ICT Indaba's missing millions.

When Pule, the minister of communications, walked onto the stage to open the ICT Indaba in Cape Town in June, she was wearing a pair of the French designer shoes – now understood to have been bought with some of the R25.7 million that sponsors pumped into the event.

The shoes were bought in Barcelona, Spain, by her romantic partner, Phosane Mngqibisa, during one of their international trips together. Mngqibisa's company, Khemano, had been hired by event organiser Carol Bouwer Productions to help stage the ICT Indaba.

The *Sunday Times* reported in June that MTN, Vodacom and Telkom – who were lobbied by Pule to pay the R25.7 million towards the event – were furious that millions in sponsorship fees were drawn from the account of the event organiser by Mngqibisa.

The sponsors are now demanding to know how their money was used, and MTN has hired the Werksmans legal firm to probe whether the R15 million it paid was looted.

The *Sunday Times* can show where some of that missing money went. Bank statements confirm that Mngqibisa took R100 000 from the bank account of Carol Bouwer Productions before flying to Barcelona, Spain, to attend the GSMA Mobile World congress from 25 to 29 February. While there, he lobbied people to attend the ICT Indaba to be held in Cape Town from 4 to 7 June.

This week Mngqibisa said that he used the "marketing allocation budget" to attend the Barcelona conference so that he could "market the inaugural ICT Indaba".

But he denied travelling to Barcelona with Pule, adding that, "I do not recall even seeing her at the GSMA conference". However, three sources independently confirmed that, in fact, Mngqibisa accompanied Pule as her official travel companion on the Barcelona trip.

Mngqibisa, who has repeatedly refused to clarify the nature of his relationship with Pule, denied buying her the Christian Louboutin shoes.

"I purchased men's shoes for myself. I have the receipt to prove this," he said. He did not reply to the *Sunday Times* when asked for a copy of this receipt.

Mngqibisa's explanation is contradicted by Carol Bouwer's spokesman, Victor Dlamini, who confirmed on Friday that the shoes were bought with sponsorship money. Several other sources confirmed this.

They said Mngqibisa had given Bouwer several invoices, one of them showing that he bought Pule the Christian Louboutin shoes from a designer shop at Placa de Catalunya in the Barcelona city centre.

Bouwer, a former TV actress contracted by Pule's department of communications to manage the ICT Indaba, told the *Sunday Times* this week that she had demanded answers from Mngqibisa about the R100 000 spent in Barcelona.

Said Dlamini: "We are not sure about why the shoes were bought."

Pule refused to answer questions from the *Sunday Times* this week about the shoes. "I have nothing to say. Thank you," she said before hanging up.

A *Sunday Times* investigation has established that Bouwer was strong-armed by Pule's department into hiring Mngqibisa's company, Khemano, as a subcontractor for the Indaba.

This took place at a meeting at Montecasino's Palazzo Hotel in Sandton in November, shortly after Pule was appointed minister. Bouwer signed the deal with Mngqibisa in January.

Bouwer told the *Sunday Times* that she would not have hired Khemano had she known of Mngqibisa's relationship with Pule.

Pule also leaned on the three companies over which she has oversight – MTN, Telkom and Vodacom – to "sponsor" the ICT Indaba to the tune of R25.7 million. Pule's own department chipped in another R10 million.

Alarmingly, Bouwer was told to give Mngqibisa access to her bank account, where Telkom and Vodacom's sponsorship money was deposited – cash he withdrew within days.

This week, Mngqibisa admitted withdrawing the cash from Bouwer's account but said: "I transferred money to pay suppliers."

Detailed financials have not been provided to prove this, and the sponsors are demanding explanations from Bouwer about how their money was spent.

MTN's R15 million was mysteriously transferred to the account of a company called ABR Consulting, rather than that of Carol Bouwer.

"It seems we were conned," said one MTN executive.

MTN was told that Carol Bouwer's account was not tax-compliant, which is why the money had to go to ABR Consulting. This was not true. Werksmans has struggled to find out how this R15 million was spent.

MTN chief human resources executive Themba Nyathi said his company was "disappointed and angry" about claims that shareholders money was looted.

"Criminal and civil charges will be laid against anyone found to have misused or abused MTN funds meant for the ICT Indaba," he said.

Vodacom executive head of division for ethics and compliance Avinash Dhanasir stated in an email that Bouwer's company must explain how much was paid to Khemano. Specifically, Vodacom wanted "answers" about who received R4.3 million billed to the organisers simply for "events management", and another R6.1 million for "event planning and delegate sourcing".

Mngqibisa said the accounts "do not take into account the payments made to suppliers after 30 June". He said the management fees were "paid out by Khemano for costs for the event, and none of it ended up with Khemano".

Telkom seems less concerned about what happened to the R10 million it contributed to the ICT Indaba. Despite earlier vowing to launch a forensic probe, Telkom refused to answer questions from the *Sunday Times* this week about what it had found.

Our investigation also discovered that Pule and Mngqibisa had made more than 20 trips around the world together and that some of Mngqibisa's bills were paid for by the department.

Early in December 2012, Pule's "intelligence operative" phoned again and requested another meeting. I met Zitha at the News Café in Woodmead on the morning of 15 December, just hours before I was to leave for Bloemfontein to attend the ANC Elective Mangaung Conference. The purpose of the meeting was to offer me another bribe.

"The minister is under fire. You guys are hammering her almost every Sunday. We have a budget. Tell us how much you need to make the story go away," said Zitha. "We have been paying other journalists. You can see, nobody is writing anything negative about the minister except the *Sunday Times*. Dina needs this job and a position in the NEC [national executive committee] in Mangaung."

I told Zitha that if the minister was offering me a bribe – she must do it in person instead of sending one of her foot soldiers. I also told him about my encounter with Themba Phiri who had offered me a bag full of money, claiming it was from Pule.

"I know about that incident but this time we are not offering you small change but big bucks," he replied.

I told Zitha he must tell Pule that my integrity and ethics were not for sale.

Weeks prior to my meeting with Zitha a man had arrived at the office while I was out on an assignment and "demanded" to see me. When he was told that I was on an assignment, he requested to speak to one of my colleagues. Our political editor Sithembiso Msomi met the man at reception, and was told there was an order that I must be killed before the ANC's Mangaung Conference. The man told Msomi that he would wait for me at the Hyatt Hotel and that I must come and see him.

When I returned to the office, Msomi told me about the man and walked with me to Hyatt Hotel where we found the stranger sitting with two other people, a man and a woman. He claimed that he was from NIA, sent to drum some sense into my head.

"We are aware that you are working on a big investigation, trying to expose President Jacob Zuma and African Union Commission chairperson Nkosazana Dlamini-Zuma before the Mangaung Conference. We have been following you around, we know the places you have been to, some of the people you have been speaking to, and some of the documents you've collected. I am here to ask you to make your choice: drop your investigation or you will die. I was asked to talk to you, take this as a friendly chat or advice but the other people just want you dead. You are the biggest problem in this country and a threat to our leaders," said the man, who refused to identify himself.

I told the man that I was not from the generation of cowards and that nobody is going to stop any of my investigations.

Trying to intimidate me, the man then mentioned some of the places I had been too – giving all the specifics – and even what I was wearing.

"We have recorded everything and we know your every move," he said.

I told them to go back to his team or principals and tell them that I was not backing down.

Then, in my presence, the man phoned one of my sources for crucial information regarding my investigation, put him on the speakerphone, and threatened him.

When I returned to the office, Msomi had already briefed my boss Ray Hartley about the threats.

The source who had been threatened now refused to talk or make any further statements.

At the Mangaung Conference, Zuma retained his position as ANC president with majority votes but Pule did not make it to the NEC.

Mangaung was a wake-up call for Pule. The writing was on the wall: her days as minister were numbered and she immediately launched a smear campaign to save her job. I was the main target.

Pule and Mngqibisa had acquired the services of a private investigator-cum-forensic auditor Bart Henderson who was being paid to dig up any dirt on me and my colleagues and use it to slander us, me in particular.

Henderson claims on his website that he has a "military background as a combat decorated paratrooper". He presents himself as a fraud specialist and forensic expert.

On 15 January 2013, just days after I returned from a holiday abroad with my family, there was an outrageous article by Henderson in which he wrote, "I have just been told that Mzilikazi wa Afrika has pictures of minister of communications Dina Pule on 'holiday' with her alleged 'lover' Phosane Mngqibisa. I have been told that he has threatened to publish these photos if we don't back off. Wa Afrika, do me a favour, write! Print your photos! Sleg moer.

"Don't you threaten me, you contemptuous little prick and don't you threaten my family, my friends or my clients. You want to threaten members of the public with war? You want to use the *Sunday Times* to wage your personal little vendettas? Go to your editor and show him or her your pictures!"

At first I was baffled by Henderson's claims as neither my colleagues nor I had ever claimed to have photos of Pule and Mngqibisa on holiday. But then I realised it was part of Henderson's smear campaign.

Henderson became an information peddler with his blog, Facebook and Twitter containing inaccurate information about my colleagues and me. I remain the main target of these statements. He was also writing newsletters and emailing them to anyone whose email he could get hold of, stating that we must, "Give back those awards! Better journalists deserved them!" And he threatened, "I'm going to be sending one of these out every day for the rest of your natural life, until every journalist worth their salt are [sic] calling for you to be fired or resign."

Henderson also added, "I been [sic] feeding earthworms on hooks since I was nine. You're not getting off my hook."

Henderson went on like this for months. After careful discussions and observations we decided to ignore him.

The Parliament of South Africa established a joint committee on ethics and members' interest to probe Pule's conduct on the 20 February 2013. ANC veteran Professor Ben Turok, who was deputised by another ANC member, Lemias Mashile, chaired the multi-party panel. Other members included

Andrew Mlangeni (ANC), Bhekizizwe Radebe (ANC), Modjadji Mangena (ANC), Dianne Kohler Barnard (DA), Jacobus van der Merwe (IFP), Thabo Makunyane (ANC), Zukiswa Rantho (ANC) and Swaphi Plaatjie (Cope). The hearing was scheduled to run from 22 to 26 April but eventually only started on 2 May 2013.

Pule started issuing press statements alleging that she was "aware for a while now that the *Sunday Times* has been running a politically motivated media campaign" against her.

"Your strategy has been to throw mud at her in the hope that something will stick. Up to this point, you have not proven any of the allegations you have levelled against her. You have also consistently sought to assign responsibility to her for other people's actions," read her public statement.

Then I received a phone call from someone on 24 March 2013 at 12:58 p.m. using Pule's official number and threatening me.

She said, "I am going to destroy you and when I am done, you won't be able even to look yourself in the mirror. You have exposed those other people but now you have reached the last number, I am going to deal with you."

The person even called me "Mr President Mzilikazi" when she said, "You are the person who decides who must be fired or hired in this country. We are tired of your shit. We had enough now."

Almost a month later, on 22 April 2013, Pule called a press conference at the Hyatt Hotel in Rosebank, a stone's throw away from our office. This was less than ten days before she was expected to appear before the ethics committee. She used it to accuse us of all the misdemeanours you can imagine including allegations that *Sunday Times* was trying to blackmail her on behalf of our "handlers".

Pule told the reporters, "The campaign was a highly sophisticated plot to blackmail me. The *Sunday Times* thought it could coerce me into a corner."

Among her wild allegations, Pule accused me of owning a cellphone company importing cheap phones from China; that I was part of a meeting between her and a soccer boss who had interest in a R2.4 billion set-top box tender in her department; that Stephan Hofstatter tried to plant a spy in her office; and that Rob Rose had friends in the telecom industry with interests in her department. She said we were running a "smear campaign" against her.

Pule vehemently denied that she was having a romantic relationship with Mngqibisa but described him as her "comrade".

Shortly after this press conference, I was called by Stephen Grootes of

Talk Radio 702 to answer Pule's accusations and I told him that Pule "was trying to circumcise a mosquito".

"She is trying to do the impossible. We are innocent of all the allegations she has levelled against us. The minister must answer questions directed to her instead of pointing fingers at other people," I told Grootes.

Our editor, Phylicia Oppelt, immediately called on Pule to produce evidence to support her allegations or apologise.

Just before 8:00 a.m. the following morning, I received a phone call from Johannesburg-based lawyer Ronnie Bokwa who said Pule and Themba Phiri, her deputy director-general, had asked him to arrange a meeting between us. She was begging for an "armistice".

At the meeting in Midrand four days later, attended by my colleagues and myself, Bokwa said Pule admitted she had "wronged the *Sunday Times*".

We told Bokwa that Pule could be forgiven if she publicly retracted all false allegations she had made during her infamous press conference, and finally came clean about what really happened at our off-the-record meeting on 19 June 2012. We asked that she admit spreading false rumours about the *Sunday Times* investigations team, especially me, to politicians and journalists, including a senior member of SANEF.

Bokwa promised that he could arrange for Pule to come in person. Her department then booked a conference room at a hotel in Sandton, but she failed to show up. Her right-hand man, Phiri, came to report that Pule could not make it as she was busy with the lawyer preparing for her appearance before the ethics committee in Parliament.

We wrote a column about her press conference on 28 April 2013:

DINA GOES TO HOLLYWOOD
**Minister has come up with an outlandish movie
script to counter allegations of wrongdoing**
By Stephan Hofstatter, Rob Rose and Mzilikazi wa Afrika

This week, journalists in Johannesburg were treated to what even the most jaded hacks must have rated a rare spectacle. The *Sunday Times* had exposed last week that Communications Minister Dina Pule was caught in yet another scandal involving her boyfriend, Phosane Mngqibisa, in one of a series of articles run by this newspaper since June last year.

This time, the report concerned a paper trail that showed how she had bullied her department into hiring a particular head-hunting firm without a proper tender process – a firm that promptly appointed Mngqibisa's cronies to several state-owned entities under her watch.

Taking a leaf out of the book of disgraced police chief Bheki Cele after he was exposed in a shady lease deal, Pule called a press conference and went on the offensive against the *Sunday Times*.

Instead of refuting the report that she had used her influence to ensure that Mngqibisa and his cronies were awarded jobs and contracts, she devoted 90 minutes to a desperate attempt at character assassination against the journalists who wrote the article.

The story she told was an equal mix of conspiracy theory and fiction.

There was an unrequited love interest (a relative of journalist Mzilikazi wa Afrika who was, the minister's story went, spurned by Pule), intercepted or "overheard" conversations of plots to plant spies in Pule's office, and secret meetings set up by powerful mandarins representing shadowy business interests intent on toppling the president.

These shady businessmen apparently threatened Pule that, unless she gave them a multi-billion-rand set-top box deal – and the president's head on a plate – they would unleash their bulldog, Wa Afrika. As Pule was, naturally, purer than the driven snow, Wa Afrika would supposedly have to invent imaginary wrongdoing.

To ensure his loyalty, Wa Afrika would be given his own deal to import vast quantities of cheap cellphones from China.

To help him, Wa Afrika roped in two trusty chihuahuas – fellow journalists Rob Rose and Stephan Hofstatter.

Rose, so Pule's story went, flits around after dark with captains of the telecoms industry who have him in their pocket.

Hofstatter is a spy master with the ability to plant eavesdroppers in a Cabinet minister's office.

It made a great fictional yarn, but bears no relationship to reality.

Let us get some facts straight: Wa Afrika has no Chinese cellphone company. Contrary to Pule's version, a meeting between her and Wa Afrika was set up by Mngqibisa – not by Wa Afrika. Moreover, he never tried to blackmail Pule into providing him with incriminating information on Zuma and a "colleague".

In fact, at the meeting, Pule, of her own volition, offered Wa Afrika damning information about the president and two of her colleagues, but without any supporting evidence. So no story ever came of it.

Pule's lies do not stop there.

The "spy" that Hofstatter supposedly deployed to ask for a job in Pule's office was actually asked by her to do "reputation management" work – not the other way around.

Rose has no "close friends" at the telecoms companies who sponsored the ICT Indaba in Cape Town – only contacts whom he speaks to regularly for comment on articles he is working on.

Most commentators could see the press conference for what it was: when you have been caught out, go on the offensive.

As former journalist Ranjeni Munusamy tweeted: "The scariest thing about Dina Pule is that she actually believes what she said. She has an altered sense of reality."

City Press editor Ferial Haffajee wrote: "As a citizen, I wish our minister would spend 1.5 hours explaining why my broadband is expensive and slow [and] why we haven't gone digital."

Hajra Omarjee of e.tv asked why, if the story was true, Pule "felt no need to report the *Sunday Times*' handlers who are blackmailing her to the police".

Writing in the *Daily Maverick*, Sipho Hlongwane said that "if the point of the exercise was to raise suspicions even more, then she accomplished that with aplomb".

Journalist Kay Sexwale, lamenting the fact that Pule had "called a presser to rant about *Sunday Times* and peddle a conspiracy theory", said that "whoever advises her on PR should be whipped".

When asked for evidence for the plot she was peddling, Pule's argument was that if the *Sunday Times* could accuse her of things without proof, what proof did she need to accuse them?

But this newspaper does have evidence.

Besides the paper trail surrounding the jobs for Mngqibisa's pals at companies such as Sentech and the SABC, the initial articles reported that she had bullied telecoms companies to sponsor the ICT Indaba – and that Mngqibisa had drawing rights to this sponsorship cash.

We have letters signed by Pule that were sent to the companies asking for cash, we have statements from conference organiser Carol Bouwer confirming that Mngqibisa had drawing rights to the money, and we have a forensic report from Werksmans Attorneys confirming that Mngqibisa was paid R6 million for working on the indaba.

When asked about their relationship this week, Pule said that Mngqibisa was "a comrade". She avoided elaborating on whether she has ever had a romantic relationship with him – a claim made by many, many sources.

This newspaper has repeatedly asked her to clarify this point and she has refused time and again. Mngqibisa has also refused to discuss their relationship – even telling Werksmans he would not answer that question.

When he complained about the *Sunday Times* to the press ombudsman – a case he lost – Mngqibisa again refused to reveal the nature of their relationship.

In ruling against Mngqibisa, the ombudsman said: "In light of their silence about the nature of their relationship, the newspaper cannot be blamed for thinking that the facts pointed to a personal one."

So the question is: Why did Pule take such a remarkable step and decide to attack the newspaper?

There are a number of theories: One is that an ethics committee hearing – since postponed – was scheduled for next week and perhaps this was an attempt to sway public sympathy.

Another theory is that perhaps it was an effort to convince Jacob Zuma not to fire her. If so, her cunning reference to how Wa Afrika was seeking information on the president seemed well placed.

Long after the press conference had ended, the disconcerting fact remains that the communications ministry is being run by somebody who clearly seems to treat off-the-wall conspiracies as fact.

Irrespective of the scandal surrounding Mngqibisa, the bottom line is that Pule is in charge of some of the most important sectors in South Africa, which are now teetering as she spends hours organising press conferences about her personal affairs.

It was Pule's failure to finalise the digital migration policy that has delayed spectrum allocation, which would translate into cheaper, faster wireless Internet. It is her pig-headed desire to fight e.tv in court over a decision already taken on digital TV that should be the headlines, as should her ham-fisted meddling at the SABC and Telkom.

We expect our Cabinet ministers to run their portfolios effectively – not make spectacles of themselves at taxpayers' expense.

Meanwhile one Sunday newspaper, *City Press*, seemed to have taken Pule's hogwash of allegations seriously and ran a front-page story on Sunday, 28 April 2013, naming Sono as "the mystery businessman at the centre of a so-called 'blackmail campaign' against Communications Minister".

City Press received so much praise for this article from one Bart Henderson, who tweeted and raved about the story, which he called a "scoop" hours before the newspaper hit the streets and for days afterwards.

We knew that the story was coming after Pule's spokesperson Siyabulela Qoza, a former *City Press* journalist, told one of my colleagues that they have "managed to plant the story in the *City Press*".

It was not the story that became the talking point among other colleagues in the industry, but a full-page advertisement on page 31 of the same edition that Pule placed with *City Press* – a full-colour advertisement with Pule's photo – singing her praises.

"Did Dina pay *City Press* for their story with a full page advertisement?" This was one of the questions many people asked me since it happened that *City Press* was the only newspaper carrying that advertisement on that specific Sunday.

These shenanigans neither stopped nor discouraged us from continuing with our investigation into Pule. Hours after Pule's press conference, we started getting calls from angry staff members in her department who were shocked and dismayed about her conduct and her abuse of taxpayers' money in calling a press conference to deny the truth and smear us. One of the callers gave us documents that proved that Pule had registered Mngqibisa as her "companion" with the department.

The documents also proved how much the department spent on Mngqibisa while he was flying around with the former minister. We published the story on 12 May 2013.

ROMANCE, LIES AND A CREDIT CARD TRAIL
By Mzilikazi wa Afrika, Rob Rose and Stephan Hofstatter

Three new questions to Communications Minister Dina Pule will blow the lid off her claim that the *Sunday Times* is running a vendetta of lies against her:

- Minister Pule, did you spend R700 000 of taxpayers' money on an overseas trip with your boyfriend, Phosane Mngqibisa?
- Minister Pule, did you live it up in the lavish Ritz-Carlton in New York, with two nights costing a staggering R35 000 – and another R10 000 blown on luxury cars?
- Minister Pule, did you state in travel documents that Mngqibisa

was your official "companion" – a term most often used to describe a romantic partner – and that his stay was at your expense in your official capacity?

The minister may try to wriggle out of answering these questions, as she has done with a string of other claims of financial abuse against her, but the *Sunday Times* knows that the answer to all three questions is YES.

The *Sunday Times* has seen the document in which she listed Mngqibisa as an official "companion" – a term used by the ministerial handbook to refer to family, spouses or long-term romantic partners who may have expenses covered by the state on foreign trips.

Pule was deputy minister of communications when she took Mngqibisa, her former personal assistant, Rebotile Zondo and a senior official, Themba Phiri, on a round trip to Monterrey in Mexico, returning to Johannesburg via New York.

Phiri, the deputy director-general of communications, has been widely regarded as Pule's right-hand man since the minister's falling-out with her director-general, Rosy Seseke.

The official reason for the Mexico trip was to attend the World Summit award-winners' gala in Monterrey from 2 to 5 September 2009.

But Pule blew an extra R270 000 by checking out of her hotel a day early, on 4 September, to fly her entourage to New York.

The unscheduled diversion to New York is unlikely to have been pre-approved in writing by the president, as is required by ministerial handbook rules that stipulate that overseas trips require approval two weeks before departure.

In New York, Pule spent R35 000 for two nights in one of the best rooms in the Central Park Ritz-Carlton and almost R10 000 to be ferried around the Big Apple in a luxury vehicle hired from Ben's Luxury Car and Limousine Service.

Pule's trip with Mngqibisa is detailed in official travel application forms, hotel and limousine service invoices, flight tickets, itineraries and credit card records.

Sources in the department of communications confirmed that soon after Pule was appointed as the deputy minister of communications, in May 2009, she had Mngqibisa – a married man and father of three – registered as her travel companion.

The ministerial handbook describes a companion as "a person who is cohabiting with the member and is publicly acknowledged by the member as a permanent companion, provided the member has informed his/her department in writing of such a companion".

The *Sunday Times* previously exposed that Mngqibisa had been on more than 20 international trips with Pule.

The new documents cast doubt on Mngqibisa's claims that he paid for all his expenses on these trips.

- The documents show that: Pule and Mngqibisa left South Africa together on 31 August 2009 on Delta Airlines flight DL 201 to Atlanta in the US. For this flight, the department coughed up R91 854 for her boyfriend's business-class ticket;

- Pule's group arrived in Atlanta the following day, spending about R4 700 on refreshments and rooms at the Marriott airport hotel;

- They arrived in Monterrey later the same day. Only three rooms were booked at the Holiday Inn Parque Fundidora, where the four spent three nights at a total cost of almost R20 000;

- The department had to pay an extra R67 497 per person to fly the group to New York on 4 September – a diversion that does not appear on Pule's official itinerary; and

- Pule and Mngqibisa landed back in South Africa on South African Airways flight SA 204 on 7 September 2009.

Mngqibisa refused to answer questions, saying it would be "extremely irregular for me to participate in what appears to be a parallel inquiry outside the parliamentary processes".

He issued a veiled threat to Parliament's Ethics Committee, which is investigating Pule's conduct: "I have taken note of the conduct of those members of Parliament who have colluded in undermining the current parliamentary process by leaking details of last week's parliamentary process despite the fact that parliamentary proceedings remain confidential until the committee has tabled its findings."

Pule declined to respond to detailed questions. Her spokesman, Siyabulela Qoza, reiterated that Pule would "no longer take any further questions on these matters to allow space for the Public Protector and

Parliament's Ethics Committee to conduct their investigations against her without any hindrance".

Qoza accused the *Sunday Times* of being "hell-bent on influencing these processes. There is nothing new in these latest allegations".

"None of these allegations will stick despite the relentless smear campaign by the *Sunday Times*," he said.

Officials in the department said Mngqibisa's name was removed from their database as an official companion when Pule was redeployed as deputy minister in the presidency in 2010. One official claimed that presidency staff told Pule she could not register a married man as her companion.

In October 2011, Pule was appointed communications minister. A few weeks after her appointment, former TV actress and businesswoman Carol Bouwer, who had been negotiating a deal with the communications ministry to organise the inaugural ICT Indaba in Cape Town, was told to subcontract Mngqibisa's company, Khemano, for the indaba.

Bouwer said Mngqibisa was imposed on her by Phiri during a secret meeting at the Palazzo Hotel in Montecasino, Johannesburg, in November 2011. Phiri was acting deputy director-general at the time.

Parliament's Ethics Committee decided to investigate Pule's conduct after the *Sunday Times* exposed that she had leaned on telecoms companies to sponsor the Indaba – from which funds Mngqibisa scored a R6 million "management fee" for six days' work.

With Mngqibisa on board, Pule got Telkom, Vodacom and MTN to donate R25.7 million for the indaba. Her department then chipped in an extra R10 million.

Telkom and Vodacom's money was paid into Bouwer's account and a R15 million donation from MTN was mysteriously diverted to ABR Consulting, a company that was subcontracted by Mngqibisa.

Bouwer was also persuaded to give Mngqibisa signing rights to her bank account to "pay suppliers".

Mngqibisa later paid himself a R6 million "management fee" and has refused to tell either the Ethics Committee or sponsor MTN how it was calculated.

It is understood that at hearings of the committee, which are not public, Pule and Mngqibisa both denied that they were romantic partners, claiming they were merely "comrades".

The hearings are expected to resume this week.

Yet more documents confirming the romantic relationship between Pule and Phosane started pouring into our office and on 2 June 2013 we published a story that proved that Pule lied:

IT'S OFFICIAL: MINISTER LIED ABOUT LOVER
By Mzilikazi wa Afrika and Stephan Hofstatter

Businessman Phosane Mngqibisa is Dina Pule's "spouse" – and that is official.

Despite the communications minister's furious public denials of any romantic involvement with Mngqibisa, official documents show she named him as her "spouse".

The new documents obtained by the *Sunday Times* this week state: "Deputy Minister Pule has nominated her spouse Mr Phosane Mngqibisa to accompany her on an official visit to Mexico [on] 2 to 4 September 2009."

Mngqibisa, a father of three, was married at the time.

Pule and Mngqibisa, who were accompanied by her former personal assistant, Rebotile Zondo, and her deputy director-general, Themba Phiri, blew R700 000 on the trip, which included an apparently unauthorised detour to New York.

The new documents were prepared by Zondo, recommended by former chief of staff Renah Lusiba and approved by former acting chief operations officer Basani Baloyi and former communications minister Siphiwe Nyanda. Pule was Nyanda's deputy at the time.

"It is recommended that the following officials accompany the Deputy Minister and her companion, Mr Phosane Mngqibisa, to attend the World Summit Award 2009 winners' event from 2 to 4 September 2009 in Monterrey, Mexico," the new documents go on to state.

Phiri and Zondo are mentioned as the officials. The trip was also authorised by Chief Director Moseamo Sebola, deputy director-general Keith Shongwe and acting director-general Gerda Grabe.

A memo refers to the relevant section of the ministerial handbook, which regulates benefits to which ministers are entitled. The handbook defines "spouse" as a "person legally married to the member [or] a permanent companion/life partner". "Permanent companion" is defined as "a person who is cohabiting with the member and is publicly acknowledged by the member as a permanent companion".

Nyanda has confirmed that he approved Pule's trips with "her spouse".

He told the *Sunday Times* this week: "I approved the trip as communications minister at the time, but I wasn't aware who the spouse was. I didn't have to ask her – it's a private matter."

Nyanda added that he had approved another trip for Pule with "her spouse", to attend an M-Net Face of Africa function in Nigeria.

A *Sunday Times* investigation has confirmed that Pule and Mngqibisa left together for Lagos on flight SA60 from OR Tambo International Airport on 4 February 2010 and returned together four days later on flight SA061.

The records show that they took 20 trips together since 2009. Their last trip together, according to documents in this newspaper's possession, was on 7 June 2012, the day the ICT Indaba ended, when they flew together from Cape Town to London on flight SA220 and returned five days later via Frankfurt on flight SA262.

Pule and Mngqibisa have repeatedly refused to clarify their relationship to the *Sunday Times* for almost a year. Instead, Pule called a press conference to accuse this newspaper of running a smear campaign against her.

In March, when *Talk Radio 702* host Eusebius McKaiser asked Pule whether Mngqibisa was her boyfriend, she replied: "No. I did say so even before." When McKaiser pressed her to clarify their relationship, she said: "I know him as a comrade, but I have nothing to do with him."

She made similar denials on Justice Malala's show on e.tv.

Last month, the *Sunday Times* exposed how Pule took Mngqibisa to Mexico in 2009, stopping off in New York for an alleged shopping spree. They stayed at the lavish Ritz-Carlton Central Park and were ferried around in luxury cars. A paper trail of receipts, invoices and travel vouchers revealed that Pule spent R35 000 on two nights at the Ritz-Carlton and R10 000 on luxury-car hire.

Pule's spokesman, Wisani Ngobeni, called a press conference to announce the department could not locate official documents for this trip, even though copies were published by this newspaper.

Pule is facing an ongoing probe by Parliament's Ethics Committee after the *Sunday Times* exposed that she leaned on telecoms companies to sponsor the ICT Indaba last year – from whose funds Mngqibisa paid himself R6 million as a "management fee".

The event organiser, Carol Bouwer, claimed she was forced to subcontract Mngqibisa by Pule's right-hand man, Phiri, during a secret meeting just days after Pule was appointed communications minister.

Mngqibisa had not responded to text messages and emails by the time of going to press.

All the highly publicised complaints that Pule launched with the press ombudsman were dismissed in their entirety on 22 June 2013. Press ombudsman Johan Retief found there were no violations of the press code and no evidence of unethical conduct by the *Sunday Times* or by our editor, Phylicia Oppelt.

In his ruling, Retief stated, "I also believe that the publication indeed acted in the public interest and I find its responses to my questions to be credible. Therefore, I simply cannot conclude that the newspaper behaved unethically."

President Zuma fired Pule during a Cabinet reshuffle on 9 July 2013.

I went on leave a week after the Cabinet reshuffle. After the break, I was scheduled to fly to Tanzania and Kenya as chair of the Forum for African Investigative Reporters (FAIR). I was driving from Bushbuckridge back to Johannesburg on 18 July 2013 when I received a text message asking for my private email address. After forwarding it, I received another text saying I must check my email. This is what the email said, "I have information that can prove that Phosane Mngqibisa (and by extension Dina Pule) had called a hit on Prof. Ben Turok so that he couldn't attend the final sit down of the Ethics Committee and therefore give the accused more time to come up with a solution for their issues with the Ethics Committee and Public Protector. I can also prove that Phosane Mngqibisa tried to create falsified documents to counter all claims sitting before the committee and the PP [public protector].

"The hit to kill Ben Turok was issued to me as a specialist consultant: I was to recruit a hitman for the job. All plans were disturbed by the Cabinet reshuffle that was made by the president last Tuesday.

I have SMSes, emails and recordings to prove my claims. Should this be published, Phosane Mngqibisa and Dina Pule will know it was leaked by me; therefore I want some compensation if I'll be risking my own safety and for the amazing ad revenue that *Sunday Times* will make from a story like this. Let me know if you'd be interested; then we can meet and get into details and I'll show you all the evidence. I'll provide my real details as we proceed. Thank you."

Since the initial email had been sent to a former *Sunday Times* editor, Mondli Makhanya, from a ghost email address, I wrote back to the author giving him my contact details and email address. He responded a day later. On Sunday, 21 July 2013, I received a phone call from a private number: it was from the same man and I persuaded him to meet me.

I cancelled my flight to Tanzania and on 23 July 2013 flew to East London. I landed there at 6:00 p.m. and drove to Butterworth, arriving late at night. I met the 21-year-old man at his house and he repeated the same allegations in his email but in more detail. I informed him that *Sunday Times* has a strict policy: we don't pay for any information and he accepted that.

Arriving back at the office the following day, I briefed my boss and colleagues about the man and his allegations. We discussed the way forward and started outlining the story. Since I was officially on leave, we agreed that we would work on the story as soon as I was back from Tanzania.

I was back at work on Monday, 5 August 2013, and revisited the Pule murder plot. The source was being elusive. The Ethics Committee released its findings against Pule two days later and the matter was highlighted in the 39-page report.

Page 27 of the report stated that, "The Panel was informed that Parliament's Head of Security Services and Management had received information of a threat to harm the Chairperson of the Panel and Registrar and to disrupt the proceedings of the Panel. These threats were reported to the authorities and appropriate measures were taken to safeguard the work of the Panel and its personnel."

The committee found Pule guilty. It claimed she had lied under oath and that she "wilfully provided the Registrar with incorrect and misleading details. The Panel finds that the evidence presented on the material aspects of the case by Hon. Pule, Mr [Phosane] Mngqibisa, Mr [Sam] Vilakazi and Mr [Themba] Phiri was unreliable and untrustworthy."

The chairperson of the committee Ben Turok said, "We also have recommended that police and the NPA investigate the breach of the Powers and Privileges Act of Parliament, which lays down severe penalties for lying."

The *Sunday Times* investigation was vindicated and Bart Henderson went silent. But for us, it was the mention in the Ethics Committee reports that Turok and the registrar of members' interests Fazel Mohamed had received threats that made us revisit our man's story. The *Sunday Times* published its story on 11 August 2013.

DINA PULE LINKED TO ASSASSINATION PLOT

By Mzilikazi wa Afrika, Stephan Hofstatter and Rob Rose

Disgraced former communications minister Dina Pule, found guilty this week of lying to Parliament after dishing out foreign trips and business deals to her boyfriend, has been linked to an alleged plot to assassinate top parliamentary officials probing her for misconduct.

The *Sunday Times* has established that a top-level police probe is under way into claims by a man who said he was hired by Pule's boyfriend, Phosane Mngqibisa, to arrange the murder of parliamentary Ethics Committee chairman Professor Ben Turok and the registrar of members' interests, Fazel Mohamed. The two were part of the team investigating Pule.

The police confirmed that they had interviewed several people with first-hand information about the threat, including the alleged plotter – although they questioned his credibility.

Turok's committee this week ruled that Pule was guilty of misconduct and lying under oath, following a *Sunday Times* exposé last year that she leaned on telecoms companies to sponsor the ICT Indaba that paid Mngqibisa's company, Khemano, R6 million in questionable "management fees", and that she flew him around the world at taxpayers' expense.

The man behind the claim, whose name is known to the *Sunday Times*, met Parliament's head of security, Zelda Holtzman, and Mohamed in Cape Town three weeks ago to confess that he had been asked to organise the hit. He said he no longer wanted to carry out his instructions.

The threats to Turok and Mohamed were taken so seriously that they were each assigned two bodyguards.

The man contacted the *Sunday Times* by email on 17 July, claiming to have "information that can prove that Phosane Mngqibisa (and by extension Dina Pule) had called a hit on Professor Ben Turok so that he couldn't attend the final sit-down of the Ethics Committee and therefore give the accused more time to come up with a solution for their issues with the Ethics Committee and Public Protector".

"I can also prove that Phosane Mngqibisa tried to create falsified documents to counter all claims sitting before the committee and the public protector," he said.

"The hit to kill Ben Turok was issued to me as a specialist consultant. I was to recruit a hitman for the job. All plans were disturbed by the Cabinet reshuffle that was made by the president last Tuesday. I have SMSes, emails and recordings to prove my claims."

He said in the email: "Should this be published, Phosane Mngqibisa and Dina Pule will know it was leaked by me ..."

The man repeated these claims in more detail at a face-to-face meeting with the *Sunday Times* on 22 July. At that meeting, he presented SMSes he said were between him and Mngqibisa, planning their first meeting at Emerald Resort and Casino in Vanderbijlpark, Gauteng, where Mngqibisa allegedly asked him to falsify documents to get him and Pule off the hook with the committee.

"I agreed to falsify documents that would have proved that Phosane paid for all his trips with the Minister. And he agreed to pay me my fee of R400 000 for the job," he said.

The man claimed he had asked Mngqibisa for a deposit and another meeting was arranged to hand him the money at an up-market restaurant in Sandton, Johannesburg. "Phosane said it was too risky to deposit money into my account and asked if I can come and collect it in cash."

He alleged that it was at this meeting that Mngqibisa asked him to organise a hit on Turok and Mohamed. He said that the request to organise a hitman made him reconsider his deal with Mngqibisa.

"I might be doing something illegal in my line of duty, but killing a person is out of my league," he said.

His claims could not be independently verified because the *Sunday Times* has not been privy to any of the recordings and documents he claimed to have.

Attempts to contact Pule for comment were unsuccessful. Mngqibisa described the claims as "nonsense".

"I meet many people all the time for business, but certainly not to plan hits or to fabricate documents," he said. He said police were investigating "rogue" individuals for "trying to extort money from me".

The Ethics Committee report on Pule, released on Wednesday, confirmed that the two members had received a threat. It stated: "The panel was informed that Parliament's head of security and management had received information of a threat to harm the chairperson of the panel and registrar and to disrupt the proceedings of the panel. These threats were reported to the authorities and appropriate measures were taken to safeguard the work of the panel and its personnel."

In an interview with the *Sunday Times* on Thursday, Turok confirmed that he had been assigned two bodyguards for the past two weeks. "I have written to the minister of police and the national police commissioner about the matter," he said.

Police minister Nathi Mthethwa's spokesman Zweli Mnisi said, "The minister was notified about the matter. He delegated it to police management to follow it up. A threat assessment or analysis will be conducted by police management that will determine the way forward."

National Police Commissioner General Riah Phiyega's spokesman Solomon Mokgale said, "We interviewed a number of people, including the person who claims to have first-hand information regarding the security threat allegations."

Mokgale refused to name those interviewed, or confirm or deny that Pule and Mngqibisa were suspects.

Mokgale said the man making the allegations "has proven to be very uncooperative and not credible. He makes allegations that he cannot corroborate. Notwithstanding, we conducted our own independent investigation. As indicated, the investigation is still continuing to assess the source and validity of the allegations."

When the *Sunday Times* contacted the man on Thursday he refused to comment further. "I am only going to speak to the police," he said.

Pule had crocodile tears dancing down her face when the former speaker of Parliament Max Sisulu rebuked her publicly in the National Assembly on 20 August 2013.

Sisulu said, "Ms Pule, the charges you have been found guilty of by this House are extremely serious. As a public representative, we are constantly aware that the people of South Africa look to Parliament and its members to display the highest ethical values and standards in what they say and how they conduct themselves.

"A great amount of trust has been placed in us as MPs to chart the course that will lead to a better life for our people. That we do by protecting our national assets and by ensuring in an open and transparent manner that these assets are used only in the public interest and not for private gain.

"Your breach of the Code of Conduct has gravely undermined the people's trust and brought this House and its members into disrepute."

After Pule asked to speak to her fellow MPs, she said, "I want to say to this House that I gave the best I could do to do my job and that if in the course of me doing my job I made a mistake, I am sorry, I apologise."

Pule was fined a full month's salary and suspended from Parliament for 15 days.

Police and the elite investigations unit the Hawks were also investigating her for the irregular employment of Mngqibisa's cronies on the boards of various entities that were under her department. She was also expected to answer some tough questions about the murder plot.

A Public Protector report released in December 2013 described Pule as a liar who squandered taxpayer's money to spoil her boyfriend on international trips.

Public Protector Advocate Thuli Madonsela found Pule guilty of unlawful, unethical and improper conduct in connection with the appointment of service providers to render event management services for the hosting of the department of communications ICT Indaba held in Cape Town from 4 to 7 June 2012.

Madonsela also advised Pule to apologise to Parliament, the communications department, and the *Sunday Times* for "persistently lying" and for her "unethical conduct". The former minister was also told to apologise to Carol Bouwer and the staff at the department of communications whom she forced to lie for her.

The *Sunday Times*, on 6 December 2013, published a story about the public protector's findings on Pule.

DINA PULE LIED LEFT, RIGHT AND CENTRE
Ex-minister must "consider vacating her seat in Parliament":
Pule must apologise to the *Sunday Times* 'for the
persistent insults and denial of the truth'
By Mzilikazi wa Afrika and Stephan Hofstatter

Dina Pule is a liar guilty of unlawful and improper conduct, and must quit Parliament and apologise to the *Sunday Times*.

That is according to Public Protector Thuli Madonsela, who investigated Pule's dodgy antics, which were first exposed by this newspaper.

In a scathing provisional report seen by the *Sunday Times*, titled "A Course in Ethics", Madonsela reveals that the former minister of communications repeatedly lied and cheated to ensure that her boyfriend, Phosane Mngqibisa, could plunder the public purse.

Pule's successor as minister of communications, Yunus Carrim, said he could not comment on a provisional report.

"This would legitimise the leaking of the report. But believe me, we are most determined to act against corruption and misconduct in the department and the state-owned companies in our sector," he said.

Madonsela's report finds that:

- Pule's R10 million sponsorship of the ICT Indaba in Cape Town, from which Mngqibisa paid himself R6 million, was an "unsolicited" and "unlawful donation" that he used to enrich himself;

- Pule admitted to Madonsela that Mngqibisa was her lover while publicly denying any romantic ties with him;

- Pule knew that her department had funded lavish overseas trips for Mngqibisa to which he was not entitled, promising to ensure the money was paid back; and

- Pule and her staff lied to Parliament, the auditor-general and the public protector's office during the investigations against her.

The report finds Pule's conduct to be "unlawful, grossly improper" and "unethical".

Pule had previously repeatedly denied the affair with Mngqibisa, a married man and father of three, and accused the *Sunday Times* at a press conference of conducting a "smear campaign" and "a highly sophisticated plot to blackmail" her.

But when Madonsela interviewed Pule on 28 June this year following allegations published by the *Sunday Times*, the then minister admitted that "she and Mngqibisa had a romantic relationship" and that "he was not her spouse as he was married to someone else under civil law and was therefore not entitled to spousal benefits".

In her report, Madonsela instructs Pule to apologise to the *Sunday Times* "for the persistent insults and denial of the truth that she eventually admitted to me on 28 June 2013".

Madonsela says department of communications "records show that Pule nominated Mngqibisa as her official companion in [its] register".

"I am satisfied that Pule knew that Mngqibisa was benefiting from privileges meant for spouses," writes Madonsela.

The public protector also reports that Pule "offered to ensure that all departmental expenditure on Mngqibisa's trips would be reimbursed before this investigation was finalised".

The report recommended that Pule should "consider vacating her seat in Parliament to minimise the damage" she caused by lying to the Ethics Committee and the South African public.

Madonsela also recommended that Pule apologise to businesswoman Carol Bouwer, who came up with the ICT Indaba concept, "for subjecting her to a hidden agenda placing her in an untenable position", to former staff members at the department she placed "in an unethical situation involving persistent lies and deceit", and to "Parliament for persistently misleading this August constitutional pillar and never admitting the truth until the end".

Madonsela's investigation confirmed the *Sunday Times* exposé of the fact that Mngqibisa benefited financially from the ICT Indaba.

The report says: "I am also of the view that the amount of R10 million provided by the Department of Communications created an excess of sponsorship money and made it possible for Mngqibisa to pay himself the amount of R6 million.

"If I am correct, it was laundered state money that Mngqibisa siphoned away, and not MTN funds."

The report finds that Pule's having solicited sponsorships for the event "per se was not unlawful or improper".

But Pule "should have been circumspect with regard to actively encouraging entities under her supervision to donate funds because they would have found it hard to say no".

MTN contributed R15 million to the event and Vodacom and Telkom chipped in R5 million each.

A total of R40 million was raised for the Indaba.

Pule, according to the report, also lied to Madonsela when she claimed that her affair with Mngqibisa had been over by the time he was involved with the event, and that "Pule's conduct in this regard was unlawful and unethical".

Their relationship created a "real and not just a potential conflict of interest" because Pule "chose Mngqibisa's interests above those of her Department and, ultimately, the state".

The public protector advised "the law enforcement agencies already seized with the matter to proceed expeditiously on the matter already referred by Parliament".

Madonsela is expected to release her final report this week.

In August, Parliament's Ethics Committee found Pule guilty of "wilfully misleading" the panel and failing "to observe the requirements of the code of conduct, both in the letter and spirit of the code".

The committee rejected Pule's evidence as "untrustworthy". She was reprimanded, fined 30 days' salary and suspended from Parliament for 15 days.

Pule later offered a half-hearted apology in Parliament, shedding what observers described as crocodile tears.

Believe it or not, Pule was number 70 on the ANC's election list of members to be sent to Parliament after the 7 May 2014 elections. She was forced to step down after a public uproar. She said in a press statement that she wanted to "be allowed to live my life in peace".

The story won us the Vodacom Journalism Award for the South African Story of the Year in 2013 and we were also named Journalists of the Year at the same event. We were also runners-up for the Taco Kuiper Investigative Journalism Award and a joint winner in the investigative journalism category at the Standard Bank Sikuvile Journalism Awards.

Chapter 20

RIVENGO: Whom God has blessed, let no man curse

"In a time of universal deceit, telling the truth is a revolutionary act."
– Unknown

A ten-year-old boy asked his father, "Daddy, what is politics?"

After scratching his head for a few seconds, his dad explained, "Let's say this house is a country; your mother, who is the administrator of the house, is the government. I would be the politician since I am the one working hard to ensure that we have food on the table.

"You shall be called the union as you are the one making all kinds of demands, like forcing me to buy you new movies, a PlayStation and plasma television set. And your three-year-old brother shall be called the future; he is still young and innocent.

"Our helper shall be called the working class. She works so hard to make our dinner, wash our clothes and keep our house clean. That, my son, is politics."

The boy went to bed disappointed because he didn't comprehend his father's convoluted explanation.

Late that night, while the boy was asleep, he heard his younger brother crying in his bedroom. He went to check on him and found out that his nappy was full.

He went to his parents' bedroom to notify his parents, but when he got there, his mother was sleeping peacefully but his father was not there. The boy decided not to bother her but get some assistance from the helper who lodged in the outside cottage.

As he walked over to the cottage, he noticed the door was half open and while peeping through he saw his father having sex with the helper. He went back to bed more dispirited.

The following morning, at breakfast, the boy said to his father, "Dad, now I know and understand what politics is."

The father, proudly, asked the boy to explain, in his own words, what politics is.

The boy said, "While the government is fast asleep, the politician screws the working class. The union sees everything but can't do anything about it. And the future is full of shit."

The father got the message loud and clear.

If the boy had asked me the same question, mine would be different from his father's lyrical answer but nevertheless close to his intelligent observation.

Politics to me is the surreal art of convincing the nation that you are proficient to milk a chicken and circumcise a mosquito every election season, and even promise to build bridges where there are no rivers.

Without being malicious, I think a politician is someone who scores an own goal then tries to convince everyone that he deserves to be named as the man of the match. And when the furious coach reminds him that his brilliant own goal would count against him, he turns around and blames the opposition for his own stupid and egregious behaviour.

Politics and I have been playing a cat-and-mouse game: there was a time in my life when I was a political activist and committed to the struggle for freedom, justice and equality. And there were also times when politics was like a jealous ex-girlfriend, just out to ruin my life and career.

There have been several times in my life when I have died: shot to death with a gun loaded with lies and left to be buried under a heap of malicious propaganda.

My obituary was poetically written by someone with an evil and twisted mind and embellished with voluminous smear campaigns.

There have been days when I was labelled a crook and a dodgy character, not because I had robbed anybody but because someone with a creative mind conjured up seeing me receiving cash stuffed in a brown envelope.

In my life and career as a journalist my integrity and conviction has never been up for sale: I have chosen to remain poor rather than to accept a bribe.

Several times some idiots have thought they could buy me. A businessman implicated in a R44 million scandal offered me R2 million to drop the story. I wrote the damn story and the man ended in jail. To this day some of my friends, who were aware of the bribe, think I was a fool not to take the cash and drop the story.

There was another attempt to bribe me with R8 million after I sued the state for my wrongful arrest. Again I turned down the offer and accepted a R100 000 settlement that was legally due to me – a matter that was discussed and agreed upon by lawyers and not settled through clandestine arrangements. When I sued the state, it was not about the money, but a matter of principle.

In my journalism career, I have always written about anybody found on the wrong side of the law or caught with their dirty fingers in the cookie jar because I do not owe anybody a favour or have allegiance to any politician or any political party. My allegiance has been to my newspaper, the *Sunday Times*.

The favour I owe is to God in Heaven because He bribed me with this life and it did not come in a brown envelope.

For my entire adult life, as a village political activist and journalist, I have lived – and still do – with the consequences of my convictions and it helps me to sleep better at night.

I am not a critic of politicians but a patriot who uses his pen, not a machine gun, to fight for his country. I am loyal to my country – politicians come and go but the country remains forever.

Life is like a marathon: you must be fully prepared for it and be ready to run the race until the end, and be ready to endure personal humiliation, prosecution and slander.

This marathon is a conundrum: when you are in the lead, those behind you will try every trick in the book to bring you down and when you are at the back, those in front will use anything to block you from getting ahead. It is a vicious cycle, brutal most of the time, and heart-breaking. In this helter-skelter world, you will never know whether your friend is a snake or a snake is your friend until one of them bites you.

Life is hard and terrible at times: the weak get eaten alive while the stronger bulldoze their way through. Life does not need a coward but a brave person who can stand the test of time.

In life, one needs a good friend: a friend in need and in deed, the one who stands by you in good times and in bad times.

Oprah Winfrey made a profound statement about friendship when she said, "Lots of people want to ride with you in the limo, but what you want is someone who will take a bus with you when the limo breaks down."

In my life, I have made all sorts of friends: those who wanted to ride in a limo with me and those who were (and still are) prepared to walk the distance with me when that limo breaks down.

I am fortunate and blessed to have met people like Nathaniel Makanete, Ripho Machate, Ronny Mkhari, Stanley Mokoena, Justin Arenstein, Jocelyn Maker and many others who came into my life when I had nothing and I was nobody – blind to the rot around me – and gave me all the wisdom and knowledge I needed to survive on planet earth.

Of course my life would be boring if those two-faced people were not there, those who tried in vain (some of them still do) to bring me down, to taint my reputation and destroy my image – not because I am a rancid human being but because my achievements and good work, which I toiled for and spent countless hours over while building my career, drives them to fits of jealousy and envy.

One day, not so long ago, I watched a movie called *The Hurricane*, a biographical film, released in 1999, about the life of Rubin "Hurricane" Carter, a former middleweight boxing champion, who was convicted for triple murder. His conviction was based on racism and not the facts.

When Carter was finally released 20 years later, he said, "Hate got me into this place, love got me out."

The movie prompted me to search for Carter's book titled *The Sixteenth Round: From Number 1 Contender to Number 45472*, which he wrote while incarcerated. Carter's movie and biography have some similarities to my life story even though I am not a criminal or an accused murderer.

In my career as a journalist, there has been a group of six gentlemen, all professional journalists working for four national publications, who have spent quality time and good resources in a racially motivated smear campaign to bring me down, taint my reputation and defame me.

These gentlemen, poisonous like snakes and burdened with hatred, have tried everything and told whoever cared to listen that I am dodgy and corrupt. They have repeated the same lie so often that many people started to believe it was the truth – an old propaganda strategy to smear a person.

At best, some of these men should be described as fiction writers instead of being called investigative journalists, which they are not.

This racially motivated smear campaign has persisted for years. The men in question have vowed that they will not stop until they "flush" me out as a no-good journalist. They do not believe that a black journalist can scoop them fair and square. No, there must be some private investigator doing it for me, or some crime intelligence operative feeding me with information. They claim I have been paid off, bribed and used as a blunt instrument by politicians and business people to expose and tarnish their rivals. In my short life, according to them, I have been an agent for the FBI, CIA, MI5 and Mossad.

My biggest mistake, I was told, was to outshine them in the game of journalism and outgun them with my colleagues at the *Sunday Times* by writing better stories and sometimes exposing some of their sources and people they like and admire.

My colleagues and I at the *Sunday Times* investigations unit have one agenda: to tell the story like it is, without fear or favour, not taking sides, to be as objective as we can – even if a friend or a relative is caught on the wrong side of the law. We will write about it as we have done so many times.

These men have constantly singled me out in their snide attacks even though the *Sunday Times* investigations unit is a team: I am the only black guy in our unit. They have, as contrarians, tried to undermine our hard work, our great efforts and the hours we spend researching complicated subjects while they are busy recycling gossip and turning it into front-page news.

Whenever my colleagues and I win an award, they boil in their anger and jealousy. Competition is healthy but professional jealousy and hatred is another thing.

Let me give you some examples of the bad experiences I have had at the hands of these men. One of them used his publication to write a series of fabricated stories about me that cast me in a bad light and quoted me verbatim from fictitious interviews. When he realised that those stories were not making the impact he had desired, his attacks took another twist and he started bad-mouthing me, even flying halfway across the world to spread his grotesque gospel.

Sometime in 2012, one of the men without any shame phoned my colleague Hofstatter and said, "Do you know that Mzilikazi is corrupt?"

When a shocked Hofstatter asked him to elaborate, the gentleman said, "He drives an Audi."

Hofstatter dismissed him and the man then phoned my former editor, Ray Hartley, and repeated the same allegation. Hartley asked him to provide proof to support his allegations or evidence that my Audi might have been bought in a corrupt deal, but there was none.

This is the man who believes that a black man or a journalist, like me, cannot afford to buy an Audi. He insinuates that someone had bought or financed the car for me. I have been driving an Audi since 2001 and still drive one today. It is my favourite car and I can afford it from my salary.

There is an explanation for this: in his company, white reporters get paid more than their black colleagues. At one point he tried to recruit me but I turned down his offer.

One of the men phoned my colleague Rob Rose in 2011 to inform him that I had driven to work in a black BMW X5 owned by crime intelligence that morning. In a spirit of fairness and transparency Rob and I went through the parking lot and found there was not a single X5 parked in the building. The security guard confirmed to us that no car of that nature had been in the building, even from visitors, for months.

Another one of these men told colleagues at his newspaper that controversial crime intelligence boss General Richard Mdluli, who was on suspension at the time of writing this book, was one of the guests at my fortieth birthday party. At the party, which was well attended by friends and family, as well as a number of journalists from different radio stations and newspapers, including some from his newspaper, nobody saw Mdluli.

I know Mdluli, who hails from Thulamahashe township in Bushbuckridge, while I come from Sibambayani village, also in Bushbuckridge, but we are not friends. Mdluli and I are Tsongas – what many prefer to refer to as Shangaans – and it ends there. Bushbuckridge is a huge area with a population of more than two million people.

With all this propaganda and these smear campaigns going around I was not surprised when Dianne Kohler Barnard, Democratic Alliance (DA) member of Parliament and the party's shadow minister of police, inboxed me via Facebook on 8 April 2012, and said, "Hi. There's this claim going around that you're related to Richard Mdluli – is this true?"

To begin with, I am not sure whether it is a crime for people to be related or if that was going to make me an incompetent or corrupt journalist if I was indeed related to Mdluli. I replied, "Not at all. He is not my relative, not even a distant cousin. He is from Bushbuckridge. I am also from Bushbuckridge but not the same area. I don't even know where his house is."

Her question implied or insinuated that I was either blocking negative stories that were to be published about Richard Mdluli in the *Sunday Times* or I was somehow protecting the crime intelligence boss. I did not know I was so powerful that I could influence my colleagues and editors.

I do not have anything against Kohler Barnard or her political party but I have serious issues with her identification of "wrongdoers".

In December 2011, when the *Sunday Times* exposed a Cato Manor police unit from Durban allegedly operating as a "hit squad" killing black people in the townships and villages around KwaZulu-Natal, the same Kohler Barnard, whose political constituency is in Durban, neither uttered a word nor issued a single press statement in this regard.

Subsequently, when 28 members of the Cato Manor police unit, including the Hawks' boss in Kwazulu-Natal who is the ultimate unit commander, General Johan Booysen, were arrested and suspended, charged with 116 counts, including 28 murders, Kohler Barnard again said nothing – not even a single press statement.

I was later told, although I do not have any documentary evidence, that some of the Cato Manor police officers implicated are DA members. The *Sunday Times* published the story.

SHOOT TO KILL: INSIDE A SOUTH AFRICAN POLICE DEATH SQUAD
By Stephan Hofstatter, Rob Rose and Mzilikazi wa Afrika

The *Sunday Times* has uncovered evidence of an alleged "hit squad" operating in KwaZulu-Natal under the ultimate command of the province's Hawks' boss, Major-General Johan Booysen.

The Cato Manor organised crime unit in Durban has allegedly committed scores of assassinations, some in retaliation for suspected cop killings and others related to ongoing taxi wars.

Booysen was previously the provincial head of organised crime. Suspended police chief, General Bheki Cele caused a stir among provincial top brass last year when he unexpectedly promoted Booysen to head the Hawks in KwaZulu-Natal, even though his unit had courted controversy through its disproportionately high kill rate of crime suspects.

Cele has been blamed for fuelling the killings of taxi bosses by making inflammatory remarks. According to court papers filed by taxi bosses fearing assassination at the hands of the unit, Cele reportedly said, speaking at the funeral of a slain police taxi task team investigator Superintendent Zethembe Chonco, "If SAPS members cannot arrest suspects and they feel that their lives are threatened they must take them to the nearest mortuary".

Police in KwaZulu-Natal, and the Cato Manor unit in particular, have been doing just that.

Official figures from the Independent Complaints Directorate (ICD) show in the past three years KwaZulu-Natal police killed 527 suspects during the commission of a suspected crime, an escape, an investigation or arrest – by far the highest in South Africa. The Cato Manor organised crime unit accounted for 45 deaths.

The ICD confirmed this week that six members of the Cato Manor unit had been investigated, some of them for killing suspects.

Captains Mossie Mostert, Eugene van Tonder and Anton Lokum and the late Warrant Officer Rakesh Maharaj are among those being investigated. None of them could be interviewed by the *Sunday Times* this week, according to police spokesman Colonel Jay Naicker.

The *Sunday Times* has, during an investigation that began last year, obtained testimony and copious evidence from dozens of people about the killings, including hundreds of death scene photographs and expert ballistics reports.

Three senior police officials, a pathologist and a ballistics expert who examined the images concluded that they appeared to have been executions. None would be named.

The *Sunday Times* has also interviewed several taxi industry bosses who claim to be assassination targets of the unit, and witnesses of at least two killings who refuse to make sworn statements to the ICD because they feared they would be killed.

Suspicious police killings linked to the unit include:

- KwaMaphumulo taxi boss Bongani Mkhize, killed on 3 February 2009 on Umgeni Road after he took out an interdict in a bid to prevent police killing him;

- KwaMaphumulo taxi boss Lindelani Buthelezi, whose wife says he was "executed by police who entered my home";

- Sandile Kinglock and Musa Qwabe, both suspects in the murder of a Durban lawyer, killed by police on 14 September 2009 in two separate incidents;

- KwaMaphumulo taxi boss Magojela Ndimande and his bodyguard Sibusiso Tembe, killed on the N3 highway at Merrivale on 16 September 2008. Witnesses say the police fabricated claims of a shoot-out;

- Five robbery suspects shot on the N3 near Camperdown on 21 January 2009, which police followed with a drink-fuelled celebration;

- Four suspected cop killers massacred together on a mattress in a house in Inanda on 13 April 2009; and

- ATM bombing suspect Lebogang Ranyali killed on 27 March 2009 in Pinetown.

In an interview with the *Sunday Times* this week, Booysen denied any knowledge of a hit squad. "I would strongly disagree with you. Their lives were at stake, they defended themselves in a shoot-out," he said.

He said it was unfair to brand the unit a hit squad because of its high kill rate of suspects, given the high number of violent criminals arrested by members. "Cato Manor only investigates murder, armed robbery, ATM bombing, serial killing and serious rape cases," he said. "They made 437 arrests in the last two years. The facts are, they do arrest very violent people."

Last month Colonel Navin Madhoe – an officer in the provincial procurement office charged with trying to bribe Booysen with R2 million to drop a R60 million corruption case – gave the Hawks boss a memory stick, hard drive and two CDs containing hundreds of photographs showing what appear to be gruesome killings of suspects at the hands of the police.

The images included several post-kill celebrations of members of the Cato Manor unit. In an affidavit, Madhoe says Booysen asked him to get the CDs as they contained "incriminating evidence of serious crimes in a unit under his direct command". Madhoe was acquitted and is back at work.

The *Sunday Times* has obtained the photographs.

Asked if he believed it was callous to hold a party after killing suspects, Booysen said there was nothing wrong with police enjoying "social events".

The Camperdown images show close-ups of three of the suspects shot in the head. "That's troubling. With head shots you want to look closely for evidence that suggests execution," said a senior pathologist. "You would expect [many] more body and limb shots."

This was confirmed by the ballistics expert and two senior police officials, who said head shots of fleeing suspects were "highly unusual".

The experts all referred to images of weapons in several of the killings, including those of Qwabe, Ranyali, Buthelezi and Mkhize, as "highly suspicious".

They cited unusually clean guns in pools of blood and improbable positioning of suspects' firearms.

In court papers ballistics expert Kobus Steyl – a former member of the ballistics section of the SAPS Forensic Science Laboratory with 19 years' experience – concluded in two of the cases that "the shooting of the suspects, as alleged by the police, is questionable in regard to the self-defence scenario".

Although questions were put to individual members of the Cato Manor unit about their role in the killings, police spokesman Naicker said the policemen "cannot speak" as the ICD investigations "have not been finalised [and] we don't want to compromise [them]".

In September, the South African Communist Party's provincial leader, Themba Mthembu, issued a public resolution calling on the government to launch a judicial commission of inquiry to probe the Cato Manor "death squad".

"The Cato Manor squad is the new Vlakplaas, they operate in the same style," he told the *Sunday Times* this week, referring to the apartheid-era unit led by Eugene de Kock that assassinated opponents of the National Party government in the 1980s.

"We strongly believe that the duty of the police is to investigate and arrest suspects. But this unit has been killing more suspects than putting them behind bars."

Booysen said he would have "no objections to something like [an official probe] – it may prove once and for all that the picture created about Cato Manor is totally wrong.

"You weren't there. I wasn't there. Let's allow these cases to be investigated by the ICD and let the prosecuting authority deal with it in the appropriate way," he said.

After the story was published, Independent Police Investigative Directorate (IPID) – a police watchdog – launched an independent investigation, assisted by the police crack unit known as the Hawks.

The outcome of this investigation led to the arrest and suspension of these police officers.

When Mdluli, a senior black police officer, was accused of one account of murder and several of fraud, Kohler Barnard issued a handful of press statements and gave interviews on different radio stations calling for his expulsion from the South African Police Service, something she failed to do with the Cato Manor police officers.

I am not saying Mdluli does not deserve to be lambasted and exposed if he is corrupt and a murderer. Let him be prosecuted and let him face the music, let him go to jail and rot there if he is found guilty; but I am questioning his treatment in comparison to other alleged wrongdoers.

In February 2013 a group of black police officers, who behaved like savages, were videotaped arresting a Mozambican national and taxi driver Mido Macia. They tied his hands to the rear of the vehicle before dragging him along a street in Daveyton, east of Johannesburg. Macia later died in a local police cell – and Kohler Barnard was quick to respond to that barbaric act.

I watched with disbelief when Kohler Barnard and her colleagues John Moodey, Mmusi Maimane and Emmah More visited Daveyton after the assault and death of Mido Macia and even laid a wreath on the spot where the 27-year-old taxi driver was attacked on Sunday.

Kohler Barnard has never visited any of the victims of the Cato Manor police unit in her own province, or laid a wreath where taxi boss Bongani Mkhize was killed in broad daylight along Umngeni Road by these rogue Cato Manor cops.

There are also Cato Manor victims in KwaZulu-Natal: women left as widows and some children left as orphans.

I have never inboxed Kohler Barnard and asked her if she is related to General Johan Booysen because there is a "claim going around", or whether any of the police officers were members of the DA.

Our Cato Manor exposé won the 2012 South African Story of the Year Award at the prestigious Standard Bank Sivukile Journalism Awards as well as the Global Shining Light Award presented at the Global Investigative Journalism Network in Rio de Janeiro, Brazil in 2013.

In Brazil, the story was selected from among 65 entries drawn from 28 countries. Winning these awards, more especially the international award, drove my racist tormentors from rival publications to fits of anger and jealousy. And again, I was singled out from my team and character-assassinated by these racist dinosaurs on social networks.

The latest slur prompted one of their readers, Khadija Sharife from Durban, to write a letter to the editor and complain.

In her letter, Sharife stated, "I am writing, specifically, with regards to the published Facebook statements, some of which are pasted below.

"I have not been following the Cato Manor story. However, the journalist appointed to cover the story has displayed significant (public) personal animus toward one of the *Sunday Times* journalists (Mzilikazi wa Afrika).

"There is no substantive mention of others on the *Sunday Times* team including Rob Rose and Stefan Hofstatter. The primary focus is Mzilikazi. Vague allusions are made to 'Leonard the Liar' as he is framed; his use of a different name is proffered as substantiating evidence of same, alongside possibly fictive and misinformed past incidents.

"The issue is not whether [publication's name withdrawn] is right or wrong in its probing of the veracity of the story, but that, as according to the defamatory (and actionable) statements published by your journalist on his Facebook page etc., he is unveiling how little it takes to condemn Mzilikazi, that allegations need not be true, and that such condemnation, as reflected, appears to be the driving factor. The smearing does not reflect well.

"In addition to being the only person worth condemning, according to [publication's name withdrawn], Mzilikazi also happens to be black. I'm not making this a race issue: rather the invisibilisation of the other (white) journalists, is transforming it into a race issue.

"Both Rob and Stefan participated as equal partners in the investigation and they should be referred to as a team, condemned or not. In summation, the coverage of Cato Manor can be seen to condemn the journalist authoring the story, rather than the people and story he focuses on."

Sharife's letter was not published by the said publication.

The Cato Manor police officers had not yet gone to trial at the time of writing this book, with the trial expecting to commence in February 2015. The thirty officers face 116 charges, including 28 of murder, 14 of unlawful possession of ammunition, 14 of unlawful possession of firearms and four of housebreaking. My colleagues and I are writing a book about how we investigated the case, as well as the threats and smear campaigns we have been through, and we will publish some of the evidence as soon as the case is finalised.

The idea to write this memoir was not to spill the beans on anyone or to reveal some family secrets, or to embarrass friends and heckle politicians, but to give a candid account of my journey from the rolling hills of Sibambayani village to the City of Gold where I became an apostle of the Fourth Estate.

The book is about my struggle and redemption, my story of triumph over darkness, of my determination over self-pity and of my victory over tragedy. In my adult life, as a journalist and political activist, I have lived with the consequences of my convictions. Just like Nelson Mandela, "it is an ideal for which I am prepared to die".

I have admitted that I was initially against the idea of opening my half-shut door to the world: the notion seemed as crass and unpleasant as being a stripper in front of a gaggle of strangers, for I have always been discrete and mysterious.

I had no motive to stoke the fire but in the end, after persistent supplications from a multitude of people following my career, I felt obliged. Even though I am not a raconteur, I decided to enter a confessional box and air my dirty laundry to the public. After all, it is therapeutic and a road map to a spiritual renewal.

I decided to chronicle my adventure with honesty before some heinous person provided a grotesque version of my career. And also to show my appreciation for the men and women who gave me a helping hand and showed me the ropes while those with rancour tried to cast me into the bottomless pit or throw me into the gutter.

I confess I am not an angel, and just like everybody, I have my own fair share of mortifying moments.

One of those moments has been misrepresented by those with little information about what really happened. It was in March 2004 and I was in Catembe, less than a ten-minute ferry ride from Maputo, Mozambique, on an assignment when I met businessman and former United Nations diplomat Koenraad Collier.

During my encounter with Collier, who helped me with my assignment, he told me that he was selling his establishment, the Catembe Hotel and Gallery, and gave me his business card asking that if I heard of anybody in South Africa looking to invest in a hotel in Mozambique I should give them his number. I took the card and returned home, and nothing happened.

About five months later, in August, while I was planning to return to Mozambique on holiday and as part of my research into my family tree, I asked

Mathews Phosa, whom I have known for years, if he could introduce me to one of his friends, Armando Guebuza, who was president of Mozambique.

Phosa, during our discussion, asked me to be on the lookout for any hotel or bed and breakfast for sale while in Mozambique as he was helping a consortium of women who were looking to invest in the tourism sector in that country.

I told Phosa about Collier's hotel and promised to look for his business card. Later I phoned Phosa to give him the details, but he suggested that I should give Collier the number of Soraya Beukes, who was heading the consortium, and gave me her number.

I phoned Collier and asked him if his hotel was still up for sale and gave him Beukes' numbers after he affirmed that his joint was still up for grabs.

I had known Beukes as one of the people under investigation by the disbanded elite investigations unit, the Scorpions, for her role in the travelgate scandal, a scam where members of Parliament colluded with travel agents to use their travel vouchers for unauthorised expenditures including hiring luxury vehicles and staying in posh hotels. In fact, it was my investigation that exposed the travelgate scandal.

A few days later after the phone call to Collier, I requested a lunch meeting with Sipho Ngwema, who was the spokesperson for the Scorpions at the time, and made him aware that I had passed on Beukes' number to a businessman in Mozambique. I told the former spin-doctor about my role as a messenger in the matter.

Days later Beukes was arrested. Collier read about it online and started bombarding me with text messages, accusing me of trying to set him up with "scams". I responded, explaining that it was his prerogative to do business with whomever he wanted and to disregard those he did not feel comfortable with.

The Scorpions approached Collier for an affidavit about possible dealings with Beukes and his statement was used to revoke her R100 000 bail.

Former Western Cape premier Ebrahim Rasool, who is now the South African Ambassador in the United States of America, and who has an axe to grind with me for, among others, getting his comrade, Tony Yengeni, into jail and exposing how the late mining magnet, Brett Kebble, was bankrolling the ANC in the province under his leadership, then got his "air force" into action. This was his team of Cape Town-based journalists who were on his payroll and who were used to "smear" his opponents.

Beukes is close to Rasool's political arch rivals Mcebisi Skwatsha and Lynne Brown.

One of Rasool's "air force" members, Ashley Smith, who was working for the *Cape Argus* in the Independent Media Group at the time, used Collier's affidavit as ammunition to write a front-page story claiming that I was linked to Beukes and had tried to help her skip the country to Mozambique.

When I was suspended from work and faced a disciplinary hearing, Ngwema came and testified on my behalf. He informed my employer that I am the one who blew the whistle on Beukes' business venture in Mozambique, which led the Scorpions to Collier. Collier submitted an affidavit confirming my account of events. Phosa also testified on my behalf, telling my employer that I was just a messenger and that he had, innocently, asked me to pass on Beukes' telephone numbers to Collier. My former boss Jocelyn Maker also testified that I had told her that Phosa had asked me to pass on Beukes' numbers to Collier.

In December 2004 there was some jubilation when I was fired from the *Sunday Times*. My employer was under the impression that I was either part of Beukes' consortium or had a financial interest in the matter.

I take full responsibility for my conduct: I made a wrong judgement call. I erred and apologised to my employer and the *Sunday Times*' readers for the inadvertent oversight on my part. One thing I am happy about though, out of this whole fracas: I never compromised my journalistic ethics and integrity.

I was prosecuted, vilified and humiliated. I served my time out of journalism for more than a year with honour and dignity. As the months went by, it became evident that my testimony was correct: I had no business interest in Beukes' consortium nor would I have reaped any financial benefit. I just made a wrong judgement call.

My employer brought me back from the cold to work as the investigations editor for *Sunday World*, a sister publication to the *Sunday Times* in March 2006, and I later re-joined the *Sunday Times* in April 2010.

Ashley Smith later made a confession in an affidavit on 28 June 2010 in which he admitted that he and his colleague, Joel Arenes, who was a political editor at *Cape Argus*, were on Rasool's payroll and had been used to trash the politician's enemies, especially Skwatsha and Brown.

In his affidavit submitted to the NPA Smith stated, "At these meetings Rasool referred to us as his 'air force', meaning his front line of attack against

266

the Skwatsha camp or his other political rivals. It was also at these meetings that [Zain] Orrie would say that it was difficult to fly the planes when the fuel tanks are dry, suggesting we couldn't do the work without payment."

The former journalist added, "By the time we had the so-called 'air force meetings', I had already regarded my integrity as a journalist being compromised."

He added that he and Arenes were paid "cash in sums ranging between R5 000 and R10 000" every time they attended an "air force meeting".

At some point, Smith and his "air force" mates submitted an invoice for R100 000 to Rasool. "By the time that the R100 000 invoice was presented to Rasool, we had already been compromised in our journalistic ethics, as we were consulting with Rasool on his media strategies in his battle with Skwatsha."

In conclusion, Smith wrote, "I also request the NPA to provide me with indemnity from prosecution for any crimes I may have committed arising out of the relationship I had with Rasool, Orrie and Aranes, while being a journalist and the consequences flowing therefrom.

"I assisted Rasool in media strategies while I was employed as a journalist with Independent Newspapers. The assistance I gave to Rasool and his allies did not relate to matters of interest to the Provincial Government, but to Rasool's political survival in the ANC."

As expected, Rasool denied all the allegations. In an email to the *Cape Argus* after the newspaper got hold of Smith's affidavit, Rasool said, "All the matters that Mr Smith is alleged to have said in his affidavit relate to things that have been dealt with in the past. They are matters that have been publicly aired, but also which have been investigated and dispensed with by a variety of bodies. I have put all of these matters behind me. In the various investigations, Mr Smith has pronounced on these matters, at least once under oath. What is consistent about his pronouncements at that time is that he strenuously denied everything he now alleges. I have consistently denied these allegations and continue to do so. I do not want to enter a battlefield that I have happily exited, nor do I want to be party to anything that is designed to damage the ANC in the Western Cape further."

Rasool was later sacked as Western Cape province premier and replaced by Brown before the DA took over control of the province.

The ANC never instituted disciplinary action against Rasool, but instead promoted him to be our ambassador to the USA.

This is becoming a standard tendency in South Africa: those found guilty of any transgression, including fraud, corruption and maladministration, are protected. As long as they belong to a certain faction of the ANC, they get redeployed. Some of them get nominated into the party's National Executive Committee, the organisation's decision-making body, and some were even on the election list for the National Assembly.

If one was to name and shame some of the ANC members who have been caught on the wrong side of the law but still hold positions of power, one could write a book revealing an intricate web of lies and corruption.

It is a shame that most of our countrymen and women have forgotten the moral principles: things fall apart when we turn a blind eye to reality, blinded by loyalty and patronage, and we let our country down.

One thing you can be certain of is that in the land of the blind, the one-eyed man is a thief – not a king. Our beloved country has become the land of the blind; many people suffer from political myopia. It has become evident that some people believe that to live like kings they must steal from the poor. Unless we do something as a collective, the thieves will continue to rob us blind, loot and pillage everything until there is *Nothing Left to Steal*.